Chaplains as Partners in
Medical Decision-Making

of related interest

Evidence-Based Healthcare Chaplaincy
A Research Reader
Edited by George Fitchett, Kelsey B. White and Kathryn Lyndes
ISBN 978 1 78592 820 8
eISBN 978 1 78450 923 1

Case Studies in Spiritual Care
Healthcare Chaplaincy Assessments,
Interventions and Outcomes
Edited by George Fitchett and Steve Nolan
ISBN 978 1 78592 783 6
eISBN 978 1 78450 705 3

Spiritual Care for Allied Health Practice
A Person-centered Approach
Edited by Lindsay B. Carey, PhD and Bernice A. Mathisen, PhD
Foreword by Harold G. Koenig, RN, MD
ISBN 978 1 78592 220 6
eISBN 978 1 78450 501 1

Ethical Questions in Healthcare Chaplaincy
Learning to Make Informed Decisions
Pia Matthews
ISBN 978 1 78592 421 7
eISBN 978 1 78450 788 6

Time to Talk about Dying
How Clergy and Chaplains Can Help
Senior Adults Prepare for a Good Death
Fred Grewe
ISBN 978 1 78592 805 5
eISBN 978 1 78450 846 3

Chaplaincy in Hospice and Palliative Care
Edited by Karen Murphy and Bob Whorton
Foreword by Baroness Finlay of Llandaff
ISBN 978 1 78592 068 4
eISBN 978 1 78450 329 1

CHAPLAINS as PARTNERS in MEDICAL DECISION-MAKING

Case Studies in Healthcare Chaplaincy

Edited by

M. JEANNE WIRPSA AND KAREN PUGLIESE

FOREWORD BY GEORGE FITCHETT

AFTERWORD BY MARTIN WALTON

Jessica Kingsley Publishers
London and Philadelphia

First published in 2020
by Jessica Kingsley Publishers
73 Collier Street
London N1 9BE, UK
and
400 Market Street, Suite 400
Philadelphia, PA 19106, USA

www.jkp.com

Library of Congress Cataloging in Publication Data
A CIP catalog record for this book is available from the Library of Congress

British Library Cataloguing in Publication Data
A CIP catalogue record for this book is available from the British Library

ISBN 978 1 78450 997 2
eISBN 978 1 78450 998 9

Printed and bound in the United States

Contents

Acknowledgements

The editors gratefully acknowledge all those who contributed to the unique focus of this book:

- Chaplain colleagues across the US whose astute observations about our role inform the conceptual framework for this work.

- The research team who designed and implemented the initial study exploring the contributions of healthcare chaplains to medical decision-making.

- Chaplain residents at Northwestern Memorial Hospital who embraced the challenge of conducting in-depth interviews.

- Case study authors who shared their skilled ministry with transparency, humility, and self-critique, and the respondents for their rich commentary on the cases.

- Northwestern Medicine, Spiritual Care and Education Departments, for recognizing the importance of chaplain research and publication.

- The inspiration and insider's perspective on case study research offered by George Fitchett and Steve Nolan, as well as the collegial support of our Netherlands' chaplain colleagues.

- Lara Boyken, for her dedication and skill in preparing this manuscript for publication.

Finally, to the patients, families, and healthcare providers whose stories—of hope and struggle, illness and healing—are included here, we are deeply indebted. We acknowledge that in their re-telling, we are standing on holy ground.

Foreword

GEORGE FITCHETT

This new book of case studies edited by M. Jeanne Wirpsa and Karen Pugliese represents an important addition to the chaplain case study literature. The first case studies were published less than 10 years ago and described chaplain care with patients with advanced cancer and Parkinson's disease (Cooper 2011; King 2012; Risk 2013). These were followed by two books of case studies (Fitchett and Nolan 2015, 2018) and a special issue of the journal *Health and Social Care Chaplaincy* (Fitchett and Nolan 2017) describing care for patients in diverse clinical contexts (Pediatrics, Psychiatry, Palliative Care, Veterans) provided by chaplains working in many different countries. The most recent advance in chaplain case studies is the Dutch Case Studies Project.[1] This multi-year project began in 2016 and involves chaplains across the Netherlands working in multiple contexts (healthcare, corrections, military), sharing and discussing cases in small groups (Walton and Körver 2017). The unique contribution of the present work is bringing together a group of cases that all focus on the same chaplaincy activity, assisting patients, families, and healthcare colleagues with medical decision-making.

Chaplains are identified as core members of the healthcare team in practice guidelines (Davidson *et al.* 2017; National Consensus Project for Quality Palliative Care 2018), but their important role in medical decision-making has not been emphasized. Nonetheless, several studies have begun to highlight the extent to which chaplains are involved in assisting with medical decision-making (Jeuland *et al.* 2017; Wirpsa *et al.* 2019). However, other research indicates

---

1   See https://ucgv.nl/case-studies-project

that chaplains are not being utilized in medical decision-making, for example, in family conferences, as often as they should be. In a study of 249 family conferences with surrogates of patients hospitalized in one of 13 Intensive Care Units (ICUs), chaplains were present in only two (Ernecoff *et al.* 2015).

The nine cases in this book, along with others that have been previously published (see Huth and Roberts 2015; Jinks 2018; Murphy 2017), provide an in-depth look at chaplains' contributions to medical decision-making. The cases demonstrate that chaplains' involvement in medical decision-making is not uncommon and is frequently substantial. The cases also allow us to identify important features of the chaplains' care. First, we see how, in these nine racially, culturally and religiously diverse cases, chaplains use their skill in building relationships to develop understanding of the patients' and families' religious and cultural background. They also use these skills to gain the trust of families who, for various reasons, do not trust the members of the healthcare team. In several cases this trust is developed over a period of weeks or months, but notably in one case it is built in a matter of hours (Alma, Chapter 12). The cases also show us how the chaplains use this trust and understanding to build a bridge with the other members of the healthcare team when communication has broken down or become strained, through informal communication with the families and the healthcare teams. We also see chaplains playing important roles in family meetings.

Second, we see the complex ways in which chaplains function as religious authorities. In several cases chaplains' ritual leadership plays a central role in the development of the case. Their ritual leadership facilitates building trust with patients and families, it sustains families who are keeping vigil at the bedside of gravely ill loved ones, it unites divided families, and it helps families name and accept the end of their loved one's life. In several cases, chaplains' religious authority allows them to reframe a families' understanding of their religious duties and hopes (such as for a miracle) which, in turn, allows these families to make decisions to focus on comfort care for their loved one. It is important to note that chaplains are the sole religious authority for several cases where the patients or families were not presently involved in a congregation. In other cases, while the family had a local religious leader, the family looked to the chaplain for guidance, perhaps because the chaplain was part of the hospital staff, understood the medical and religious complexities of the situation, and could bridge communication with the healthcare team. The chaplains in these cases rarely share the religious affiliation, if there is one, of the patients and families for whom they care. While questions have been raised about inter-religious chaplaincy care (Cadge and Sigalow 2013), these cases suggest that the absence of faith concordance is not an obstacle to the chaplains' effectiveness, most remarkably so in the case of Ayesah (Chapter 13), where a Presbyterian chaplain provides care for an immigrant Muslim patient and her family. In at least one case (Bob, Chapter 3), the patient was "not a particularly religious man," but he "hit it off" with the chaplain when during a long inpatient stay she helped negotiate the opportunity for him to visit his dog in the hospital's outdoor lobby.

Third, the cases allow us to see the outcomes associated with the chaplains' care. These include improved communication between the families and the healthcare teams caring for their loved ones. They include withdrawing painful, unwanted treatment. They also include avoiding initiating non-beneficial treatment for patients near the end of life and thus avoiding the ICU stay that frequently accompanies that treatment.

There are several additional reasons why case studies, and especially a case series such as this, are important. First, they support research that may lead to improvements in chaplaincy care. By permitting close observation of the role of the chaplain in medical decision-making, this case series allows us to ask whether there are ways any of these chaplains could have been more effective. Are there cases in which the chaplain should have been consulted sooner? Are there cases where the chaplain could have been more assertive in engaging the family or healthcare team or in initiating family conferences?

Second, cases such as these can play an important role in educating healthcare colleagues about chaplains' contributions to medical decision-making. Other members of the healthcare team often have limited education about religion or spirituality or the role of the chaplain. Cases such as these provide memorable examples of chaplains' contributions in situations where medical decision-making has become difficult. Cases in which families cite hope for a miracle in the context of intensive, non-beneficial end-of-life care are notably challenging for physicians and other health professionals (Cooper *et al.* 2014; Lo *et al.* 2002). Case studies like these will help healthcare colleagues understand the important role that chaplains can play in such situations.

Finally, a case series such as this can play an important role in chaplain education, by identifying medical decision-making as an important arena for chaplaincy practice and by illustrating effective ways in which chaplains contributed to medical decision-making in complex cases. Being familiar with these cases may help chaplains with less experience identify ways in which they can be effective partners in medical decision-making. This important book helps make the case for the important role of case studies in advancing healthcare chaplaincy (Fitchett 2011).

George Fitchett, DMin, PhD, BCC
Professor and Director of Research
Department of Religion, Health and Human Values
Rush University Medical Center, Chicago Illinois

References

Cadge, W. and Sigalow, E. (2013) 'Negotiating religious differences: The strategies of interfaith chaplains.' *Healthcare Journal for the Scientific Study of Religion 52*, 1, 146–158.

Cooper, R.S. (2011) 'Case study of a chaplain's spiritual care for a patient with advanced metastatic breast cancer.' *Journal of Health Care Chaplaincy 17*, 1, 19–37.

Cooper, R.S., Ferguson, A., Bodurtha, J.N. and Smith, T.J. (2014) 'AMEN in challenging conversations: Bridging the gaps between faith, hope, and medicine.' *Journal of Oncology Practice 10*, 4, e191–195.

Davidson, J.E., Aslakson, R.A., Long, A.C., Puntillo, K.A., *et al.* (2017) 'Guidelines for family-centered care in the neonatal, pediatric, and adult ICU.' *Critical Care Medicine 45*, 1, 103–128.

Ernecoff, N.C., Curlin, F.A., Buddadhumaruk, P. and White, D.B. (2015) 'Health care professionals' responses to religious or spiritual statements by surrogate decision makers during goals-of-care discussions.' *JAMA Internal Medicine 175*, 10, 1662–1669.

Fitchett, G. (2011) 'Making our case(s).' *Journal of Health Care Chaplaincy 17*, 1–2, 3–18.

Fitchett, G. and Nolan, S. (eds) (2015) *Spiritual Care in Practice: Case Studies in Healthcare Chaplaincy*. London: Jessica Kingsley Publishers.

Fitchett, G. and Nolan, S. (eds) (2017) Special Issue of *Health and Social Care Chaplaincy 5*, 2.

Fitchett, G. and Nolan, S. (eds) (2018) *Case Studies in Spiritual Care: Healthcare Chaplaincy Assessments, Interventions and Outcomes*. London: Jessica Kingsley Publishers.

Huth, J. and Roberts, W. (2015) '"I Need to Do the Right Thing for Him" – Andrew, a Canadian Veteran at the End of His Life, and His Daughter Lee.' In G. Fitchett and S. Nolan (eds) *Spiritual Care in Practice: Case Studies in Healthcare Chaplaincy* (pp.201–222). London: Jessica Kingsley Publishers.

Jeuland, J., Fitchett, G., Schulman-Green, D. and Kapo, J. (2017) 'Chaplains working in palliative care: Who they are and what they do.' *Journal of Palliative Medicine* *20*, 5, 502–508.

Jinks, P. (2018) '"She's Already Done So Much" – Sarah, Diagnosed Prenatally with Trisomy 18, and Her Family.' In G. Fitchett and S. Nolan (eds) *Case Studies in Spiritual Care: Healthcare Chaplaincy Assessments, Interventions and Outcomes* (pp.52–70). London: Jessica Kingsley Publishers.

King, S.D. (2012) 'Facing fears and counting blessings: A case study of a chaplain's faithful companioning a cancer patient.' *Journal of Health Care Chaplaincy 18*, 1–2, 3–22.

Lo, B., Ruston, D., Kates, L.W., Arnold, R.M., *et al.* (2002) 'Discussing religious and spiritual issues at the end of life: A practical guide for physicians.' *JAMA 287*, 6, 749–754.

Murphy, J. (2017) 'The chaplain as the mediator between the patient and the interdisciplinary team in ethical decision making: A chaplaincy case study involving a quadriplegic patient.' *Health and Social Care Chaplaincy 5*, 2, 241–256.

National Consensus Project for Quality Palliative Care (2018) *Clinical Practice Guidelines for Quality Palliative Care*, 4th edition. Richmond, VA: National Coalition for Hospice and Palliative Care.

Risk, J.L. (2013) 'Building a new life: A chaplain's theory based case study of chronic illness.' *Journal of Health Care Chaplaincy 19*, 3, 81–98.

Walton, M. and Körver, J. (2017) 'Dutch case studies project in chaplaincy care: A description and theoretical explanation of the format and procedures.' *Health and Social Care Chaplaincy 5*, 2, 257–280.

Wirpsa, M.J., Johnson, R.E., Bieler, J., Boyken, L., *et al.* (2019) 'Interprofessional models for shared decision making: The role of the health care chaplain.' *Journal of Health Care Chaplaincy 25*, 1, 20–44.

Introduction

M. JEANNE WIRPSA AND KAREN PUGLIESE

In *Paging God: Religion in the Halls of Medicine*, sociologist Wendy Cadge (2012) broke new ground by exploring the interface between the culture of medicine and the professional identity of healthcare chaplains. Dr Cadge observed and interviewed physicians, nurses, and chaplains in 17 academic healthcare organizations to demystify the relationship between increasingly high-tech medical care and the enigmatic role of religion and spirituality in medicine. Cadge spent a year learning what and how chaplains do what they do, and described how hospitals shape chaplains' professional tasks. Her book provided new insights and perspective for the profession, and challenged chaplains to describe their competency in terms and methods understood by their medical colleagues.

George Fitchett and Steven Nolan reinforced this message by encouraging chaplains to discuss the complexities of their role and the impact of contributions via the art of Narrative Medicine in the form of clinical case studies (Fitchett and Nolan 2015, 2018). Long-recognized in the fields of psychiatry, psychology, and social work as valid research as well as a vehicle for training members of the profession, case studies present and evaluate spiritual care, thereby contributing to a growing body of research in the field of professional healthcare chaplaincy. In the last several years, professional chaplaincy organizations have committed to joint efforts to strengthen and advance the profession, issuing a unified call for research describing the work of chaplaincy care and the difference it makes to patient care outcomes (ACPE *et al.* 2018).

This book owes a debt of gratitude to Fitchett and Nolan, as well as chaplain colleagues in the Netherlands (Walton and Körver 2017), for promoting the use of the case study to advance the profession of chaplaincy and inspiring us to follow in their footsteps as well as blaze a new trail. We chose to focus on an area of chaplaincy often overlooked in describing what chaplains "do" (Damen *et al.* 2018). Chaplains are invited into controversial and ethical dilemmas in Catholic teachings about artificial nutrition, Pentecostal beliefs in faith healing and miracles, and Jewish law and teachings about fertility or pregnancy termination decisions. Proficient in Family Systems Theory and conflict mediation, chaplains are often called upon to clarify values and beliefs impacting treatment options, and to facilitate the direction of care conversations and issues related to goals of care. By slowing down the pace and creating safe sacred space, healthcare chaplains address underlying factors that impact—and sometimes impede—decision-making, such as emotions of guilt or fear, unresolved family dynamics, or misunderstanding of medical terminology. As our recently published study of the chaplain's role in medical decision-making attests, chaplains report high levels of involvement in this area in spite of barriers to their full integration (Wirpsa *et al.* 2019).

For this volume, we have chosen comprehensive cases instructive in demonstrating the role of the chaplain in assisting adult patients and families with serious or life-limiting illnesses in medical decision-making. Our studies are drawn from diverse settings and purposefully feature cases in which a variety of religious traditions and beliefs are major themes so that our interdisciplinary team colleagues, as well as interested readers, can experience chaplains' unique approaches and contributions.

Conversations with healthcare colleagues from other disciplines—begun here with the responses from a psychologist, Palliative Care physician, and family medicine resident—are another desired outcome of publishing this particular set of case studies. We know very little at present about how non-chaplains perceive our specific contributions to medical decision-making, where they would ask us *not* to tread in this process, and what value is added in their minds by fully integrating the chaplain into the process of shared decision-making. As models of interprofessional shared decision-making are developed and evaluated for their ability to promote patient-centered care, the perspective of each discipline as well as that of patients and families will need to be included.

Like previously published case studies in healthcare chaplaincy this volume does not purport to represent ideal chaplain care or even best practice. We are certain some of you reading these case studies will take umbrage with a chaplain's specific response to a situation or with the intervention selected out of the many possible ones available. Each of these chaplains themselves would make slightly different choices with the wisdom gained from seeing the whole picture and reflecting critically on their own biases, transference, or missed opportunities. One of the objectives of publishing case studies is to invite debate, dialogue, and conversation among chaplains, both novices and experienced practitioners.

We wish to express our gratitude to the nine chaplains who humbly and boldly share the details of the care they provide, as well as their analysis and critique of their work. Such transparency, and the willingness to receive the commentary offered by the respondents, provides a rich foundation for dialogue.

Origin and structure of this volume

In the process of designing a mixed-method study to document chaplains' perception of the extent to which and how they support medical decision-making with adult patients and their families facing serious or life-limiting illness, the research team ambitiously added case studies on that topic to our research protocol. When chaplains completed their online survey, they were offered the opportunity to be contacted if they were interested in (1) participating in a semi-structured follow-up interview and/or (2) contributing a case study for possible publication in a journal or book. Over 150 of the 700+ respondents indicated an interest in writing a case study. They were provided with guidelines for content and confidentiality concerns and asked to write an 800-word summary of their case. Twenty-five chaplains submitted a summary case for consideration and the team of reviewers chose nine. Selection criteria included clarity of writing, how well the case addressed the central themes of the book, and evidence of the ability to reflect critically on one's own work. Finally, we chose case studies to represent the diverse and multifaceted ways chaplains support the medical decision-making process.

The book is divided into three major sections. Each focuses on key contributions chaplains make to the medical decision-making process with patients and their families facing serious or life-limiting illness.

Part I, Story Matters: Patient as Person features three cases where the chaplain's focus on the patient narrative—personal, familial, religious, and illness narratives—informs and frames the goals of care, adjudicates the timing of medical decisions, and impacts the specific outcome of the medical decision faced. Chaplains Galchutt, Hogg, and Wirpsa offer cases involving long-term relationships with patients and their families, thus allowing us to see the shared story of patient, family, and chaplain unfold. Responses to these cases are offered by a professional healthcare chaplain with expertise in literary methods and a Palliative Care physician who uses poetry in her clinical practice with patients.

Part II, Emotions and Family Dynamics that Impact Medical Decision-Making includes three cases by Chaplains Goheen, Swofford, and Vilagos illustrating the impact of the chaplain's attention to emotions and family dynamics on the medical decision-making process. Whether feeling so overwhelmed as to be unable to process information or struggling with anger, guilt, or grief, patients and families benefit from a clinician trained to assist them in processing the affective aspect of the decision-making process. Patients rarely make decisions in isolation; their concerns for family members or the history of their relationships are factors that exert considerable influence on the direction of care they choose. Disagreements between family members who find themselves in the burdensome role of making life and death decisions for a loved one are also common and can have deleterious impacts on the health and well-being of those decision-makers, as is well-documented in the literature (Sharma *et al.* 2011; Sulmasy and Snyder 2010; White 2016). Chaplains in these cases attend to these complex relational and emotional dynamics as they support patients and families in the decision-making process. An experienced chaplain with a background in family systems and a healthcare psychologist reflect critically upon these cases.

Finally, **Part III, Negotiating Religious and Cultural Differences** features three cases by Chaplains Axelrud, Kirby, and Rosencrans. These cases uphold the conclusion made by Timmins *et al.* (2018, p.95) in their review of research documenting the role of the healthcare chaplain: "[These cases] demonstrate the sensitivity with which an experienced chaplain carefully negotiates within religious and cultural boundaries to support patients effectively." The boundaries negotiated in these cases include specific religious beliefs that conflict with medical recommendations, as well as spiritual explanations for illness that defy the rational, biomedical interpretative framework of the medical team. A Jewish healthcare chaplain with extensive experience negotiating boundary crossings and a family physician with a research background in religion and medicine engage the major themes raised in this section.

What do we know about the role of the chaplain in medical decision-making?

Prior to publication of our article, "Interprofessional models for shared decision making: The role of the health care chaplain" (Wirpsa *et al.* 2019), chaplain contributions to the medical decision-making process were acknowledged in disparate studies as valued and expected by patients and families, healthcare administrators, and chaplains themselves (Carey and Cohen 2008, 2010; Galek *et al.* 2007; Piderman *et al.* 2008). While the frequency of involvement was cited as relatively high in two separate studies (26% in Massey *et al.* 2015; 30% in Johnson *et al.* 2016), little was known about what this involvement actually entailed. Insight into both the specific ways chaplains support medical decision-making of adult patients and families facing serious or life-limiting illness and the approach and training that makes such support possible was gained through a survey of US chaplains. Activities foregrounded by our study included clarification of values, communication of patient preferences to the healthcare team, completion of advance directives, and pastoral blessing of religiously informed choices, among others. Barriers to the integration of the chaplain into interprofessional shared decision-making identified by participants in that study included staffing ratios, the biomedical focus of healthcare, and the narrowing of the chaplain role by other providers.

In a series of follow-up semi-structured interviews (Phase II of our research protocol; $n=14$), we gained additional insight into how chaplains perceived the complex team dynamics, professional training, and system-level factors that either promote or impede their ability to contribute meaningfully to medical decision-making. A purposeful sampling of chaplains was divided into two groups:

those with high levels of integration into medical decision-making and those with low levels of integration.

In a textual analysis informed by both content and linguistic methods (Frey, Botan and Kreps 1999), chaplains in the high integration group were noted to be proactive in their involvement, making themselves aware of family meetings and claiming their place at the table even if not directly invited. They sought out colleagues for curbside conversations when they had significant insights to offer. They were skilled at educating others about key aspects of their training that positioned them to contribute, and cited building relationships of trust over time and with key people such as the attending physician as key to their success. They used language endemic to the culture of medicine with frequency and familiarity; their examples demonstrated their position betwixt and between two cultures, rather than a position standing outside gazing onto a foreign world.

In contrast, the chaplains with self-reported low levels of integration into medical decision-making showed a striking lack of recognition of terminology outside of what might be called chaplain "code language" (de Vries, Berlinger and Cadge 2008; Lee, Curlin and Choi 2017). Specifically, they did not see themselves included in the domain of "medical decision-making." The terms "medical" and "medicine" were reserved for physicians, nurses, and others who practice medicine. This group demonstrated a notable inability to answer questions about medical decision-making as a result. Even when asked to focus directly on their contributions to decision-making or to provide concrete examples of how they supported this process, they talked about other aspects of chaplain care such as provision of prayer, making sure the patient was treated as a person, or using empathetic presence to resolve spiritual distress (not related to a medical decision per se). They indicated that involvement in medical decision-making was outside the scope of their responsibilities or belonged solely to the physician. Their lens was narrowly focused on the domains of care widely attributed to chaplains by others—meeting spiritual and religious needs and the provision of general emotional support to help patients and families cope with the impact of illness on their well-being.

At the end of the in-depth interviews, in response to the question "Is there anything else you'd like to offer?" several chaplains commented that merely by taking the original survey they found they were made aware of and now paid more attention to their role in medical decision-making. Others expressed feeling empowered to claim their role and be more assertive in what they had to offer. Still others advocated for additional training during residency and in the early years of professional employment.

Interprofessional Shared Decision-Making (IP-SDM)

Shared decision-making pairs patient values and preferences with the expertise of the medical provider. This approach to decision-making in healthcare has been recognized as key to the effective delivery of patient-centered care for over 20 years (Charles, Gafni and Whelan 1997). Originally conceived in terms of a dyad model between a primary physician and the patient, increased specialization in care with multiple providers has led to an emergence of models of shared decision-making that incorporate various disciplines and members of the healthcare team. Trained decision coaches or navigators are recommended; flexibility on who serves as the initiator of process of a decision is called for; and valuation for contributions of each discipline is cited as integral to the provision of whole person care in emerging models of IP-SDM (Dogba *et al.* 2016; Legare *et al.* 2011).

The majority of chaplains who responded to open-ended questions in our survey about barriers and those with whom we delved more deeply into team dynamics through the interview process named and affirmed the key elements that support interprofessional collaboration, though none used the term directly. If the following elements were present, the chaplain more easily claimed "a place at the table" in medical decision-making: shared vision of how decision-making occurs; mutual trust and respect; collaborative relationships; recognition that output is greater than the sum of input from each member; symmetry of power; consistent interactions among players over time; mutual understanding of roles; communication tools; and a supportive system or environment (D'Amour *et al.* 2005; Lewis *et al.* 2016).

When one or more of these elements were significantly lacking, a sense of frustration and powerlessness emerged in the responses of chaplains who participated in the study. Specifically, chaplains discussed heavy caseloads and coverage assignments as major impediments to full participation in IP-SDM. The lack of time to build relationships, lack of recognition of the importance of interdisciplinary collaboration, and non-synchronistic schedules of team members were raised as factors impeding their participation, a direct correlation with the key elements in the IP-SDM literature. Asymmetry of power—with control over communication and care claimed by the attending physician—was also cited as a significant barrier to IP-SDM by chaplains in our study.

Chaplains also noted mutual understanding and valuation of roles of each member of the team as key to integration, mirroring the importance of these concepts in the IP-SDM literature. Respondents consistently observed that other members of the healthcare team— with the exception of bedside nurses—do not understand or value the potential of chaplains to contribute meaningfully to the decision-making process. As summarized in previous work on this topic, chaplains in our study report that members of the healthcare team compartmentalize the role of the chaplain, view the chaplain as a pastor and not a medical clinician, and persist in "only calling the chaplain at the time of death, for patients who self-identify as religious, or for request for prayer or ritual" (Wirpsa *et al.* 2019, pp.14–15). Notably, even in an article written in 2018 advocating for interprofessional care and teamwork in the Intensive Care Unit (ICU) setting, the physician authors limit the contribution of the spiritual care provider to attending to spiritual and religious needs and providing "support," with no mention of chaplain role in values clarification or as a bridge to communication between the patient and family and medical team when critical decisions are faced (Donovan *et al.* 2018).

A consistent conclusion in the IP-SDM literature is the need for education to ensure the "mutual understanding of roles" requisite to interprofessional collaboration. While the literature suggests various pedagogical methods including didactics, interdisciplinary case presentations, and even shadowing, in our study chaplains place the onus of responsibility for teaching others about the full scope of chaplaincy practice on themselves. Chaplains with the highest level of integration into interdisciplinary team decision-making issue a strong call, if not a mandate: chaplains must take a proactive rather than passive stance for their contributions to be fully appreciated and incorporated into patient care. Chaplain administrators, in turn, must address the underlying system barriers that preclude chaplains from claiming their place as a full partner in decision-making.

Making our case for chaplains as partners in medical decision-making

Why use case studies, in addition to previously published research, to "make a case" for chaplain integration into the medical decision-making process of patients and families facing serious or life-limiting illness? First, case studies provide a process-oriented, thick description of chaplain involvement in medical decision-making without the level of abstraction found in research published to date. This enables insights into the relationship between therapeutic presence and specific activities or interventions, between the "who" and the "what" of chaplaincy care as it relates to medical decision-making. Second, the cases included in this volume represent chaplain involvement in medical decision-making in which barriers to their full integration into team processes and communication have been minimized, if not removed entirely. We witness the stance chaplains take toward other members of the medical team, how their authority is exercised and respected, and what enables them to promote interprofessional collaboration.

Finally, and perhaps most significantly, the impact of the chaplain in promoting patient-centered care may best be appreciated in this genre: in each case, we see how the chaplain was key to aligning the approach to decision-making or the specific outcome of decisions with patient values or frameworks. As one chaplain so eloquently put it, because "chaplains live in the balance between religion, culture, and medical best practices and are the skilled weavers who help make all these elements function together to bring about safe and effective *patient-centered decisions*" (Wirpsa *et al.* 2019, p.15; original emphasis). In its landmark report *Crossing the Quality Chasm*, the Institute of Medicine offers the following definition for patient-centered care: "respectful of and responsive to individual patient preferences, needs, and values...[and ensures] that patient values guide all clinical decisions" (2001, p.40). Patient-centered decisions start and end with the patient; patient-centered decisions are made by the patient or someone who knows and loves them; patient-centered decisions fully appreciate patient values formed through a unique life history and embedded in culture and relationships; patient-centered decisions account for the undercurrents of emotions at play; patient-centered decisions ask a team of expert clinicians to see the person they are treating, not just the disease (Institute of Medicine 2001, pp.48–51).

In contrast to this relational, holistic, considered, person-specific approach to medical decision-making, the process for patients who are seriously ill in our complex healthcare system increasingly resembles that of a speeding train. J. Kruser and her colleagues (2017) coin the term "clinical momentum" to describe this unrelenting, fast-paced process of medical care and decision-making that takes place throughout medicine, but that is seen especially in the intensive care setting. The system of critical care medicine seems to have a life or mind of its own; one small clinical decision drives the next clinical decision, and so on. Though seemingly insignificant in the larger course of events, Kruser contends that each clinical intervention—adjusting blood pressure medication, treating a new infection, adding another arterial line—drives care toward a goal that is no longer informed by a weighing of risks and benefits, consequences and alternatives (2017). Drawing upon a framework informed by behavioral economics, Kruser cites the "sunk cost effect" as another factor that drives the clinical momentum: once the family and medical team have invested a certain amount of energy, resources, emotions, and time into this course, stopping to re-evaluate if the plan aligns with patient goals becomes increasingly difficult. "We've come this far, we can't stop now" is the unspoken narrative that drives continued investment in care. The clinical momentum of critical care medicine may explain why anywhere between 25–50 percent of patients receive end-of-life care that is discordant with their previously expressed preferences (Kruser, Cox and Schwarze 2017).

Making our case for the involvement of the healthcare chaplain in this decision-making process is less about making a case for chaplaincy care or added value to the institution per se; it is more about making a case that chaplains have a unique role to play in promoting patient-centered care. Case studies, as a research genre, have the significant benefit of examining chaplain care as it relates to medical decision-making as a step-by-step process that unfolds in slow motion, allowing insight into the following questions: How do healthcare chaplains significantly challenge, impact, or alter the reigning model of decision-making in contemporary healthcare captured in the "speeding train" metaphor? Do healthcare chaplains interrupt the "clinical momentum" of an entire system or environment? Are healthcare chaplains positioned to promote decision-making that is truly patient-centered? These questions can only be answered if (1) chaplains are helping to define how medical decision-making is studied and (2) we know more about what difference their involvement in the decision-making process makes. The current volume of case studies is a starting place to answer these questions, not the final destination.

Case study research

In his 2018 address to the Joint Annual Conference of the Association of Professional Chaplains (APC) and the National Association of Catholic Chaplains (NACC), Steve Nolan argued that case studies provide rich and compelling data (Nolan 2018). Not only do they provide rich material to formulate more specific research questions in a similar way to other qualitative studies, he made an even bolder claim. Case studies challenge the false dichotomy between chaplaincy care as "presence" and chaplaincy care focused on outcomes. The verbatim account plus analysis by the chaplain that constitutes the case study form reveals chaplaincy care as a particular kind of therapeutic intervention. To apply Nolan's insight to our volume of cases: the relationship each chaplain establishes with patients, families, and other healthcare providers is the intervention that promotes patient-centered medical decision-making. These case studies provide insight into three significant ways chaplains promote patient-centered decision-making: by ensuring who the patient is as a person drives the timing and outcome of medical decision-making; by acknowledging patients and families as affective and relational beings and not just disembodied minds that make decisions; and by locating patients, families, and clinicians within cultures that frame, sometimes consciously and more often unconsciously, what is taken into account in the decision-making process. Again, as Nolan has so persuasively and insightfully argued, it is the relational skill, empathy, healing presence, and "professional person" of the chaplain in each case that grounds a specific "activity" or aspect of supporting medical decision-making (Nolan 2018).

Do these cases provide "evidence" that a chaplain's involvement ensures medical decisions align with patient values? Do these cases support the claim that the chaplain's involvement in end-of-life care leads to less aggressive, life-prolonging interventions or a shorter length of stay? Do these cases demonstrate the chaplain's impact on lessening moral distress and burnout of healthcare providers? What do these cases reveal about elements that promote interdisciplinary collaboration? As you read these cases and the responses by our chaplain and non-chaplain colleagues, consider not only how case studies provide rich data, but also what counts as "evidence" in our profession and in academic medicine as a whole. Finally, consider what kinds of research questions these case studies raise that might be tested through experimental methods more widely recognized and accepted by our academic medical colleagues. In so doing, chaplaincy as a profession can help shape the research questions that are asked (or not asked) in this area even as we claim a place at the table of shared decision-making.

References

ACPE: The Standard for Spiritual Care & Education, Association of Professional Chaplains, Canadian Association for Spiritual Care/Association canadienne de soins spirituels, National Association of Catholic Chaplains and Neshama: Association of Jewish Chaplains (2018) *The Impact of Professional Spiritual Care*. A joint publication. Available at www.spirit-filled.org/documents/APC18_Report.pdf

Cadge, W. (2012) *Paging God: Religion in the Halls of Medicine*. Chicago, IL: University of Chicago Press.

Carey, L.B. and Cohen, J. (2008) 'Religion, spiritualty and healthcare treatment decisions: The role of chaplains in the Australian clinical context.' *Journal of Health Care Chaplaincy 15*, 1, 25–39.

Carey, L.B. and Cohen, J. (2010) 'Health care chaplains and their role on institutional ethics committees: An Australian Study.' *Journal of Religion and Health 49*, 2, 221–232.

Charles, C., Gafni, A. and Whelan, T. (1997) 'Shared decision-making in the medical encounter: What does it mean? (or it takes at least two to tango).' *Social Science & Medicine 44*, 5, 681–692.

Damen, A., Labuschagne, D., Fosler, L., O'Mahony, S., Levine, S. and Fitchett, G. (2018) 'What do chaplains do: The views of palliative care physicians, nurses, and social workers.' *American Journal of Hospice and Palliative Medicine*, Available at https://journals.sagepub.com/doi/abs/10.1177/1049909118807123# Doi:10.1177/1049909118807123

D'Amour, D., Ferrada-Videla, M., San Martin Rodriguez, L, and Beaulieu, M.D. (2005) 'The conceptual basis for interprofessional collaboration: Core concepts and theoretical frameworks.' *Journal of Interprofessional Care 19*, Suppl. 1, 116–131.

de Vries, R., Berlinger, N. and Cadge, W. (2008) 'Lost in translation: The chaplain's role in health care.' *Hastings Center Report 38*, 6, 23–27.

Dogba, M.J., Menear, M., Stacey, D., Briere, N. and Legare, F. (2016) 'The evolution of an interprofessional shared decision-making research program: Reflective case study of an emerging paradigm.' *International Journal of Integrated Care 16*, 3, 4.

Donovan, A.L., Aldrich, J.M., Gross, A.K., Barchas, D.M., Thornton, K.C., *et al.* (2018) 'Interprofessional care and teamwork in the ICU.' *Critical Care Medicine 46*, 6, 980–990.

Fitchett, G. and Nolan, S. (eds) (2015) *Spiritual Care in Practice: Case Studies in Healthcare Chaplaincy.* London: Jessica Kingsley Publishers.

Fitchett, G. and Nolan, S. (eds) (2018) *Case Studies in Spiritual Care: Healthcare Chaplaincy Assessments, Interventions and Outcomes.* London: Jessica Kingsley Publishers.

Frey, L., Botan, C. and Kreps, G. (1999) *Investigating Communication: An Introduction to Research Methods*, 2nd edition. Boston, MA: Allyn & Bacon.

Galek, K., Flannelly, K.J., Koenig, H.G. and Fogg, S.L. (2007) 'Referrals to chaplains: The role of religion and spirituality in healthcare settings.' *Mental Health, Religion & Culture 10*, 4, 363–377.

Institute of Medicine (2001) *Crossing the Quality Chasm: A New Health System for the 21st Century.* Washington, DC: The National Academies Press.

Johnson, R., Wirpsa, M.J., Boyken, L., Sakumoto, M., *et al.* (2016) 'Communicating chaplains' care: Narrative documentation in a neuroscience-spine Intensive Care Unit.' *Journal of Health Care Chaplaincy 22*, 4, 133–150.

Kruser, J.M., Cox, C.E. and Schwarze, M.L. (2017) 'Clinical momentum in the Intensive Care Unit. A latent contributor to unwanted care.' *Annals of the American Thoracic Society 14*, 3, 426–431.

Lee, B.M., Curlin, F. and Choi, P. (2017) 'Documenting presence: A descriptive study of chaplain notes in the intensive care unit.' *Palliative and Supportive Care 15*, 2, 190–196.

Legare, F., Stacey, D., Pouliot, S., Gauvin, F.P., *et al.* (2011) 'Interprofessionalism and shared decision-making in primary care: A stepwise approach towards a new model.' *Journal of Interprofessional Care 25*, 1, 18–25.

Lewis, K.B., Stacey, D., Squires, J.E. and Carroll, S. (2016) 'Shared decision-making models acknowledging an interprofessional approach: A theory analysis to inform nursing practice.' *Research and Theory for Nursing Practice 30*, 1, 26–43.

Massey, K., Barnes, M.J., Villines, D., Goldstein, J.D., *et al.* (2015) 'What do I do? Developing a taxonomy of chaplaincy activities and interventions for spiritual care in intensive care unit palliative care.' *BMC Palliative Care 14*, 10. doi:10.1186/s12904-015-0008-0.

Nolan, S. (2018) 'Lifting the lid on chaplaincy: A first look at findings from chaplains' case study research.' *Journal of Health Care Chaplaincy.* doi:10.1080/08854726.2019.1603916.

Piderman, K.M., Marek, D.V., Jenkins, S.M., Johnson, M.E., Buryska, J.F. and Mueller, P.S. (2008) 'Patients' expectations of hospital chaplains.' *Mayo Clinic Proceedings 83*, 1, 58–65.

Sharma, R.K., Hughes, M.T., Nolan, M.T., Tudor, C. *et al.* (2011) 'Family understanding of seriously-ill patient preferences for family involvement in healthcare decision making.' *Journal of General Internal Medicine 26*, 8, 881–886.

Sulmasy, D.P. and Snyder, L. (2010) 'Substituted interests and best judgments: An integrated model of surrogate decision making.' *JAMA 304*, 17, 1946–1947.

Timmins, F., Caldeira, S., Murphy, M., Pujol, N., *et al.* (2018) 'The role of the healthcare chaplain: A literature review.' *Journal of Health Care Chaplaincy 24*, 3, 87–106.

Walton, M. and Körver, J. (2017) 'Dutch case studies project in chaplaincy care: A description and theoretical explanation of the format and procedures.' *Health and Social Care Chaplaincy 5*, 2, 257–280.

White, D.B. (2016) 'Strategies to support surrogate decision makers of patients with chronic critical illness: The search continues.' *JAMA 316*, 1, 35–37.

Wirpsa, J.M., Johnson, R., Bieler, J., Boyken, L., *et al.* (2019) 'Interprofessional models for shared decision making: The role of the health care chaplain.' *Journal of Health Care Chaplaincy 25*, 1, 20–44.

PART I

STORY MATTERS: PATIENT AS PERSON

KAREN PUGLIESE

ALTHOUGH among the most ancient of art forms, a contemporary understanding of the craft of story-telling and story-receiving has emerged as a core competency for professional healthcare chaplains. Chaplains understand patients' narratives as both a reflection and symbol of their human experiences. When integrated into a medical team, chaplains can facilitate insightful perspectives vital to deepening therapeutic relationships and promoting value-concordant care.

Advanced theological degrees and the clinical pastoral education (CPE) process prepare chaplains to address medical decision-making and skillfully bridge the divide between the medical team, patient and family. Board certification in chaplaincy requires expertise in religious, ethical, and cultural frameworks as well as clinical pastoral approaches and processes to compassionately and therapeutically attend to patients' stories. Honoring the stories people share demands rigorous attempts to accurately capture their meaning (Brown 2010). Respect for how medical decisions are made, and who makes them, requires patience and an authentic acceptance of ambiguity in the process. As experienced communicators, chaplains serve as liaisons to the healthcare team who, for the most part, are unprepared to professionally address the complexity of patient and family understandings and responses to suffering, or have little time or capacity to interpret the values and hidden meanings in patient narratives.

Partly in response to these barriers, Narrative Theorist Rita Charon (2006, p.12) provided a framework for physicians to understand "truth" from an existential point of view: "It is as if the heads of the teller and the listener are bowed over the suffering that happened in the attempt to interpret and understand it." Although each field of study defines and adapts narrative knowledge uniquely, narrative craftsmanship is "a magnet and a bridge, attracting and uniting diverse fields of human learning" (Charon 2006, p.11).

Highly praised as a pioneer in theological education and training, Anton T. Boisen believed that a direct study of theology through encounters in human experience was a necessary supplement to academic training (Asquith 1982; see also ACPE nd). At the time, theology students were not utilizing scientific methodologies. In 1944, Boisen wrote that his new approach to empirical theological inquiry was to begin with the study of *living human documents*. In developing the case study method as a *written* human document for systematically reflecting on the human condition, both psychologically and theologically, Boisen's work is one of the precursors to today's practice of Narrative Theology. Boisen founded the CPE movement and started the first CPE program in 1925. CPE programs continue to use verbatims, case studies, spiritual and theological reflection, and students' own stories as tools for developing proficiency in unearthing the values embedded in a storyline.[1]

In theological circles today, there is intensified interest in making sense of life through the art of story-telling. The discipline of chaplaincy benefits from the seminal work of theologian and theological ethicist H. Richard Niebuhr, credited as providing the conceptual groundwork for Narrative Theology. Philosopher Steven Crites and theologian John Shea posited that human life is rooted in myth, metaphor, and ritual, inevitably creating stories that, when reflected upon and interpreted, promote coherence and meaning-making (Crites 1971; Shea 1978).

French philosopher Paul Ricoeur (1984) asserted that the study of ethics first turned to narrative more than 24 centuries ago when Aristotle wrote in his *Poetics* that every story told well teaches something. The chapter "Deliver Us from Certainty," in *The Principles and Practice of Narrative Medicine* (Charon *et al.* 2016), describes the emergence of a deepening relationship between Narrative Medicine and Narrative Ethics. In a recent article, Hille Haker (2009) contends

---

1   See www.acpe.edu

that healthcare chaplains are uniquely positioned to link the two. The *Common Qualifications and Competencies for Professional Chaplains* include the ability to "incorporate a working knowledge of ethics appropriate to the pastoral context" (BCCI 2017, ITP6, Integration of Theory and Practice Competencies) and "support, promote, and encourage ethical decision-making and care" (BCCI 2017, QL4, Organizational Leadership Competencies). These skills are essential in embracing the ambiguity and inconsistencies inherent to complex decision-making, and using narrative to manage conflicting principles and beliefs. Collective narration can help to hold competing values in creative tension until ultimately unifying patients and families by linking stories of the past to present and future possibilities.

Chaplain Galchutt characterizes Keith's "well told" narration of his experiences of illness as often focusing on what he was "learning" about himself. During his first chemotherapy infusion treatment after deciding to pursue a clinical trial, Keith states: "I just want to learn from this experience." As Galchutt and Keith engage in Mutually Expressive Writing together, Keith gains greater insight into his disease process and learns more about "what mattered to him." Each time Keith engages in narrating and writing his experience, he "found language to lift to consciousness and name his increasing awareness and integrate it into his treatment decisions."

Certified chaplains must "formulate and utilize spiritual assessments in order to contribute to plans of care" (BCCI 2017, PPS10, Professional Practice Skills Competencies) and "Document one's contribution of care effectively in the appropriate records" (BCCI 2017, PPS11, Professional Practice Skills Competencies). Galchutt develops a Scope of Practice template to "create an interpretive narrative of the patient's illness understanding and sense of future while describing the moment in time in which the chaplain was a character in the patient's story." Thus, Galchutt creates an "interpretive narrative" to facilitate the healthcare team's understanding of his interventions and perspectives, and to communicate Keith's illness-understanding and sense of future.

Chaplain Hogg's three-month journey with Glen focuses on the patient as a "self-reflective man whose faith was his foundation" and whose "reflective spirit informed our conversations as he shared his story, values, and what really mattered to him, which impacted his medical decision-making process." Glen, however, believes that he could help others through illness by sharing his own learning. Throughout his mutually meaningful relationship with Hogg, *storying* is essential to Glen's making sense of and communicating the meaning of his life.

During a care conference, Hogg intervenes as physicians address goals for Glen's care to empower and safeguard both Glen and his wife's ability to give voice to the values underlying their wishes for his treatment. Story-telling, Hannah Arendt (quoted in Jackson 2002, p.36) maintains, transforms personal meaning to communal meaning, and Hogg deftly facilitates a transformational moment. Glen's life is, as Ricoeur suggests, "an activity and a passion in search of a narrative" and ultimately, Glen's search and mission are accomplished (Ricoeur, "Life in Quest of Narrative," p.29, quoted in Irvine and Charon 2017, p.110).

As Anne Windholz notes in her response to "Bob's case," Chaplain Wirpsa "highlights the importance of character analysis for chaplains as they assess and choose interventions that will empower patients facing painful decisions." Windholz further notes, "to do this effectively, the skilled chaplain perceives constituent and recurring indications of a person's character." Wirpsa's narration of her role in assisting Bob and his family in making challenging medical decisions illustrates the ways in which chaplains' insightful assessments of character enable value-concordant care planning and meaningfully effective interventions. In suggesting to Bob that visiting patients with similar diagnoses might motivate and inspire them, Wirpsa demonstrates the benefit of intentional value-concordant ministry. She extends that strategy in ministry to Bob's family and ultimately to Bob himself. Wirpsa tells us that her role "was consistently reflecting back to Bob the way he was growing and engaging him in deeper thought regarding questions of value, purpose, self-image, and identity" and this, in turn, impacted the value-based decisions he made for himself and for his family.

Patient-centered care is defined by the Institute of Medicine (2001, p.4) as "Providing care that is respectful of, and responsive to, individual patient preferences, needs and values, and ensuring that patient values guide all clinical decisions." Value concordance, then, would appear to be synonymous with patient-centered care, and anchored in the conviction that medical decisions agreed upon between healthcare providers and those in their care should, ideally, be a therapeutic alliance between equals. However, even when patients and families feel heard by healthcare providers, they often weigh the benefits and risks of treatment differently than the importance assigned by physicians and clinicians.

In these three cases, each chaplain assists in aligning the medical plan with patient values through their creative and sensitive attention to the patient's story. However, the process is neither static nor unidimensional. None of these patients enters into the decision-making process with a clearly delineated healthcare preference documented, as some might wish, in an advance directive. Hogg's patient Glen is arguably the clearest about his goal—to complete his "mission"—and the chaplain ensures the timing of moving toward comfort care coincides with this goal. As described by Galchutt, Keith engages in a process of "discerning" what matters to him in the context of his life-threatening illness. As his illness advances and begins to take a toll on his quality of life, he is able to draw upon the insights gained through writing about his experience to better articulate what really matters to him. In Wirpsa's case, Bob and his family wrestle with competing values—his independence and dignity versus the value of family and his identity as their protector. It is over time and with painful attention to Bob's multiple storylines that the chaplain ensures that specific medical decisions are patient-centered.

These cases suggest that "value concordance" in medical decision-making occurs on multiple levels: with a patient's well-defined goal; with a patient's individual decision-making process, both relationally and culturally; and with the timing of decision-making. Each of these cases illustrates that chaplains are tasked not merely with the identification of patient goals embedded within an already written life narrative; chaplains are also skilled diagnosticians and facilitators in the alteration, adaptation, and clarification of patient values and goals, an ambiguous, non-linear process, to say the least. Chaplains form therapeutic relationships and enter the patient and family narrative at life-threatening junctures, skillfully respecting the role of decision-makers as well as the process by which decisions are made. In addition, advocating for value concordance while patiently holding competing values in creative tension, and bringing closure through meaningful ritual, characterizes the essential role Galchutt, Hogg, and Wirpsa play on their medical teams.

References

ACPE (Association for Clinical Pastoral Education, Inc.) (no date) 'The Biography of Anton Theophilus Boisen.' Available at www.acpe.edu/pdf/History/The%20 Biography%20of%20Anton%20Theophilus%20Boisen.pdf

Asquith, G. (1982) 'Anton T. Boisen and the Study of "Living Human Documents."' *Journal of Presbyterian History (1962–1988) 60*, 3, 244–265.

BCCI (Board of Chaplaincy Certification, Inc.) (2017) *Common Qualifications and Competencies for Professional Chaplains.* Available at www.professionalchaplains. org/files/2017%20Common%20Qualifications%20and%20Competencies%20 for%20Professional%20Chaplains.pdf

Brown, B. (2010) *The Gifts of Imperfection: Let Go of Who You Think You're Supposed To Be.* Center City, MN: Hazelden.

Charon, R. (2006) *Narrative Medicine: Honoring the Stories of Illness.* Oxford: Oxford University Press.

Charon, R., DasGupta, S., Hermann, N., Marcus E.R. and Spiegel, M. (2016) *The Principles and Practice of Narrative Medicine.* Oxford: Oxford University Press.

Crites, S. (1971) 'The narrative quality of experience.' *Journal of the American Academy of Religion 39*, 3, 219–311.

Haker, H. (2009) 'Narrative Ethics in Health Care Chaplaincy.' Medical Ethics in Health Care Chaplaincy. Münster: LITVerlag, 143–174.

Institute of Medicine (2001) *Crossing the Quality Chasm: A New Health System for the 21st Century.* Washington, DC: The National Academies Press.

Irvine, C. and Charon, R. (2017) 'Deliver Us from Certainty: Training for Narrative Ethics.' In R. Charon, S. Dasgupta, N. Hermann, C. Irvine, *et al.* (eds) *The Principles and Practice of Narrative Medicine* (Chapter 5). Oxford: Oxford University Press.

Jackson, M. (2002) *The Politics of Storytelling: Violence, Transgression and Intersubjectivity.* Copenhagen: Museum Tusculanum Press.

Ricoeur, P. (1984) *Time and Narrative.* Chicago, IL: University of Chicago Press.

Shea, J. (1978) *Stories of God: An Unauthorized Biography.* Chicago, IL: Thomas Moore Press.

Chapter 1

KEITH'S STORY

"It was an easy choice. I'm not ready to die"—Keith, a
59-year-old living with Stage IV bladder cancer

PAUL GALCHUTT

Introduction

I met Keith on the first day of his outpatient chemotherapy. His nurse referred him because he had shared with her that his Christian faith was a significant source of coping. I was privileged to know Keith for a period of nine months. He identified as African American, a husband, and a father of two young adult children. I never met Keith's family, as his children lived out of state and his wife was working when he came in for his appointments. He was a former corporate executive and an entrepreneur. At the time of his diagnosis and throughout his treatment he held a position as a director with a local non-profit organization. He was also a former college and professional football player. Being a "grill master" was also among his many accomplishments.

I identify as male, white, middle-aged, a husband, father, and a Lutheran (Evangelical Lutheran Church in America) pastor. I have been a healthcare chaplain for over 14 years, 10 of which I served as the chaplain on an inpatient Palliative Consult service. I have worked in the outpatient clinic setting for approximately three years.

Much of my work as an outpatient healthcare chaplain occurs within an advanced cancer infusion clinic that is part of an academic healthcare system located in the Midwest region of the US. Many of the people I've come to know in this position are enrolled in a clinical trial, and it is in this treatment trajectory that Keith and I met. Prior to our meeting, Keith had an extensive oncologic surgery, and it was during his recovery that his community-based oncologist had recommended the clinical trial. Keith knew his only other option was to palliate his symptoms and possibly enroll in a hospice. Keith's decision to pursue the trial was based upon the hope he might yet be cured.

I met with Keith 10 times. The location of our visits—in the outpatient rather than inpatient setting—supported this establishment and lengthening of our relationship. I experienced him to be ever-reflective, working on his self-awareness about what his scans, tumor markers, symptoms, and prognosis meant for his sense of future. In addition, he was in touch with his emotions regarding the impact of treatment on his body and life. When narrating stories about his illness experience, he would often talk about what he was "learning" about himself. He possessed a keen ability to focus on his present awareness. Keith stayed rooted in those aspects of his self that had formed him up until that moment, while simultaneously maintaining a vision toward the future.

From our first handshake to his last breath, I cherished knowing Keith. I grieved his physical decline and mourned his death. Per his family's wish, and with their permission, I have not disguised his identity or any facts about his illness and treatment. The dialogue in this text is from my recollection of our conversations over time.

Case

Throughout the following case study, I reflect on how healthcare chaplaincy helped Keith with medical decision-making. I used two different means of supporting his decision-making, both of which are premised on a belief that "as narrative is constructed, narrative constructs" (Mattingly and Garro 2000, p.16). First, medical decision-making emerged through the conversations we shared and the stories Keith told in response to my wondering about his understanding of his future and what it meant for him. The other way his decision-making emerged was through an intervention called Mutual Expressive Writing. This intervention is a good fit for chaplains, as it requires a vocation wired for narrative, exploration of meaning, and our interpersonal caregiving skills. It also requires time—a minimum of 20 minutes—within a patient care encounter.

My initial encounter with Keith lasted approximately 45 minutes. A small portion of our conversation is recreated below.

Initial encounter: first day of chemotherapy infusion

Keith: "I've had a rough go of it lately. With my diagnosis of bladder cancer, then surgery and then recovery from that...it was harder than I thought it was going to be. After my surgery recovery, I met with my community oncologist. He told me there was nothing he could do for me. What he really said is that I had two choices—I could either come here to pursue being a part of this trial, which I'm starting today, or I could prepare to die. It was an easy choice. I'm not ready to die."

Chaplain: "Though the choice was 'easy,' was it hard to be forced into choices?"

Keith: "The surgery and the waiting to be enrolled in this trial has been hard. The decision to pursue the trial wasn't."

Chaplain: "You mentioned the waiting was hard..."

Keith: "Yeah, each day I wasn't here getting chemotherapy, the cancer has been growing. That concerns me, but now that I'm here starting this [pointing to the infusion bag], my mind is more at ease. I have a sense of peace."

Chaplain: "Speaking of peace, your nurse mentioned that you had said your Christian faith is pretty significant for you while you go through this."

Keith: "I couldn't be doing this without God."

Chaplain: "Over the years, I've been amazed with the variability of how people of faith talk about and understand how God is present and active in their lives while living with some tough illnesses."

Keith: "When this all started, I used to ask God, 'Why me? Why now?' That was difficult. The story of Job has been a comfort to me. I figure if Job went through it, I can go through this too. I just want to learn from this experience."

The intertwining of these themes of Christian faith as a source of coping and Keith's evolving perspective on his future would recur throughout our time together.

When I first meet patients, I delineate ways I might be of service to them, including chaplaincy interventions of reflective conversation and story listening (Galchutt 2016). I speak of being able to offer non-pharmacological, integrative interventions such as meditation, energy work, and contemplative prayer. Keith enthusiastically accepted my invitation to join me in one of these interventions, called Mutual Expressive Writing.

Mutual Expressive Writing is a practice based on and adapted from the Amherst Writers & Artists (AWA) method developed by Pat Schneider (2003). Central to this writing method is the belief that every person is a writer with a unique voice. The Mutual Expressive Writing process involves reading a pre-selected prompt twice, writing for five minutes, and if comfortable, reading what was written aloud. Essential to facilitating this are three mandates I follow closely. First, true to the AWA method, I only affirm what I find meaningful, powerful, and memorable. Second, I hold fast to the promise that I am not an editor and I will not critique any writing. Third, I mutually write. In other words, instead of looking at patients as they write, I write alongside them. Most people want to hear what I've written as well, but this is not universal. For patients with advanced cancer, this intervention is particularly helpful, as it allows them to hold the tension between giving voice to the deleterious and disruptive aspects of serious illness while at the same time, giving them a means to attribute meaning and coherence to an experience that defies both (Conway 2013).

Keith and I wrote together on three separate occasions over the course of our nine months of knowing one another. Following each session, Keith wept. He possessed an immense capacity to be fiercely present and vulnerably transparent to his current understanding of what his life, his treatments, his emotions, and his future meant to him. This writing experience offered an intentional portal for Keith to name his experience and process the medical decisions he faced.

Below I offer a brief reconstructed dialogue following the first time we wrote together.

Second encounter: writing together, recreating and making sense

Keith: "[Crying] That was amazing. I can't believe how filled I was with thoughts and memories of how much I wanted to write."

Chaplain: "Your emotions…?"

Keith: "Yes [laughing and crying]. I can be a pretty emotional guy. This writing surfaces stuff and thoughts I didn't anticipate having before you read that poem [the prompt]."

Chaplain: "Perhaps an understatement, but I'm guessing you liked it."

Keith: "Liked it? Loved it! When are we going to do this again? This was great."

Chaplain: "Yes, I'd love to do this again sometime soon. For now, would you be willing to read what you wrote? I, too, as I mentioned before, am happy to read what I wrote as well."

Keith yielded to intermittent tears as he read. He then stood back and commented on how meaningful it was to him to have a concrete expression of his experience in the form of creatively written words. He expressed how remarkable it was that this moment and this creation had not existed prior to our encounter. I observed how the experience of writing with one another deepened the caregiving relationship and further solidified our trust.

Shortly after having engaged in two longer chaplaincy care encounters with Keith, I received a corporate email from my healthcare system's director of advance care planning. It was addressed to everyone trained to facilitate healthcare directives (HCDs). The purpose of her email was twofold: first, to inform us that a local television station was planning on doing a series of stories concerning the importance of advance care planning amid medical decision-making; and second, to ask if we had a patient who might consider being interviewed about their advance care planning experience. Keith came to mind in part because I believed the focus on writing HCDs would complement the writing he was already doing.

When I approached Keith with this request, he said he was hesitant to participate because he had not created an HCD. He made himself available, however, citing his hope that he might motivate others to engage in conversations with loved ones about their wishes and put into writing their end-of-life preferences. Keith reflected that completing an HCD meant more than making some jottings in a document. He confessed that he had not yet created his own HCD out of fear that by putting words on paper in this format, he was acknowledging that he was dying and "wasn't going to make it." Once he faced this fear, Keith was free to clearly articulate what he would want should he be unable to make his own medical decisions in the future. His advance care planning process and reflections on facing his own mortality aired on television. What follows is part of the conversation we had about that experience and the responses of his friends and family to that segment.

Third encounter: approximately halfway through the chemotherapy regimen

Keith: "I got a bunch of calls and emails from my family, friends, and co-workers about the television segment. Many of them I hadn't talked to in years. A lot of these people didn't even know I was sick and most assumed I was dying."

Chaplain: "What was that like?"

Keith: "It was horrible in some ways. Beautiful in other ways. I mean, it was pretty amazing to know that all these people love me and that I have made a difference in their lives. But, it was weird to talk to many of them when they initially thought I was dying. What I usually brought our conversations back to was the reason I consented to being interviewed."

Chaplain: "Advance care planning and those conversations?"

Keith: "Yes. So, I had those conversations, and went on to tell them to complete those documents and have their own conversations with family. I also told them I was not dying, that I was still doing treatments and that I planned to be around for a while. My prognosis is pretty good."

I continued to see Keith with some regularity for approximately two more months as he completed his scheduled chemotherapy infusion regimen as stipulated by the clinical trial. He continued to speak about the possibility of his treatment leading to a potential cure. Following the trial, he experienced some short-lived gains with the shrinking of his tumors and the lessening of his symptom burden.

We also shared in a ritual of treatment completion on the day of his last infusion. The ritual purposefully utilizes language for recognizing the disruption to life with the arrival of an advanced cancer diagnosis, the initiation of treatment(s), and the days and associated anxiety (often referred to as "scanxiety") of coming to clinic with lab work, diagnostic scans, and appointments. The ritual culminates in a transitional point of hope—that the cancer will either go away, shrink, stay the same the size, or at least not recur.

It was several weeks before I would see Keith again. When I was walking through the large cancer center waiting area looking for someone else, I peripherally noticed Keith.

Last encounter: "I don't think it is in me to do more chemo"

Keith informed me that he was undergoing radiation therapy and was there for a follow-up appointment with his physician. Though dressed for work, Keith was visibly more worn-down than in any previous encounters. The usual light in his eyes was dimmer. They conveyed a lurking uncertainty awaiting him, the abyss he had hoped to avoid. He paused. Breathed. He began...

Keith: "The cancer is now on my spine. They also said that I've now got lesions on my liver. If that weren't enough, I've been dizzy lately. They're afraid. I'm afraid that I've got brain mets too."

Chaplain: "That's really difficult to hear."

Keith: "Yes, after my last infusion appointment, I was physically feeling the best I'd felt in months since beginning the infusions. I was back to working my full schedule and taking back most of the duties I had to give away. Then my symptoms, especially the physical pain, started coming back, and they started me on radiation. [Pause] It doesn't look good."

Chaplain: "This is devastating news. [Pause] I'm guessing this puts a different light on everything in your life right now. What's your oncology team, the doctor, saying about next steps?"

Keith: "They're talking about doing more chemo. [Pause] But, I don't think it is in me to do more chemo. I've got my son's wedding in a few weeks. I've got to do whatever I can to be out there for it."

Chaplain: "Yeah, absolutely. [Pause] When we've talked in the past, I know you've talked about paying attention to your emotions. What are you sensing, perceiving through all this?"

Keith: "That's exactly what I've been doing. I'm paying attention and everything about me doesn't want to do chemo. [Pause] If it is my time to die, I'm ready for that. If it isn't, I want to keep on living. I've just got to take it day by day."

The shifting of Keith's perspective from "I'm not ready to die" to "If it is my time..." was a weighty shift, made possible in part by our ongoing writing about his illness experience. For example, he reflected on the trauma of receiving care in the Emergency Department. He recounted, "I didn't know where I was. I was so disoriented. It was horrible." Keith was not offered additional chemotherapy and did not seek a second opinion, but, as I was later to learn, did finish his course of radiation.

A few weeks after our conversation, I was reviewing charts and examining the list of people I regularly see. Instead of Keith's age being listed by his name on the census, the word "Deceased" appeared. In reading "Deceased," I could see nothing else on the page. It felt enlarged and bolded as it struck me with a knock-you-off-the-chair strength. I was stunned.

The clinical story was that Keith had once again returned to the Emergency Department for care. This time it was determined that due to Keith's deteriorating functional status, he should be admitted. I was on vacation during this brief acute care hospitalization. The discharge note, the story of what happened, provided me a strange sense of comfort as it gave me the final chapter of the story of Keith's life. I was comforted as well because the discharge note quoted Keith as stating, "It is time" to transition to hospice, and "I want to be comfortable." Reading the discharge note triggered rich memories: Keith talking about something sublime after we wrote with one another or discussing his sense of faith about God's care for him throughout his cancer trajectory. I pictured his face; his voice and laughter returned un-beckoned. My recall was made possible only because of my good fortune of having become part of Keith's story.

Analysis

Keith welcomed me as a character into his evolving story in which he remained the author. Atul Gawande writes, "All we ask is to be allowed to remain the writers of our own story. This story..." (Keith's story) was "...ever changing" (2014, p.109). His story changed because his emplotted (Ricoeur 2008) future changed during the final nine months of his life. Not uncommon for people living with advanced cancer, Keith's death awareness increased in an inverse relationship to his physical condition; as his condition worsened, he was able to consider the possibility he might die. His sense of future and decisions related to it vacillated based on what his oncology team was telling him mingled with what he imagined or desired to be possible. Most of us, frankly, "...need to tell ourselves whatever is necessary" (Strauss 2010, p.122) to cope with an unbidden and unwelcome uncertainty we are barreling toward, knowing there is no detour, brake, or way to stop. Through our conversations and writing sessions, Keith found language to lift to consciousness and name his increasing awareness and integrate it into his treatment decisions.

When chaplains pull up the chair and sit opposite those in our care, stories emerge (Cassell 2004). Patient stories emerge when chaplains engage in reflective conversations. Philosopher Alasdair MacIntyre writes of conversations and human actions as "enacted narratives" (2007, p.211). The interventions of reflective conversations and story listening need to be viewed as the active, and not passive, processing of a patient's narrative.

Mutual Expressive Writing is a spiritual intervention that is, by design, active. Psychologist and Episcopal priest, James W. Jones, wrote, "...understanding requires doing. And understanding something new requires doing something new. A deeper spirituality requires a deeper spiritual practice" (2003, p.1). As noted above, Mutual Expressive Writing was a new spiritual practice for Keith; it afforded him insight into his illness and what mattered to him and became the form his medical decision-making embodied.

What a patient reads from what they wrote can never be predicted. It is neither objective nor linear. Neither is decision-making. The often recursive and vacillating experience of decision-making can be assisted with a safe, creative environment to foster the emotional and meaning-based components of decision-making. Mutual Expressive Writing is neither life review nor legacy work, per se. The primary goal is to provide a present moment creation of one's self. Arthur Frank explains: "People remember by telling stories of times past, but they tell in response to the needs of the reassembly at the time when the story is told" (2013, p.84).

Much of the work of healthcare chaplaincy involves caring for people facing serious or life-threatening illness. Chaplaincy care in this context is a constant stream of decision-making about treatments, appointments, and next steps, both those feared and welcomed. In the act of listening to and reflecting back their stories, we assist patients in the creation of their decision-making narratives—past, present, and future. These stories, like any story, are "...the source of all values" (Frank 2010, p.69). Paying specific attention to values embedded in life stories and to the specific story (or stories) of the future elicits goals of care.

Given the centrality of narrative and narrative methods to chaplaincy care, it makes sense that chaplains employ narrative methods to document their care, unlike most other disciplines in healthcare (with the exception of Palliative Care and Psychiatry). To capture a person's understanding of their illness and its impact on their coping and spirituality, I utilize a Scope of Practice template I designed drawing upon other recognized spiritual care approaches to documentation (Galchutt 2013, 2016). It contains the following sections: Illness Circumstances/Understanding, Religious/Spiritual Coping, and Goals of Care. I find it useful for representing to interdisciplinary partners the interventions and perspective chaplains bring to care. The intent is to create an interpretive (Lee, Curlin and Choi 2017) narrative of the patient's illness-understanding and sense of future while describing the moment in time in which the chaplain was a character in the patient's story.

Conclusion

Being able to accompany, absorb, bear witness, and attend to patients and their stories will always be at the heart of healthcare chaplaincy. Whether through conversation, story listening, or the innovative method of Mutually Expressive Writing, chaplains are positioned to hear a patient's values, meaning of their illness, and their desired future, and come alongside them to integrate this complex, ever-evolving story into the medical decisions they face. In so doing, we give "people an opportunity to hear themselves tell their own stories, and probably to tell stories repeatedly, with minor variations, until they find a version they can live with, at best a version worth living with" (Frank 2014, p.S18). For those of us privileged to work with people revising the plot of their lives based on illness, the task is to help them get to a decision themselves (Frank 2014), as Keith did.

References

Cassell, E. (2004) *The Nature of Suffering and the Goals of Medicine*, 2nd edition. New York: Oxford University Press.

Conway, K. (2013) *Beyond Words: Illness and the Limits of Expression*. Albuquerque, NM: UNM Press.

Frank, A.W. (2010) *Letting Stories Breathe: A Socio-Narratology*. Chicago, IL: University of Chicago Press.

Frank, A.W. (2013) *The Wounded Storyteller: Body, Illness, and Ethics*, 2nd edition. Chicago, IL: University of Chicago Press.

Frank, A.W. (2014) 'Narrative ethics as dialogical story-telling.' *Hastings Center Report 44*, s1, S16–S20.

Galchutt, P.A. (2013) 'A palliative care specific spiritual assessment: How this story evolved.' *OMEGA-Journal of Death and Dying 67*, 1–2, 79–85.

Galchutt, P.A. (2016) 'Chaplaincy scope of practice note: The evolution of a specific palliative care spiritual assessment.' *PlainViews 13*, 12.

Gawande, A. (2014) *Being Mortal: Medicine and What Matters in the End*. New York: Metropolitan Books.

Jones, J.W. (2003) *The Mirror of God: Christian Faith as Spiritual Practice – Lessons from Buddhism and Psychotherapy*. New York: Palgrave Macmillan.

Lee, B.M., Curlin, F.A. and Choi, P.J. (2017) 'Documenting presence: A descriptive study of chaplain notes in the intensive care unit.' *Palliative & Supportive Care 15*, 2, 190–196.

MacIntyre, A. (2007) *After Virtue*, 3rd edition. Notre Dame, IN: University of Notre Dame Press.

Mattingly, C. and Garro, L. (eds) (2000) *Narrative and the Cultural Construction of Illness and Healing*. Los Angeles, CA: University of California Press.

Ricoeur, P. (2008) *From Text to Action: Essays in Hermeneutics, II*, Vol. 2. New York: Continuum.

Schneider, P. (2003) *Writing Alone and with Others*. New York: Oxford University Press.

Strauss, D. (2010) *Half a Life: A Memoir*. New York: Random House.

Chapter 2

GLEN'S STORY

"Glen's mission"—a 72-year-old man, living
until his sense of purpose was fulfilled

JIM HOGG

Introduction

This case study records my three-month journey with Glen during my work with Palliative Care patients. My encounters with Palliative Care patients were generally short-term, with little or no follow-up possible post-discharge. My time with Glen, however, was extended due to multiple factors, which I describe below.

Glen was an engaging, self-reflective man whose faith was his foundation, as it had been throughout his life. He affiliated with the United Methodist Church. Glen's life was one of faith, family, work, awards, and service. He was a decorated Vietnam War veteran, where he had served as a Captain in the US Army. He was awarded three Bronze Stars (one for valor) and two Purple Hearts. After the war, he and his wife Betty purchased a local photography business where he invested his life for over 35 years, winning several awards. He was married for 60 years, and together they had three children and multiple grandchildren. Glen was active in his community as a volunteer in several different organizations.

My time with Glen was extended over a three-month period due to several factors. One factor, and the one I believe is the most important, was our relationship. We seemed to connect from the very first visit, though it was not his first encounter with a chaplain. During my first visit he commented that he had a "long and wonderful visit" with one of my chaplain colleagues the previous day. I was grateful for his introduction to chaplaincy in this way. This reflective spirit informed our conversations as he shared his story, values, and what really mattered to him, which impacted his medical decision-making process.

His primary medical service team requested that the Palliative Care service have conversations with Glen about his chemotherapy, pain management, prognosis, and to form his goals of care. Palliative Care is a specialized discipline for patients and families dealing with chronic, life-limiting illness. The focus is on the management of symptoms, complications, and quality of life. Soon after our Palliative Care team began to work with Glen, they asked if I would get involved to see if my chaplaincy interventions would be helpful in addressing these concerns.

Another factor in my extended time with Glen was his multiple hospitalizations, which fostered this relationship. I was an inpatient Palliative Care chaplain. His repeated hospitalizations were the means by which our conversations could develop. Glen was oriented and alert throughout his hospitalizations.

A third factor was the continued referrals I received from Palliative Care to provide care to Glen. I am deeply grateful for my excellent colleagues in Palliative Care who were appreciative of the unique specialization of professional chaplaincy.

Glen's case is an example of how his religious beliefs and human values influenced his medical decision-making. I was aware that his wife Betty was struggling with Glen's medical decisions, which he confided to me. Most of our visits were one-to-one, but Betty was present during a limited number of our encounters. I never had the opportunity to meet any of his children or grandchildren.

During this case study I was a full-time Palliative Care chaplain. I worked at a large tertiary academic medical center in the Midwest region of the US. I am endorsed for ministry as a chaplain by the Southern Baptist Convention and am board-certified through the Association of Professional Chaplains (APC). The Palliative Care service at this hospital consisted of staff physicians, physician residents, physician fellows, nurse practitioners, physician assistants, social workers, nurses, a pharmacist, a chaplain, and people from other specialties.

My role on this team was to conduct spiritual assessments and facilitate and/or provide chaplaincy care. I initiated visits and received patient referrals from Palliative Care. As an active member of the interdisciplinary team, I communicated insights gleaned from my spiritual assessments, interventions, and outcomes to the rest of the team as we worked together to meet Glen's needs.

Preparation and publication of this case study was approved by the hospital where I worked. Glen is deceased, and I was not able to contact his spouse. Thus, in keeping with the hospital's policy where I work, I have changed the name, circumstances, and any identifying features while keeping intact the integrity of the visit and my interventions. This case study was not reviewed by our Institutional Review Board because a case study involving one individual is not considered research.

This was such a meaningful experience that I wrote detailed notes about my interventions and shared my learning with our Palliative Care service. I am now honored to share his story with you. This case demonstrates the unique role a chaplain can have with patients, including those approaching end of life, in medical decision-making. In addition, it is my hope that this case study communicates how existing literature can inform and impact clinical practice and guide our patient interventions and outcomes.

Case

I am including five visits that are representative of the 10 total visits I had with Glen over a three-month period. At the time of the visit indicated below, I had already seen Glen three times. I was mindful of trying to understand Glen's own goals as his disease progressed and how aggressive he wanted to become in his care. I have edited these conversations so that the reader may hear Glen's story, his values, and his desired outcome(s), in his own words.

Glen had been moved to the Medical Intensive Care Unit (MICU). When I was on my way to visit him, I was unsure how this visit would go and if he would be able to talk or how critical his situation might be. When I entered his room, I noticed that Betty was not present. I was glad to see that Glen was receptive to a visit as I entered the room. In this visit, Glen introduced his "mission."

Glen: "… You know, I've been doing a lot of thinking."

Chaplain: "I would love to hear more about that."

Glen: "Oh, I've just been thinking, reflecting really, on my life. I have really had a good life [he recounted some of his life]. I'm not ready to go just yet. I just feel like there's more I need to do."

Chaplain: "Thank you for sharing that with me, I feel honored that you have told me that. I am curious about your statement of not yet being ready to go. Can you tell me more about that?"

Glen: "I believe I'm still alive because I still have a mission, something I still need to do. When I complete this, I think then God will call me home. You know, I think I might have found my mission actually. I think that I can help others through their illness as I share what I'm learning through mine. I think I can help people."

Chaplain: "That sounds very beautiful."

Glen: "I think I want to write something. People tell me I'm a good writer."

Soon after the visit, Glen was discharged. About a month later, I learned from Palliative Care that he was hospitalized again. When I arrived, he was alone. He smiled and welcomed me into his room for an update and additional conversation.

Glen: "Hi Jim, it's good to see you again."

Chaplain: "It sure is good to see you too, Glen, but I'm sorry you have to be hospitalized again for us to reconnect."

Glen: "Oh, that's okay. That's all part of my illness. I accept it... [Changing the subject] Well, I think I have it figured out now."

Chaplain: "What do you think you have figured out?"

Glen: "What I'm still here for. [At this point, he talked at length about some of the things he had learned through his illness, such as talking to doctors, advocating for oneself, being grateful for caregivers, being thankful for every day, trusting in God, etc.] I have learned so much through all of this."

Chaplain: "I see that you indeed have much to share with others."

Glen: "Yes, I do, and I so want to share [looking pensive] and I don't think I will be able to return home now. I am hoping to go to a nursing home half a mile from my house so Betty can come and visit me often."

Chaplain: "How do you feel about this, Glen?"

Glen: "I am truly okay with it. [I noticed that Glen seemed to be optimistic about many things and I was curious about this.] I know one thing, I'm not ready to give up. Palliative Care was in here earlier and asked if I would be willing to talk to someone about hospice. They think that I could use the additional support. I told them that I'm not ready to give up yet but I would be willing to talk about it [referring to hospice]. They said that maybe I could stay home that way. So we'll see what comes of that."

Chaplain: "You have a lot on your plate right now, and now with a conversation about hospice too…lots of things to consider. How are you with it all?"

Glen: "Well, I don't like people trying to talk me into giving up. I'm not there yet. I still have much to do. I mean, I'm not afraid to die. I've already planned my funeral."

Chaplain: "Who is trying to talk you into giving up? [I was impressed by his statement of already having planned his funeral and was prepared to come back to this a bit later.]"

Glen: "Oh, I don't know any names, I just feel that way sometimes."

Chaplain: "Can you tell me more about that?"

Glen: "I don't know, I guess I just feel that people are not really listening to me."

Chaplain: "Can you help me understand who these people are and maybe what you are wanting them to hear?"

Glen: "I have had several people in my room that don't always seem to listen to me. I am not ready to give up. I still have a reason to live. I want someone to hear what my reason is, and to maybe help me."

Chaplain: "[I decided not to pursue any further the issue of who is not listening to him.] I would love to hear more about that reason if you want to share it."

Glen: "I'll try. I do have a lot to say to my family, to my church, to my friends, and to others. I have had a good life, I am thankful for them all, and want them to listen to some of the advice I have learned. You know, for example, to keep one's faith in God, to recognize the importance of keeping a good attitude during life, to love each other, forgive each other, things like that."

Chaplain: "Thanks Glen. That is important for me to hear. I so honor that...and you have planned your funeral?"

Glen: "Yes, I have. Betty already knows what I want. So I am not afraid to die. I just know I'm not ready yet. [We continued to talk about his funeral for a while, and he shared the songs he wanted in his funeral, the scripture, who he wanted to do his funeral, who would speak, etc.]"

In this visit, I felt that Glen went a bit deeper and moved away somewhat from optimism to express his frustration at feeling "like people [are] trying to talk me into giving up." I was truly grateful that Glen opened up and shared more of his feelings. I intentionally addressed his feelings of "people trying to talk me into giving up." I offered to advocate on his behalf but honored his wishes. We did not talk much more about his "mission," but I felt as though I had a better sense of who he was after this visit, which was a person who was grateful for his life and who wanted to share lessons from his life with others.

The following day, during Palliative Care rounds I learned that there would be a care conference later that morning. I was asked to attend by a Palliative Care physician colleague. This care conference took place in Glen's hospital room and was also attended by Betty. This was a two-hour meeting, much of which was dedicated to the physicians explaining Glen's condition, some of their concerns, and Glen and Betty providing feedback. I am including here the portion of my involvement during this conversation.

At one point, the physicians began to address Glen's goals for his care. I decided to intervene in the conversation to reframe it since I was the only one from the Palliative Care team who had been present during our previous conversations.

Chaplain: "Glen, you and I have had many conversations about what is important to you, would you mind sharing that?"

Glen: "Yes. I feel as though I have so very much yet to offer. I am not afraid to die nor am I in denial about the course of my illness. I know that I am dying, but I feel as though I still have a mission. I feel as though, because of what I'm going through, I can truly help other people. I love to write. I'm wanting to write some of the lessons I'm learning that I think might help others."

Betty: "I also am not ready for Glen to move toward hospice. I'm just not ready for that yet [crying]. We've been married for 60 years."

There was a moment of empathy from all present at this time. I think everyone in the room was aware of the sacredness of what had just been shared by both Glen and Betty.

Doctor: "[After answering more of Glen's and Betty's questions] Thank you both for sharing with us today. I feel like we know you better now. I know these are hard decisions and we want to be with you and help you to achieve your goals. Why don't we think about our conversation for a few days and revisit?"

Glen was discharged not long after our meeting. He was hospitalized 12 days later. This time he was back in the MICU. I was accompanied by a senior physician fellow, Dr S, as he had asked if he could come along. During this meeting, Glen told us that another care conference was scheduled for later that day and he asked me to attend. It is important to note that Glen had a very supportive pastor who was not able to attend care conferences at the hospital due to her schedule.

Chaplain: "Hi Glen, I would like to introduce to you Dr S, one of the doctors working with Palliative Care. [Dr S greeted Glen.] We stopped by for a visit if you feel up to it."

Glen: "Oh, sure. I've been mulling over in my mind about the placement of a feeding tube. We've been talking about that for a while and it still bothers me. [I knew that this subject had come up in the previous care conference.] I really want to address this today at the care conference. I am not feeling like people are listening to me and I have a lot of questions."

Chaplain: "What do you think they are not hearing?"

Glen: "I just have lots of questions."

Chaplain: "Dr S is here, and perhaps he can begin to address some of your questions. [This seemed to be helpful to Glen as he opened up with Dr S and shared his fears about the feeding tube placement, how it would happen, what kind of pain to expect, the risks of infection, benefits, etc. During this time, I sat quietly as the two of them engaged in conversation.]"

Glen: "[After his conversation with Dr S was winding down] Last night was scary."

Chaplain: "What happened?"

Glen: "Well, I was at home and all of a sudden I got this incredible pain. Betty had to call an ambulance at 3am and they brought me to the hospital. I am feeling much better now though."

Chaplain: "Last night does sound very scary, to have to call an ambulance at 3am. You have been through so much already."

Glen: "Yes, it feels that way too… [Changing the subject] Oh, let me tell the two of you what happened at church yesterday! I almost forgot. Remember that I talked about my mission and wanting to write something to help others? Well, I did, and my pastor read it at church yesterday. I couldn't be there but Betty was. She said that there 'weren't too many dry eyes.' I brought several copies with me and I'd like you both to have one."

Chaplain: "Thank you so much, Glen. [We both read it and noticed that Glen was tearful.]"

Glen: "I really feel like I was able to help people by writing this."
Below is the copy of what Glen wrote:

A Message to First Methodist friends:

God hears prayer. Your petitions are heard, but God remains mysteriously in charge. Thank you for caring, praying and your messages of hope. I wish I could hug each of you.

I willingly accept whatever events God lays in my path. My confirmation hymn included, "…and lead thou me." I have always asked to discover and be a part of God's will…it matters not what it is… Often it is not written boldly on the wall so I stumble forward the best I can. Even Martin Luther said if you are going to sin, sin boldly.

It is our faith assumption that God knows what is best for us. We believe and we trust. Our faith has made us whole. My faith has matured over the years—first it was sort of an early home school. Then it was a more formal school and eventually advanced to a more absorbent, confident belief. Now I don't engage in prayer as much as I am prayer. I am not God but I hope when you look at me you see God because I am transformed. Take from me hope; see in me love.

I have no doubt I have survived the last 18 months lifted by your prayers to the gentle wings of God. We know our life and death are not predetermined. We know God can be persuaded, Always leave room for the miracle. Bishop Tutu says, "I am the prisoner of hope."

Each of us is different, but we are a wonderful family of believers in our journey with Jesus. Bishop Johnson told our confirmands a few years ago to hang on tight to Jesus because you never know where the journey with him will speed you. I agree...and with anyone at any age.

God bless you and let us keep the faith.

Chaplain: "Glen, this is so very powerful. What especially spoke to me was your comment, 'now I don't engage in prayer as much as I am prayer.'"

Glen: "I feel that every breath is a prayer. I no longer feel as though I need to spend a certain amount of time in formal prayer, but that my very life is a prayer. It is something that has grown on me over the years."

Chaplain: "That really speaks to me. I am very grateful that you wrote this and then your pastor shared it with the congregation. [We continued to go over each sentence, with him explaining what he wanted to say. I was cognizant that Dr S was listening as Glen shared.]"

Glen: "Yes, I feel very good that I was able to do this and that Pastor Susan read it. My wife said how well it was received...feel free to share it with others if you wish. [Glen asked if I would close this visit in prayer.]"

Chaplain: "God, thank you for these beautiful words, straight from Glen's heart to his friends, family, and church. I pray for Glen and Betty that you would hold them, especially during this time. You promise to 'walk with us through the valley.' Thank you for walking with Glen and Betty and his family. I also pray for guidance as they make decisions about their future. Glen, you are the beloved son of God and I pray that you can sense this within your very heart. Thank you, God, for your presence in Glen's life. Amen."

I attended the care conference later that day, which lasted close to two hours again. Glen was able to ask his questions regarding the placement of a feeding tube. Based on what he and Betty heard, they were open to receiving a feeding tube if it would help him gain more quality to his life. I spoke with Glen and his wife after the meeting, as is my practice, to evaluate how they thought the meeting went and if they had any concerns. Glen expressed "guarded expectations" based on his previous experience with treatment options.

My last time with Glen was one week later, and was brief. This was at my own initiative. He was on a regular floor and said that he planned to be discharged soon. I sensed that this would be my last encounter with him as he had decided to go home on hospice care and to stop all treatment options. This was news to me, and was different from my understanding. I was conscious of my thoughts and questions in this regard, but sensed that we also needed to just "be" today.

Glen: "Thank you for coming again. I've chosen to go home with hospice and I am now ready. I'm tired of all of the treatments and changed my mind on the feeding tube."

Chaplain: "Thank you for sharing this with me Glen. What helped you to come to this decision?"

Glen: "Well, I guess because I have done what I wanted to do. I was able to help other people. I am ready now... I sure would like a prayer though!"

Chaplain: "I'm happy to offer a prayer. Great God, I thank you for Glen and Betty, and for the opportunity for Glen to share his heart with his church and family. I know that Glen will forever be in their hearts. I place Glen in your care and know you will always be there for them, wrapping them in your love. Amen."

Glen: "Thank you."

Chaplain: "You are most welcome. [Sensing I still needed closure from this relationship] Glen, this may be the last time we see each other. I just wanted you to know how much you have meant to me over our time together, and that you have touched me deeply. Thank you."

Glen: "I feel the same way, Jim. Thank you for being there. I wish the best for you. [Our eyes connected and we were in silence for a few moments. I felt the sacredness of the moment and feel it again as I write this.]"

We then said our goodbyes and I walked out of the door. He died 13 days later at home.

Analysis

My approach to the care of Glen was informed primarily by the integration of *The Minister as Diagnostician* (Pruyser 1976) and the 7 by 7 model for spiritual assessment (Fitchett 2002), as well as the theoretical frameworks of Narrative Medicine (Charon *et al.* 2017) and Dignity Therapy (Chochinov 2012).

An overarching question in spiritual assessments is, "What is the patient's desired outcome (if any) from this visit?" (VandeCreek and Lucas 2001). For example, in Glen's story, his stated outcome is best expressed in his own words: "[I believe that] I'm going through this for a reason; I have a mission to fulfill. I think I can help others because of what I am going through." The natural progression over the course of several visits was that Glen was able to eventually write his "mission." His pastor later shared Glen's words with the church where there "weren't too many dry eyes," to quote his wife Betty. This integrated spiritual assessment model, used within a therapeutic chaplain–patient relationship, helped to meet his desired outcome, which, in turn, naturally led to his medical decision-making.

Within spiritual assessments, it is my philosophy that the relationship informs at what level the spiritual assessment will take, as well as its depth. I found that Narrative Medicine and Dignity Therapy frameworks informed my spiritual assessment because I had a prolonged and deep relationship with Glen, which is not the case with all patients I see. These theoretical frameworks helped me pay attention to Glen's story, values, and what really mattered to him. This most certainly impacted his medical decision-making.

Narrative Medicine helps patients, families, and healthcare professionals in the telling and listening to the "alchemy of illness" (Duff 1993). It invites healthcare providers to ask themselves the illuminating question, "Where am I in this patient's story?" If we can find ourselves within a patient interaction and open ourselves to the curiosity of a learner, then we can truly become "human sanctuaries" for another, as one colleague recently put it.

Rita Charon, a leader in the field of Narrative Medicine, offers this insight:

> Since illness and injury are among the most exposing experiences of the mortal life…narrative medicine is present when a person urgently comes to face or question or embrace his or her identity. Who am I now suffering, now recovering, now dying? What matters to me now? In the face of this illness or injury, what is the best way forward in my life? (Charon *et al.* 2017, pp.110–111)

I noticed that Glen began to touch on these themes during one of my initial visits. Somehow, I knew his mission would touch me, too. As I visited with Glen, I often asked myself one of the pivotal questions of Narrative Medicine, "Where am I in this patient's story?" Glen impacted me with his kindness, self-awareness, self-reflection, and faith in the midst of questions, and his desire to help others through his illness and death.

Dignity Therapy also helped to inform some of my questions and interventions. Dignity Therapy was designed by Dr Harvey Max Chochinov (2012) to address some of the psychological, existential, and spiritual challenges that patients and families may encounter as they face the end of life. Like Narrative Medicine, it is an approach that listens closely to the patient's story and empowers through an intentional writing of that story.

Dignity Therapy (2012, p.71) informed some of my interventions:

- "Tell me a little about your life history; what parts do you remember most or think are the most important?"

- "When did you feel most alive?"

- "What do you want your family to know about you?"

- "What are some of your accomplishments in life? Why are they important to you?"

- "Is there anything that you feel you still need to say to your loved ones?"

- "What do you hope for your loved ones?"

- "What have you learned about life that you would want to pass along to others?"

This case study shows the value of a chaplaincy that is attentive to narrative and how that can help patients as they face important healthcare decisions.

Conclusion

Part of my own theology may have been evident during this encounter. It is my belief that each person is beloved. This "belovedness" can come from many different sources. For example, it can come from a relationship with the divine, from one's sense of self, nature, music, art, etc. The sources of this "belovedness" are limitless. It is this belief that informs how I encounter people. I know inherently that each person is beloved and of value. I attempt to create a human sanctuary where this can be expressed and received.

I would now like to share some of the areas for further improvement or reflection, based on my encounters with Glen.

I noticed during this case study that I did not invite Glen to talk more about his relationship with God, what that meant for him, what his view of God was, or how God has helped him over the course of his life. I noticed that I followed his lead entirely in these conversations and was not very directive in exploring more of this walk with God. I am also aware that this was intentional.

Another area that I believe was underdeveloped was Glen's family. Although Betty was present for a couple of visits, she was not a major part of my conversations with Glen. He would share about her and his 60 years of marriage, but she was not specifically addressed in his "mission." His mission was to "help everyone." I noticed that he did not address his family in his "mission" to his church. I would have liked to have been more curious about that.

Finally, I could have been more directive regarding his understanding of hospice. Several times Glen said that he "did not want to give up." Could I have taken that as a cue to explore further, as in,

"Help me understand what you mean by not giving up?" Perhaps if I had offered some education on hospice or invited Palliative Care to provide additional information, this may have helped with his level of distress. I do not feel as though I adequately addressed his concerns about hospice.

In closing, I am grateful to have had the opportunity to explore the mysteries throughout our conversations and to have been a part of the unfolding of Glen's medical decision-making process. Most of all, I am grateful that he entrusted me with his story.

References

Charon, R., DasGupta, S., Hermann, N., Irvine, C., *et al.* (2017) *The Principles and Practice of Narrative Medicine.* New York: Oxford University Press.

Chochinov, H.M. (2012) *Dignity Therapy.* New York: Oxford University Press.

Duff, K. (1993) *The Alchemy of Illness.* New York: Bell Tower.

Fitchett, G. (2002) *Assessing Spiritual Needs.* Lima: Academic Renewal Press.

Pruyser, P. (1976) *The Minister as Diagnostician.* Philadelphia, PA: The Westminster Press.

VandeCreek, L. and Lucas, A. (2001) *The Discipline for Pastoral Care Giving: Foundations for Outcome Oriented Chaplaincy.* Binghampton, NY: Haworth Press.

Further reading

Byock, I. (2004) *The Four Things that Matter Most.* New York: Simon & Schuster, Inc.

Fowler, J. (1981) *Stages of Faith: The Psychology of Human Development and the Quest for Meaning.* New York: HarperCollins.

Marin, D.B., Sharmam V., Sosunov, E., Egorova, N., Goldstein, R. and Handzo, G.F. (2015) 'Relationship between chaplain visits and patient satisfaction.' *Journal of Healthcare Chaplaincy 21,* 1, 14–24.

Massey, K., Fitchett, G. and Roberts, P. (2004) 'Assessment and Diagnosis in Spiritual Care.' In K.L. Mauk and N.K. Schmidt (eds) *Spiritual Care in Nursing Practice* (pp.209–242). Philadelphia, PA: Lippincott, Williams & Wilkins.

Peck, M.S. (1978) *The Road Less Traveled.* New York: Simon & Schuster, Inc.

Piderman, K., Brietkopf, C.R., Jenkins, S.M., Lovejoy, L.A., *et al.* (2015) 'The feasibility and educational value of Hear My Voice, a chaplain-led spiritual life review process for patients with brain cancers and progressive neurologic conditions.' *Journal of Cancer Education 30,* 2, 209–212.

Piderman, K., Egginton, J.S., Ingram, C., Dose, A.M., *et al.* (2017) 'I'm still me: Inspiration and instruction from individuals with brain cancer.' *Journal of Health Care Chaplaincy 23,* 1, 15–33.

Piderman, K., Radecki, B.C., Jenkins, S.M., Lapid, M.I., *et al.* (2015) 'The impact of a spiritual legacy intervention in patients with brain cancers and other neurologic illnesses and their support persons.' *PsychoOncology 26,* 3, 346–353.

Puchalski, C. and Romer, A.L. (2000) 'Taking a spiritual history allows clinicians to understand patients more fully.' *Journal of Palliative Medicine 3*, 1, 129–137.

Wheatley, M. (2006) *Leadership and the New Science.* San Francisco, CA: Berrett-Koehler Publishers.

Chapter 3

BOB'S STORY

"I don't want to put them through anything more. They've already done enough for me"—Bob, a middle-aged husband and father as he faces treatment decisions for his second life-threatening cancer

M. JEANNE WIRPSA

Introduction

This case study describes the role of the chaplain in assisting Bob and his family in making difficult treatment decisions over the course of a seven-year relationship. It highlights two specific juncture points in that journey, when Bob faced decisions that directly challenged his understanding of who he was as a man, a firefighter and electrician/ electrical contractor, and a provider for his family. Bob was in his fifties, a middle-class Caucasian man of Italian descent who was spiritual but not religious. He resided in a suburb of Chicago with his wife of 35 years. They had raised three children together, all of whom, at the time of his illness, were young adults with careers and relationships. One moved back home and was centrally involved in the care of Bob throughout the long course of his illnesses.

Bob was diagnosed with his first cancer—acute myeloid leukemia (AML)—at the age of 52. Always an active, physical, and extremely independent man, he suddenly found himself feeling flu-like and became short of breath while engaging in simple tasks. His skin tone grew pale and he started to discover bruises on his arms and legs. His wife Phyllis, who worked in healthcare throughout her career, pushed Bob to go see the doctor and get checked out. The doctor took note of the bruising and small red dots on Bob's lower legs. He drew blood and said he would call Bob with the results. The preliminary diagnosis of leukemia came as a shock to their ears. Bob was instructed to return to the hospital where he was immediately admitted to the Oncology inpatient ward.

For adults, AML is a life-threatening disease. Recent advances in treatment hold great promise, unlike a few years ago, when the mortality rate was near 50 percent. Patients undergo intensive chemotherapy for an extended period of time in an inpatient acute care hospital. If the initial course of treatment does not significantly reduce their cancer burden, they are required to remain as inpatients for another round of aggressive chemotherapy. In total, patients may be hospitalized for one to three months during their initial stage of treatment. During treatment, they are not allowed to leave the unit, though visitors are welcomed and encouraged. In Bob's case, he spent three months in the hospital, and was able to go home for just over a week before he returned for another month-long stay for an even more intensive round of consolidation chemotherapy. He then received the gift of a second chance at life through an anonymous donor's stem cells, which would rebuild his depleted bone marrow. The treatment was considered successful, but like many stem cell transplant recipients, Bob suffered from mild to moderate graft vs. host disease, where the donor cells attacked not only hidden leukemia cells but also his own system. His skin, eyes, and gut all suffered from this assault. In addition, the chemotherapy caused him to suffer from neuropathy—numbing of the hands and feet—such that he needed to walk with a cane (and later a walker) and was in constant, low-grade pain.

As if having and surviving leukemia were not enough, Bob was diagnosed with a second, unrelated colon cancer about three years after his first diagnosis. At the time of diagnosis this cancer was treatable, but not curable. The oncologist recommended surgery to remove the section of colon affected and, if needed, to take out sections of his liver to which the cancer had already spread. Bob was still followed by his primary oncologist at the time. When he expressed resistance to pursuing any treatment options for this second cancer, she was concerned and asked him talk to the clinic psychologist—which he refused. Aware that Bob had a long-standing relationship with the inpatient Oncology and Stem Cell Transplant chaplain (me), she offered him that resource—to which he agreed.

I first met Bob when he was inpatient for his leukemia treatment. I was the chaplain serving the Oncology and Stem Cell Transplant

Units at a large, academic teaching hospital that receives patients from around the region for specialized and advanced treatments not available elsewhere. I am a board-certified chaplain with over 20 years of experience in end-of-life care, chronic illness, pediatrics, and oncology. I am a progressive Episcopalian who entered chaplaincy through "the back door" after pursuing a doctoral degree in ethics and determining that academics was too removed from the concrete lives of ordinary people. I am Caucasian, married with two young adult children, a martial artist, and cyclist—someone who, like Bob, prides herself on putting others first and being active and independent.

Throughout the course of our relationship, Bob felt a pressing need to "give back." He wanted to use his experience to help others faced with similar circumstances. On numerous occasions, Bob visited consenting patients newly diagnosed with leukemia. Usually these patients were men of about his age, struggling with being cooped up in the hospital, desperate for a break, feeling useless and scared that they would not survive this ordeal either physically or emotionally. In the last year or so of his life, Bob dreamed that together we would write a book about what he had learned over the course of his cancer journey to help others navigate this unknown territory. That book never came to be, but I know that Bob would be pleased that his story might yet benefit others. Bob's family directly reviewed and edited this case study. They provided permission for it to be published.

Case

Bob had been in the hospital for three weeks when he started making passing comments to the staff about calling "Dr Kevorkian." Instead, they called me. Bob was stir crazy. He had changed from a man who always engaged actively with any member of the staff who entered into his room to someone who barely looked up from his chair, responding to questions about his well-being with only with one or two words. I could see the toll this lengthy stay was taking on his spirits. He wept when I asked him how he was really doing. Not a particularly religious man at the time, Bob found strength primarily in his family, friends, and connection with his dog. We hit it off when I negotiated with the inpatient team to let him go down to the outdoor lobby—to see his dog. I remained in contact with Bob throughout the next few years—I saw him through his stem cell transplant, and met up with him, his wife, and daughter when he came for follow-up appointments. I connected him with patients who needed someone who had walked in their shoes and could relate to what they were experiencing.

Medical decision #1

I vividly recall meeting Bob by the Dunkin Donuts in the pavilion where I worked after he had been diagnosed with his second cancer. I approached him with great affection and concern, offering a warm embrace as he shuffled up with his walker. I thanked him for trusting me enough to talk about the hard decisions he now faced. Bob jumped in, quickly telling me he had already survived the impossible. He expressed confusion about why God had kept him here this long only to put him through this again. He reminded me about the friend he had made during his lengthy inpatient stay for leukemia treatment who had died. "Why am I still here? I shouldn't have survived, but I did. And now this?"

As we wrestled with these unanswerable questions, Bob honed in on one thing that was really bothering him. He could not tolerate the thought of having a colostomy. The surgery that would remove a large portion of his colon would most likely require he live with a bag attached to his side for the rest of his life. The very thought of this was off-putting to him. As he spoke about the details of the colostomy, Bob looked like he might actually throw up. He grew tense even as he hung his head, as if in anticipatory shame. It was a visceral reaction, grounded in a deeply rooted self-image. Though he was no longer the fit and active man he had once been (age and leukemia had taken its toll), he retained a sense of pride about his body. He reminisced about working on projects around his house, overseeing jobs at work, chartering and cleaning his boat in Michigan, and rushing into fires fearlessly and ready to face death at any moment. He could not endure one more assault, one more limitation, or one more indignity.

I recall spending a good deal of time acknowledging Bob's reaction, using phrases like "that sounds unbearable for you" and "I can see the very thought of a colostomy disgusts you." I took both of Bob's hands in mine and was silent for a few moments. I noticed that Bob began to return to a more centered place—he was sitting upright again and he looked directly at me and wiped the tears from his eyes. I saw Bob's quirky half smile begin to appear again. He shrugged and commented: "What can you do? It is what it is. You just have to deal with it."

I decided to risk broadening his perspective. I invited Bob to step back from these fears and to reflect with me on how he had dealt with the many changes to his body, functioning, and self-image from the time he was diagnosed with leukemia to now. I had seen Bob nearly defeated by the many restrictions placed on him through the course of his treatment, only to come through with greater strength, compassion, and openness. A formerly reserved man who rarely talked about his feelings and experiences, he had begun to cultivate a dimension of his person that had received little attention until then. It seemed to me that the losses he had suffered in his physical being and functioning (he no longer drove, worked independently, or served as a firefighter) had created space for a greater development of his emotional and spiritual being (though I did not say this to him directly until he began naming this for himself).

Bob's daughter, Elyse, joined us at some point during that meeting. With Bob's permission, I asked for her thoughts about his resistance to treatment and a bit later in the conversation, for her perspective on who her father had become and what role he played in her life. Always forthright and to the point, Elyse said, "Whatever he decides we will accept and support, because it's his life. He's been through so much already—no one can ever really understand how hard it has been." She added with tears in her eyes, "But I can't imagine him not being here. I want as much time with him as I can get. My mom, on the other hand, is angry and hurt that he is even considering not undergoing treatment. Dr M says he could have a few good years yet and they have so many plans."

Bob's position and body began to soften. I asked him if hearing what his daughter said in any way changed his thinking. He grew somber and said something I'd heard him say repeatedly: "I don't want to put them through anything more. They've already done enough for me. They need to be able to move on and live their lives. I'm just holding them back." I turned back to Elyse. I knew Bob and his family well enough by this point in our relationship to be able to speak frankly. "Elyse, I think he's saying he doesn't want to be a burden to you guys. Sound like something we've heard before?" She rolled her eyes and reiterated her thoughts on some of the positive aspects of his long battle with cancer. She had gotten to spend so much more time with him as she drove him to many of his appointments, enjoyed their long talks in the car, and felt like helping him made her life more meaningful. She boldly asked him to not rob them of more time if the only reason he did not want to do surgery and chemotherapy was out of concern for the impact it would have on them.

Bob made decisions never thinking only of himself; rather, he defined himself in relationship to his family. He began to concede to his family's wishes to give treatment a shot, saying, "Let me think about it more, talk to Dr M to see if she thinks I'll get some good time and not just be in bed with you all having to take care of me." I affirmed his consideration for his family and named that this was consistent with the man I had come to know over these years. But I also reminded him of what his daughter had said: that they would support him in not pursuing treatment if the benefits did not outweigh the potential complications that came with treatment.

I then returned to his concerns about the dreaded colostomy. This was the remaining hurdle, I could tell. I was tempted to share with him my mother-in-law's experience living with a colostomy for 20 years (a mixed bag of grace and repeated indignities) but held back. Instead, I wondered aloud if he might be open to speaking with other men who had undergone a similar surgery and lived with a colostomy—to which he agreed. I also encouraged him to fill the surgical oncologist in on his visceral reaction to having a colostomy. I explained that not everyone thinks of it as such an assault on their dignity as he did; that in fact, surgeons would argue it is better to have the bag than have the patient die.

Bob decided to have the surgery. I was with Phyllis and Elyse when the surgeon came out unexpectedly about an hour into the procedure. The metastases to the liver were more extensive than they had originally thought. The surgeon was not convinced that taking out part of the colon would therefore change the outcome, as the cancer could have spread to nearby lymph nodes and be present in other areas of the body. Would Bob want him to proceed given his strong resistance to having a colostomy? They did not hesitate. No. Bob would be furious if he woke up with a colostomy and the grim news that removal of his colon was not going to make that much difference in the long run.

Medical decision #2

Bob and his family bought almost three years with various chemotherapy agents. Bob was fortunate to be in the hands of Dr M, an oncologist who did not shy away from goals-of-care conversations (and in fact introduced these at the outset of treatment), was realistic about what treatment could and could not accomplish, and spent time exploring what quality of life meant to her patients and their families. She also valued interdisciplinary teamwork and was aware of the long-standing relationship of trust I had with Bob and his family.

When the scans revealed that the fourth line therapy was no longer "containing" the cancer, Dr M paged me asking if I would join her in the clinic when she delivered the news to Bob and his wife. Bob and Phyllis reacted with resignation and sadness rather than surprise or anger. They knew this day would come. Dr M reviewed Bob's history, observing warmly how good it was that Bob and his family had used this time wisely and how inspired she had been by Bob's resilience and care for his family throughout. Although she did not think another chemotherapy would be very effective, if he wanted to try, she had one more agent in mind.

Bob and Phyllis looked confused and started hemming and hawing. I strategically decided to intervene by posing a question to Dr M on their behalf: "Given what you know of Bob and his concern for quality of life, and given what you know about the side effects of this new agent, do *you* recommend they try it, or not?" Dr M paused, then without the slightest bit of ambivalence said, "No. Bob, I think you should go home, do the things you love and spend time with your family. We'll keep your appointments to every two weeks so I can monitor your symptoms and give you something for pain if you start to have any. We should probably connect you to the Palliative Care doctors as well."

After Dr M left, I remained with Bob and Phyllis. We, too, reviewed the past few years of his life, gave thanks for the relationship we had enjoyed, and explored how I might support them moving forward. Bob asked if I would do his funeral. I said that I would be honored and would have offered if he had not asked.

Then Bob launched into a line of reasoning that I had not heard before, but later found out that Bob's family knew well. Bob expressed how he should just spare them all the burden of caring for him and end his own life. After all, he argued, they had already given up seven years of their lives taking him to countless doctors' appointments, visiting him in the hospital, accommodating their schedules, and lifestyles, to his condition. His job, he explained, was to care for his family, to sacrifice for them. Instead, they were doing that for him.

My response surprised Bob (he later shared). I did not judge. I did not tell him he would go to hell if he ended his own life. Instead, I acknowledged the deep existential suffering present as his core identity as a provider and protector was challenged. I hesitated, then decided to push a little. I wondered if he also could not tolerate the idea of being dependent, of seeing his own body deteriorate, of being less than the man he saw himself to be. He wept. Phyllis wept. I wept. Phyllis reassured Bob first. Caring for him in his last days would be a gift to her. Caring for him would be hard, yes, but it would give her peace later knowing she did the hardest thing a spouse can do, that she had seen him through to the very end.

As I had done previously in our encounters, I offered back to Bob an image of the man he had always been—a man who would risk his life for those in danger; a man who would do almost anything for others, especially for his son, daughters, and wife. I also lifted up the man he had become during this long journey with cancer—a man who had endured countless physical challenges yet remained caring and generous; a man who had experienced growth in relational intimacy as he had opened up to share more of his inner self with those around him; a man who had come to trust that God had a purpose for his life even when he could not see it; a man who had impacted and would continue to touch and teach those around him, even from his bed, sick and dying.

Bob died peacefully in his own bed a few weeks later. He was mercifully spared some of what he would have considered to be indignities of dying—he was calm, in bed for only a day or two, and clear enough to enjoy visits from long-time friends and firefighters, offer words of wisdom to his children, and love and gratitude to his beloved wife.

Analysis

Two interrelated conceptual and therapeutic frameworks informed my approach to Bob and his family as they faced important medical decisions. First, Narrative Medicine—an approach that values the patient and family story and seeks to overcome barriers within medical care to ensure that the patient story is appreciated and fully integrated into all medical decisions. Second, I am steeped in the body of research on shared decision-making (SDM) in the medical setting—what promotes SDM, barriers to SDM, and emerging conceptual frameworks for Interprofessional Shared Decision-Making (IP-SDM) that incorporate the perspective of a diverse patient population as well as contributions of members of the healthcare team other than the physician.

Narrative Theory and Narrative Medicine

It is over the course of time that a chaplain comes to know who a patient is, not as a patient but as an individual, embedded in a specific culture, relationships, and roles. Rita Charon (2006), one of the leaders of Narrative Medicine, argues that healthcare systems and processes are designed not to regard patients as people but rather as "cases." The training of physicians requires they categorize patients according to disease type and the protocols in place for diagnosis and treatment (Charon 2006). The format for securing information from the patient, the History and Physical ("H & P"), structures interactions in such a way to potentially preclude the introduction from the patient about what is of utmost concern to him or her, what informs their understanding of illness and healing, and what is realistic in terms of follow-through with treatment recommendations (Charon 2006).

Charon proposes a new paradigm for medicine—Narrative Medicine—that fully teaches and incorporates into practice "narrative skills of recognizing, absorbing, interpreting, and being moved by the stories of illness" (Charon 2006, p.4). Narrative Medicine holds promise for improved health outcomes through more accurate diagnosis, attention to somatic manifestations of emotional or spiritual injury and distress, adherence to treatment plans that take into account the social context of the patient, and end-of-life care as the medical team and patient and their family become allies in difficult goals-of-care discussions, because the story is being constructed together (Charon 2012; Holmes and Chambers 2005). Narrative Medicine has the potential to re-humanize medicine (Halpern 2001) through empathetic engagement and by "recognizing and respecting those afflicted with [disease] and in nourishing those who care for the sick" (Charon 2006, p.4).

My love of Oncology chaplaincy arises from the long-term relationships it affords. Although my primary location as a chaplain is in the inpatient acute care setting, I am able to follow patients in the outpatient clinic setting if I have an established relationship and they agree this would prove beneficial. Following Bob and his family for seven years, I admit, was the exception, not the norm, and for that I am extremely grateful. Chaplains located in the outpatient Oncology clinic setting (of which there are few) enjoy this privilege with much greater frequency.

Healthcare chaplains are trained in narrative methods. Verbatim reports of encounters with patients and their families are the main method by which we gain self-awareness, competence in skills, and the ability to reflect theologically, psychologically, and philosophically on our work. We listen carefully for clues not only to who the person has been before becoming ill, but to the way in which the illness is transforming their narrative or, more proactively, how they are re-writing their story and their identity in the face of the life-altering event of an illness (Kidd 2012; Mundle and Smith 2013; Osborn 2012). We have the luxury of time in our encounters that few clinicians have. We humbly become part of their story and assist in its creation. The chaplain approach and training, in this way, closely aligns with the Narrative Medicine approach. At the heart of our practice is the experience described by Charon:

> Receiving our patients' stories mobilizes material deep within ourselves, transforms us, situates us at the threshold of illness with patients, humbly recognizing the patient and appreciating the magnitude of what must be done by that person, now at least not alone. (Charon 2006, p.67)

Bob and his family invited me into the fullness of their shared narrative. With little effort, the Bob who prided himself on being the provider and protector of others emerged. It was easy to appreciate the Bob who located himself in his body—who saw himself as a physical person who depended upon a body that worked for his independence, his livelihood, and his recreational activities. Bob's relational self—his commitment to his wife of 35 years, his long-term relationships with friends and co-workers, and his identity as someone who cared more about the well-being of others than himself—was a consistent, defining thread of his life story. When critical decisions were to be made, I had the insight into what mattered to Bob and who he was at the core of his identity so as to lift these up for consideration and integration.

Individuals faced with serious or life-threatening illness, if fortunate enough to survive, rarely emerge from the experience unchanged. Existential or spiritual distress is a common occurrence. Existential, personal, or spiritual growth is less likely to be noticed or tracked, but is an outcome chaplains hope to see emerge from their interactions with patients and their families. In the midst of a crisis, patients may begin to ask questions of meaning and look for opportunities to evaluate their lives, shift their priorities, and question "what really matters."

Narrative Theorist Arthur Frank (1995) invites clinicians to recognize a variety of illness narratives embedded in the patient experience and imposed upon patients from family, medicine, and culture at large. When Bob was stuck in hospital undergoing treatment for his leukemia, despairing and ready to bolt and, later, when he could not make sense of his second life-threatening cancer diagnosis, my role was to bear witness to what Frank names the "Chaos Narrative" defining his experience (1995). I knew better, in both instances, than to look for a larger good, purpose, or meaning. Bearing witness to suffering and providing a container so the chaos did not engulf Bob, an approach recommended by Frank, proved to be the pastoral intervention that supported Bob, when he was ready, to search for meaning and purpose (1995).

With Bob, the process of transformation and growth took place over the course of many years as he was supported in reflecting on his purpose in life, as he opened himself to explore with deeper intimacy the relationships in his life, and as he perhaps unwittingly, or perhaps of necessity, shifted his energy to the underdeveloped spiritual dimensions of his personhood. Arthur Frank (1995) uses the paradigm of the Quest Narrative to describe the shift that occurred in Bob's relationship to his illness. Rather than let the cancer bat him around or control who he became, with the encouragement of his family, Bob began to claim agency and purpose. As he had been a "hero" rescuing people from flames as a firefighter, so now he would become a "hero" in the eyes of his family and friends by how he faced his illness and death. My role in this process was consistently reflecting back to Bob the way he was growing and engaging him in deeper thought regarding questions of value, purpose, self-image, and identity. This emerging narrative in turn impacted the medical decisions he ultimately made for himself and his family.

Shared decision-making models in medicine

SDM stands on the premise that patient and family values—their story, their location, their economic and social realities, and relationships, what really matters to them—will be attended to by the medical team. Historically framed within the doctor–patient dyad, SDM joins the experiential expertise of the patient (or substitute decision-maker) with the medical expertise of the physician (Charles, Gaffni and Whelan 1997, 1999). With the fragmentation of the doctor–patient relationship, increased specialization in medicine, and economic pressures leading to shorter and shorter visit times, many physicians are no longer able to attend fully to their patient's hopes, concerns, and values. For SDM to succeed in the current healthcare system, it must include other members of the healthcare team with the time and training to attend to the psychosocial dimensions of the patient and family experience (You *et al.* 2015). Social workers, nurses, psychologists, ethicists, and chaplains are all potential contributors to this process. For IP-SDM to work, trust and a common language between disparate disciplines are essential ingredients to effective communication and outcomes. (D'Amour *et al.* 2005; Dogba *et al.* 2016; Sohi, Champagne and Shidler 2015).

My lengthy tenure as the Oncology chaplain afforded me trusting relationships with oncologists who recognized and valued my contributions to patient care, not merely in providing spiritual counsel or religious ritual, but in identifying the values, wishes, and concerns of patients and their families that impact their medical care and decision-making process. The physicians involved in Bob's care wisely assessed that there was always "more going on" throughout various stages of his battle with leukemia and colon cancer that impacted Bob's ability to continue or pursue treatment. They welcomed me to the table of shared decision-making as an equal and valued member, one who had established trust with Bob and his family, and who had the skillset to understand the emotional, relational, and spiritual factors that were impacting his decisions.

My lengthy tenure in Oncology also meant I had learned their discursive framework. I knew what it meant that a patient was receiving third- or fourth-line chemotherapy agents. I understood what it meant to live with GVHD (graft versus host disease). I had an insider's knowledge of how oncologists struggle in offering clinical trials or emerging (yet relatively untested) therapies. I was able to pose questions to the physicians that actually made sense within their medical lexicon and cultural expectations.

Conclusion

As I conclude this story, I am gratefully and humbly aware that who I am—as a chaplain, as a family member, as an incarnate being—is forever changed as a result of walking alongside Bob and his family. Though my role as a chaplain is multifaceted (it includes teaching, mentoring, research, staff support, and patient care), connecting with and caring deeply for people in their most vulnerable times is what makes this work holy. I do not have the luxury or the emotional resilience to become even a minor character in the stories of all my patients. Bob, his family, and I became not merely characters in each other's stories, but co-creators of a story of mutual trust, vulnerability, resilience, and love.

References

Charles, C., Gafni, A. and Whelan, T. (1997) 'Shared decision-making in the medical encounter: What does it mean? (or it takes at least two to tango)'. *Social Science & Medicine 44*, 5, 681–692.

Charles, C., Gafni, A. and Whelan, T. (1999) 'Decision-making in the physician–patient encounter: Revisiting the shared treatment decision-making model'. *Social Science & Medicine 49*, 5, 651–661.

Charon, R. (2006) *Narrative Medicine: Honoring the Stories of illness*. New York: Oxford University Press.

Charon, R. (2012) 'Our heads touch: Telling and listening to stories of self'. *Academic Medicine 87*, 1154–1156.

D'Amour, D., Ferrada-Videla, M., San Martin Rodriguez, L. and Beaulieu, M.D. (2005) 'The conceptual basis for interprofessional collaboration: Core concepts and theoretical frameworks'. *Journal of Interprofessional Care 19*, Suppl. 1, 116–131.

Dogba, M.J., Menear, M., Stacey, D., Briere, N. and Legare, F. (2016) 'The evolution of an interprofessional shared decision-making research program: Reflective case study of an emerging paradigm'. *International Journal of Integrated Care 16*, 3, 4.

Frank, A.W. (1995) *The Wounded Storyteller: Body, Illness, and Ethics*. Chicago, IL: University of Chicago Press.

Halpern, J. (2001) *From Detached Concern to Empathy: Humanizing Medical Practice*. New York: Oxford University Press.

Holmes, M.S. and Chambers, T. (2005) 'Thinking through pain.' *Journal of Literature & Medicine 24*, 1, 127–141.

Kidd, R. (2012) 'Foundational Listening and Responding Skills.' In S. Roberts (ed.) *Professional Spiritual and Pastoral Care: A Practical Clergy and Chaplain's Handbook* (pp.92–105). Woodstock, VT: SkyLight Paths Publishing.

Mundle, R.G. and Smith, B. (2013) 'Hospital chaplains and embodied listening: Engaging with stories and the body in healthcare environments.' *Illness, Crisis & Loss 21*, 2, 95–108.

Osborn, N. (2012) 'Life Review.' In S. Roberts (ed.) *Professional Spiritual and Pastoral Care: A Practical Clergy and Chaplain's Handbook* (Chapter 11). Woodstock, VT: Skylight Paths Publishing.

Sohi, J., Champagne, M. and Shidler, S. (2015) 'Improving health care professionals' collaboration to facilitate patient participation in decisions regarding life-prolonging care: An action research project.' *Journal of Interprofesional Care 29*, 5, 409–414.

You, J.J., Downar, J., Fowler, R.A., Lamontagne, F., *et al.* (2015) 'Barriers to goals of care discussions with seriously ill hospitalized patients and their families: A multicenter survey of clinicians.' *JAMA Internal Medicine 175*, 4, 549–555.

Further reading

Charon, R. (2001) 'Narrative medicine: A model for empathy, reflection, profession, and trust.' *JAMA 286*, 15, 1897–1902.

Chapter 4

CRITICAL RESPONSE TO STORY MATTERS: PATIENT AS PERSON CASE STUDIES

A Chaplain's Perspective

ANNE WINDHOLZ

As the case studies shared by Chaplains Galchutt, Hogg, and Wirpsa reveal, decision-making foregrounds issues of patient identity and agency. I approach these cases as a published literary scholar and as a professor of English for over 20 years. During my transition into professional chaplaincy, I realized that literary analysis offers a fresh way to look at the patient story, its plot, and characters. Taking the patient as a protagonist, one working toward a goal while facing antagonistic forces, the chaplain enters the patient's story as an aid with power to reframe and (sometimes) guide the course of narrative events as well as interpret character.

Galchutt's case study

Chaplain Galchutt's case study highlights the power of words to transmit emotion, work through problems, and facilitate decisions. Galchutt is attentive to the power of writing to construct reality. The "expressive writing" he models has gained currency in the last few years as a way of promoting physical and psychological health. Popular magazines as well as more scholarly journals and studies have documented its positive effects, even its ability to impact the trajectory of an illness (Colino 2016; Evans 2012; Pennebaker and

Evans 2014). Indeed, Rita Charon's work in Narrative Medicine, with its emphasis on physicians writing about their own feelings as they deal with patients, can be seen as underscoring the healing power of words (Charon 2006). Such writing also inevitably introduces the question of power relations. As Michel Foucault and other twentieth-century theorists noted, discourse—the stuff of any narrative text, from clinical pastoral education (CPE) verbatims to chart notes—can be both liberating and repressive, able both to impose order and to disrupt (Foucault 1980). Galchutt's interventions with patient Keith highlight the liberating possibilities as well as the power to control that chaplains wield as they support patients making choices.

The case study genre itself is a prime example of the chaplain's power. The chaplain chooses words to construct what readers know about the patient, the illness, or situation that necessitates intervention, and the characters and settings in the patient's story. Whoever controls discourse holds ultimate power because they select the words that shape reality. How a chaplain uses the patient's words—when responding to them in the presence of the patient, presenting them to the medical team, or writing them down for spiritual care colleagues—can affect how the patients perceive and define themselves, how the team responds to them, and how chaplains use case studies in the care of their own patients. Words are like fire—excellent at providing light, but also capable of harm.

Keith's own reluctance to create a healthcare directive (HCD) speaks to the dangerous power of a text to legislate reality or our perception of it. On the other hand, *naming* what he fears gives Keith some measure of control; he determines how he contextualizes the reality of his death. Galchutt offers Keith the chance to put his decision-making within the context of a story *he* tells in a television interview.

Of course, the interviewer determines the parameters of the interview even as the camera person chooses how to frame Keith on the screen. In a similar way, Galchutt paints our protagonist, defining Keith as "ever-reflective," "in touch with his emotions," and equipped with a "keen ability to focus." He is the one who constructs the narrative we receive about Keith and the words attributed to him. He is also the one who adheres to the guidelines for the practice of Mutual Expressive Writing, including the prerogative for the teacher to affirm what they find meaningful and memorable.

My deconstruction here of Galchutt's interactions with Keith is not to question the excellence of his care or the great sensitivity he brought to every visit. It is, however, meant to raise awareness in chaplaincy that the words we choose, the words we use, *and the words we decide to omit*, matter. How we frame a question, compose a progress note, or describe a patient in an interdisciplinary team meeting can affect how a patient is perceived, how a patient is led to interpret a healthcare decision, and even what treatment is given. For a man like Keith who values his faith, the chaplain's power is accentuated by the chaplain's alliance (actual or assumed) with spiritual authority and their role as intermediary with God. This allied power is often palpable in crises, whether they occur in hospital rooms or outpatient settings. To help a patient in what Galchutt calls the "creation of their decision-making narratives—past, present, and future" is an awesome responsibility.

Galchutt uses reflective listening to good effect in his conversations with Keith; he is able to repeat back what he hears Keith say for possible corroboration, correction, or extrapolation. He helps Keith name his fears, rewrite his plot (shifting his goal from defeating the cancer with a clinical trial to living long enough to attend his son's wedding), and eventually learn to take what happens "day by day."

Galchutt opens his final analysis stating that Keith "welcomed [him] as a character into his evolving story in which he remained the author." This is true—up to a point. Part of the trauma for patients, and most especially for the critically ill and dying, is that much of their agency is lost. Forces beyond the control of the patient and the medical team intrude and, unlike fiction writers, patients do not have the power of an author over their story. They do not, ultimately, control plot events the same way an author does who creates a make-believe world. Their decisions are often less proactive assertions of self-determination than reactions to a story that happens *to* them rather than being chosen *by* them.

This is not to say that patients are powerless. The ability to shape experience into a form that may be read, seen, or heard is no small gift. But the story of any life is, as Galchutt's example shows, a mutual endeavor. A patient's narrative in the quest for health and life is only one among many. The chaplain's professional art is to ensure that, amid the plethora of competing narratives and texts that comprise a medical history, the individual patient's voice is nurtured and preserved in its sacred singularity.

Hogg's case study

Narrative Medicine, as Chaplain Hogg notes, originated as a method for training physicians to get in better touch with their feelings, reactions, and role in the story of their patients. It lends itself well to the work of chaplains, whose very métier is story. A chaplain's spiritual assessment is strengthened by drawing upon the insights of Narrative Medicine, as we see in Hogg's case. I argue that focusing on the basic building blocks of plot also has much to teach us, not just about the patient's goals and the chaplain's role, but also the arc of illness and the efficacy of intervention.

Because Glen is so conscious about wanting to tell his story and so unequivocal about his goal, his narrative exemplifies how a chaplain can use plot analysis to both assess and intervene on a patient's behalf. A successful businessman, civic leader, and decorated war veteran, Glen is, in narrative terms, a fairly typical or traditional "hero." As a professional photographer, capturing the essence of people and places has been Glen's life. He now seeks to capture in words the essence of what it means to live and die well, and has the skills necessary to accomplish his mission. Glen's goal is to talk about his learning, to share his wisdom, to give the gift of hope to others who suffer like him. Hogg comes into the relationship intentional about understanding and honoring Glen's goals.

To do so, a chaplain needs the ability to identify what I call "narrative knots"— kinks in a patient's storyline that indicate potential or actual distress (Windholz 2018). These include:

- Inability to identify *goal*, a goal based on impossibility or delusion

- Inability to identify *protagonist "aids"* (support, community, and coping)

- Denying or inflating *obstacles*/power of *antagonist*

- Loss of identity/sense of self as agent, as *protagonist* in their own story

- Inability to *revise* their story or life narrative in light of illness, loss, death—or hope

- Gaps in story signaling distrust, trauma, or lack of awareness

- Having their story "stolen" through the imposition of others' interpretations

- Dissatisfaction with their story, a sense that all has been (or will be) *tragedy* or *catastrophe*; inevitable fate

- Fear that they have no choice or fear of making the wrong choice: *climax or crisis* that will not end

- Not being allowed to *narrate* their own story; disempowerment.

By Hogg's second visit, "knots" are beginning to complicate Glen's hopeful rewriting of his experience. The disease is worsening. Although Glen names the positive lessons learned about self-advocacy and gratitude, Hogg astutely observes Glen's pensiveness when others suggest he consider hospice care. Facing mounting obstacles to his goal, Glen reiterates that he is "not ready to give up." Hospice represents a failure; in military terms, it is a surrender. His sense of being under attack is amorphous, ill defined, and hence, especially frustrating.

Glen is faced with a second, potentially more devastating, "knot" when he complains he is not being heard. This observation underscores the value of the listening gift that Hogg is able to give his patient. Through narrative, Glen is able to wrest away from disease the power to dominate his story; he is able to control the role disease has in his life rather than the other way around. Like the photographer that he is, Glen is able to frame his subject, ensuring that he, the lessons he has learned, and his love for family and church are at the center. The disease is in the background, not the focus, and certainly not the central character. Despite cruel obstacles, he produces the narrative statement of faith with which he intends to give his life and death meaning. Glenn achieves his goal. His mission is accomplished, the battle won. This change in story marks its *denouement*, a happy ending: "I have done what I wanted to do. I was able to help other people."

While Narrative Medicine gives chaplains a new way of under-standing our role in a patient's story, attention to plot does much more than that. As Hogg's case study of Glen reveals, it also gives us a way to *hear* (and, in some cases, *read*) the stories to which we are witness. Knowing a patient's goals, we can spot narrative knots, understand the roles of other people in a patient's story, and be attentive to times of stress—climax and crisis—as well as resolutions of meaning in a patient's life. We can imagine and assess interventions within the play of plot. We can grow in attentiveness to the stories within stories, the alternative stories, and the changes in storyline that impact the spiritual well-being of our patients and their families.

Wirpsa's case study

Chaplain Wirpsa's narrative about her seven-year journey with Bob and his family underscores the asset that a long-term relationship can be for both patient and caregiver. It further highlights the importance of character analysis for chaplains as they assess and choose interventions that will empower patients facing painful decisions. A proponent of shared decision-making, Wirpsa places a premium on partnership. Wirpsa's personal identification with the patient as one who "takes pride in putting others first" is a credit to Bob's character and Wirpsa's powers of insight and affirmation. That identification is also, however, a potential boundary-breaker, raising questions about how the reification of a character trait may have unintentionally legislated that Bob put others first yet again when he actually asked something for himself.

Wirpsa's focus on character delineation as a means of entering into relationship is evident from the opening of her case study. Narrating Bob's story, she uses a series of descriptors to sketch Bob's outline: man, firefighter, electrician, provider. To this she adds adjectives that serve as social markers: middle-aged ("fifties"), middle-class, Caucasian, Italian–American, husband, and father. As she introduces his initial diagnosis of leukemia, she focuses on personal descriptive adjectives—"active, physical, and extremely independent"—to form the overall baseline of his character. Against this baseline she gauges his emotional and spiritual health throughout the history of their relationship and his various illness narratives.

Character delineation and analysis is a narrative art that enables a chaplain to draw out, assess, and ultimately decide upon interventions with a patient. To do this effectively, the skilled chaplain perceives constituent and recurring indications of a person's character. Such traits transcend time, unlike "feelings, thoughts, temporary motives, [and] attitudes" (Chatman 1978, p.126). This does not mean that traits cannot change or develop, but that they are often deep-seated, profoundly "of" the person. When Wirpsa participates in decision-making discussions, she stresses her ability to offer "back to Bob an image of the man he had always been—a man who would risk his life...do almost anything for others...caring and generous." In other words, she defines and reinforces throughout their relationship these character traits.

While empowering, such an intervention must be done carefully to ensure that the patient does not become captive to the illness narrative, turned into a one-dimensional hero with no option but to sacrifice himself for others. That Bob is not a flat character is evident from his capacity to "surprise" both his chaplain and his medical team, most notably when he expresses a desire to give up or die. Bob reminds those around him that his decisions are not to be imposed or predicted, that his motivations are not necessarily all rooted in (or limited to) the role of self-sacrificing first responder and family man.

Whenever Bob mentions wanting to die, the chaplain is called in. Reading his spiritual distress, Wirpsa intervenes, in part by recalling him to his "hero" self. She fosters his helper identity by having him talk with and encourage cancer patients suffering similar challenges. His subsequent actions reinforce and return him to the stable role of helper, which gives him strength.

However, the dangers of a reductive character reading become evident when Bob, diagnosed with a second cancer, wants to reject further treatment, specifically the colostomy. His deeply rooted self-image is shamed by the prospect of defecating in a bag. Wirpsa reframes that shame within the context of an emotional and spiritual growth she has been able to chart. She focuses with compassion on the reality of his disgust, his survivor's guilt, his acutely felt loss of dignity, while also recalling the heroic narrative of winning and overcoming. She offers him, potentially, the freedom to be something less than a perfect hero, something more than a static figure of self-sacrifice.

When Bob's daughter Elyse joins their conversation, Wirpsa supports the family's need for him to not give up by again affirming the part of his character focused on putting family first over his own needs. Her affirmation lends spiritual authority to his self-conception. Bob acts in accord with the chaplain's and the family's understanding of his character by unselfishly agreeing to a treatment and surgery he dreads. Their reading of his character has swayed his choice. To be sure, Wirpsa reminds Bob that the family will not ask him to bear the unbearable. This is an important intervention, not least because it proves true later when the discovery is made that a colostomy can make no difference in Bob's prognosis.

For Bob, the narrative of generous, self-sacrificing hero gives meaning to a suffering that is otherwise meaningless. Even his desire to stop that suffering is couched in the familiar narrative of other-oriented self-sacrifice rather than personal yearning for freedom from pain. Here the chaplain plays an important counter role, using her spiritual authority to give Bob the opportunity to look back at *himself*, at *his* feelings and *his* needs. With non-judgmental compassion and astuteness, she both acknowledges the challenge to his core identity as provider and protector that dying represents and wonders about his aversion to being dependent, weak, "less than the man he saw himself to be." The weeping that follows seems cathartic; he is allowed to embrace his own self-concern and self-care, able to mourn who he has been and loved being *for himself*.

Whatever its moral implications, Bob's suicide would also have been an act of autonomy and independence, giving him active agency as one who decides his own fate. Bob's calm death and his lucid goodbyes suggest that, if not exactly a free choice, his decision to die a natural death was nonetheless graced, satisfying the narrative urge for a heroic end and testifying to the chaplain's role in ushering him to a place of peace.

References

Charon, R. (2006) *Narrative Medicine: Honoring the Stories of Illness.* Oxford: Oxford University Press.

Chatman S. (1978) *Story and Discourse: Narrative Structure in Fiction and Film.* Ithaca, NY: Cornell University Press.

Colino, S. (2016) 'The health benefits of expressive writing.' *US News and World Report,* August 31. Available at https://health.usnews.com/wellness/articles/2016-08-31/the-health-benefits-of-expressive-writing

Evans, J.F. (2012) 'Expressive writing, what's on your mind and heart.' In 'Write Yourself Well.' *Psychology Today,* August 15.

Foucault, M. (1980) *The History of Sexuality, Volume 1: An Introduction.* New York: Vintage Books.

Pennebaker, J. and Evans, J. (2014) *Expressive Writing: Words that Heal.* Enumclaw, WA: Idyll Arbor Inc.

Windholz, A.M. (2018) 'Meaning Making and the Patient Story.' Paper presented at APC/NACC Conference, Anaheim, CA.

Chapter 5

CRITICAL RESPONSE TO STORY MATTERS: PATIENT AS PERSON CASE STUDIES

A Palliative Care Physician's Response

NORA SEGAR

I am a Palliative Care physician and general internist. In this dual role, I see patients at many stages of health and illness. I work at two very different practice sites. The first is the Jesse Brown VA Medical Center, where I see patients on the Palliative Care inpatient service. The second is at a federally qualified health center, Erie Family Health, where I see primarily Spanish-speaking patients in an outpatient setting.

To review, Palliative Care is specialized medical care for people with serious, often end-stage, illness. It is focused on relief from the symptoms and stress of illness with the primary goal of improving quality of life. It is provided by a specially trained interdisciplinary team of doctors, nurses, social workers, and chaplains (CAPC 2018). By focusing on symptom relief and patient priorities it has been shown to improve quality of life, advance care planning, and possibly survival (Smith *et al.* 2014). In my capacity as a Palliative Care provider I have the great fortune to work with our chaplain team on a daily basis. This case series strengthens my understanding of the mechanisms underlying their key role in patients' medical decision-making.

I choose to work in Palliative Care because the practice necessitates learning about the patient as an individual, asking "What is their story? How can we match a medical care plan with this story?" I did not grow up thinking I would go into medicine. My parents are both visual artists. I did my undergraduate degree in Spanish Language and Literature and came to medicine through the Humanities and Medicine track offered by the Icahn School of Medicine at Mount Sinai (2018). Along this path, I became interested in Narrative Medicine. I wrote my undergraduate thesis on representations of illness in Latin American literature, and during my residency, I also had the opportunity to participate in Yale School of Medicine's Workshop (2018). I subsequently organized a similar writer's workshop for my Palliative Care colleagues, and continue to write about my experiences in medicine (Segar 2013, 2016). Additionally, together with a small group of colleagues at Northwestern, we have developed an ongoing collaboration with the Poetry Foundation. We started our work reading poetry and reflecting within our multidisciplinary care team, and have since expanded it to include reading poetry with students and patients on our Palliative Care service.

I would like to introduce two key concepts that will serve to guide my comments on this case series. The first is that of *narrative competence*, and the second is that of *negative capability*. Rita Charon defines *narrative competence* as the ability to listen to the patient's stories of illness, recognize a clinical narrative, and establish a therapeutic alliance (2001, 2004; Charon *et al.* 2017). By reading literature and engaging in reflective writing, students and providers practice understanding narrative. This recognition helps us to bear witness to unfair losses and convey empathy for the patient experience. This work is central to medical practice as a Palliative Care physician and also to the work of the medical chaplain, as this case series deftly illustrates.

Negative capability is a term coined by John Keats (a physician poet). He defines negative capability as, "The ability to hold and cherish opposites in one's mind at the same time" (quoted in Coulehan and Clary 2005, p.384), to "live in uncertainties, mysteries, and doubt without any irritable reaching after facts and reason" (Coulehan and Clary 2005, p.384). This is something that we need particular help with as physicians who often, "irritably reach after facts and reason" (Coulehan and Clary 2005, p.384).

Literature in general, but poems more specifically, ask us to hold and cherish opposites in the mind at the same time. One stanza often contains two contradictory meanings or different meanings to different readers. Take the patient who can't swallow. He wants to live no matter what but also doesn't want a feeding tube placed. Or the patient's family who understands that their loved one will not make it out of the Intensive Care Unit (ICU) but holds out hope for a miracle.

In this, I am reminded of Chaplain Galchutt's shared writing experience with his patient Keith. Keith is able to use his writing to articulate his feelings, hopes, and fears, facilitating his medical decision-making. Galchutt writes that this was, "an often-vacillating experience, neither linear nor objective." Writing creates a safe space for the patient to express his conflicting hopes, for him to, "hold and cherish opposites in the mind at the same time." Narrative Theorist Arthur Frank attests to the power of writing in the face of complex, often conflicting, emotions and goals: "We give people an opportunity to hear themselves, tell their own stories, and probably to tell stories repeatedly, with minor variations until they find a version they can live with" (2014, S17). In trying on a variety of sometimes contradictory narratives, Keith is able to come to the decision that feels best for him.

How can two different stories be true at same time? How can a vacillating narrative help us to make medical decisions? These are sometimes foreign concepts to the biomedically trained. While contradictory facts are difficult for us as doctors to hold in the mind at once, if we can do so, it greatly increases our capacity for empathy with our patients and our ability to stand with them in the uncertainties they face at the end of their lives.

While reading and writing can help a clinician cultivate their own narrative capacity, these cases show us that writing can also do this for our patients. There has been very little work like this in medicine, even in the domain of Palliative Care, which often uses non-traditional therapeutic strategies. Additionally, this is not something we are trained to do in medical school. With the help of the Poetry Foundation, we have worked to curate collections of poetry and a corresponding discussion guide. We are currently reading these poems with patients on our Palliative Care consult service. I have found the reflections of our patients when reading these poems to be moving and profound. It has opened up spaces for non-medical conversations, and leveled the playing field between the patient and myself.

The importance of personal narrative is central to each of the cases in this section. In Glen's case, he is able to express his personal narrative in the form of a message to his congregation. In writing and delivering this message, he is able to frame his illness for himself and continue to feel useful and vital. As he says, "he still has a mission." He is able to help others, though he is losing much of his independence. This feeling of completion, or of purpose, in the chaplain's description, also seems linked to his decision to forgo feeding tube placement.

Chaplain Wirpsa's understanding of Bob's personal narrative leads her to recognize his need to give back to others. Bob accepts her offer to speak with other newly diagnosed cancer patients, an activity that is therapeutic for him. This activity becomes a means by which Bob incorporates his illness into his identity as provider and giver of comfort.

In Galchutt's case study, the Mutually Expressive Writing exercise that Keith and the chaplain perform together also illustrates the therapeutic power of narrative articulation. The formality of the written word serves to amplify Keith's unique voice. He comments on how meaningful it was for him to have a concrete creative expression of his illness experience. Illness has the potential to destroy an individual's creativity and sense of utility. In contrast, reading poetry with patients, writing with them, or simply hearing their story also allows us as providers to see the patient as an intellectual with creative capacity.

As providers, many of us enter into medicine with at least some capacity to elicit narrative. Yet the pressures of the job and the training involved can erode these skills. Sometimes we have to *unlearn* some of the interview techniques modeled in biomedical practice. The medical interview is a very agenda-focused interview. We are taught to collect answers to a checklist of questions in order to create a very specific note in the chart and a very specific style of communication with our colleagues. This style of communication tends to truncate open-ended questions; it often prioritizes what the doctor needs to know over what the patient wishes to discuss. We have to *unlearn* some of the interview techniques or, as these cases also illustrate, we have to learn to lean on the skills of our interdisciplinary colleagues.

For example, in Wirpsa's case, when Bob initially refuses treatment for his colon cancer, the oncologist's instincts are to refer the patient to a psychologist and to Wirpsa. Though one could argue that the oncologist should also be trained to elicit the underlying narrative for this decision-making, she shows skill in identifying other people on the care team who would provide the best longitudinal narrative insight. In seeing Bob over time, the chaplain is able to understand how Bob's illness has robbed him of his identity and help him to articulate and shift this narrative—and ultimately to shift his medical decision-making.

I often find myself tempted to prioritize my own agenda in the medical interview. The time pressures of a busy clinical schedule add another layer of pressure. In contrast, the dialogue of these case studies demonstrates a more patient-centered, active-listening interview technique. Lines like "tell me more..." or "I would love to hear more about that;" reflective statements like "sounds like...," "that sounds beautiful," or "that sounds unbearable" are common throughout these case examples. It is this open-ended, reflective interviewing style that elicits a personal narrative from the patients and facilitates their complex end-of-life decision-making. It takes practice, mentorship, and collaboration to maintain these skills.

Many providers would be able to employ a narrative approach to the medical interview given they had additional time and training. In the outpatient setting this is especially challenging, as visits are often 20 minutes long (including clinical documentation, ordering of necessary tests, and executing a medical plan.) While these extreme time pressures harm patients and providers alike (Wright and Katz 2018), in our current clinical context shared decision-making relies heavily on our interdisciplinary teams. These teams increase our effectiveness and also our capacity for joy in practice.

These cases remind us of the importance of patient-centeredness in a few key ways. First, the chaplain interview reminds us of the centrality of the question, "What is the patient's desired outcome (if any) from this visit?" (VandeCreek and Lucas 2001, quoted in the Hogg case study). In contrast, the overarching question from most medical interviews would read more like, "What does the doctor need to know so they can develop a treatment plan?" As medical practitioners, we could benefit from considering that first question more often. Second, we learn that being patient-centered does not require us to remove ourselves from the patient encounter. In contrast, we benefit from asking ourselves, "Where am I in this patient's story?"

Each of these cases involves self-reflection and disclosure on the part of the chaplain. For example, Galchutt writes, "the patient identified as African American, a husband and father of two young children. I identify as male, white, middle-aged, a husband, father, and a Lutheran pastor." One rarely sees this type of self-identification from medical doctors, though our identities are integral to our clinical encounters. Instead, we can project an illusion of objectivity, which negates how our own identities affect our relationships with our patients, or implies that these identities can somehow be surmounted.

Self-removal from the clinical encounter can erode our sense of meaning in our work over time. It also diminishes the role that race, class, and culture play in developing (or impeding) an effective and trusting therapeutic alliance. The majority of my work is with patients whose identity differs significantly from my own, a young, white woman. In listening for personal narrative with my patients, I am often aware of these differences and how they inform the types of stories I hear or don't hear. I have found that reading poetry with patients often opens up a space for my patients to discuss their personal identities. By reading together, I am also allowing myself to be present (and sometimes vulnerable) as an individual in the clinical encounter.

Removing our identities and emotions from the clinical encounter also negatively impacts physician wellness. It robs us of the opportunity to grieve the losses of our patients and amplifies the distance between us. In contrast, I am struck by the frank acknowledgement of grief by the chaplain discussants in these cases. Medical practitioners would benefit from a more complete acknowledgement of their own grief. First, though, we must acknowledge ourselves as individuals present in our clinical relationships, in both our strengths and our own personal biases.

The mutual nature of the expressive writing exercise that Galchutt does with Keith allows for the kind of appropriate self-disclosure and self-awareness I am referencing. It is not just the patient writing then sharing; the chaplain also participates in writing and sharing his part in the story, deepening and solidifying the trust in this relationship. Similarly, Wirpsa discloses aspects of her own identity in understanding her relationship with Bob. Her conclusion acknowledges this co-creation of their story, and her unique identity in the relationship. This acknowledgement of self in the patient–provider relationship, though often neglected, has the potential to nourish both patient and clinician.

In allowing patients to speak, be fully heard, and write their own stories, the patients in these cases are able to construct a narrative that makes sense and meaning out of the chaos of their medical illness. In other words, "As narrative is constructed, narrative constructs" (Garro and Mattingly 2000, p.16). Galchutt frames the completion of advance directives in terms of the writing experience he does with Keith. By default, if the patient does not specify otherwise, medical practitioners will provide a patient with every possible intervention to extend the quantity of life. This can come at the expense of quality of life and can lead to unnecessary suffering at the end of life. In completing advance directives, we ask our patients to consider the difficult questions of what they would want for their own healthcare if they were to become sicker. By choosing what he does and does not want for medical interventions, Keith acts as the author of his own medical future. He regains some control in an otherwise chaotic and confusing experience. In this way, completion of advance directives becomes a way that Keith can shape his own narrative.

Similarly, it is Wirpsa's narrative work with Bob that shapes many of his medical decisions—first, his decision to undergo surgery and then his family's decision to advise the surgeon to stop, when Bob could no longer speak for himself. In the second major decision juncture, a Narrative Medicine approach also allows Bob's oncologist to make a recommendation to forgo ongoing chemotherapy. Though additional chemotherapy can lead to unnecessary suffering and harm at the end of life (Greer *et al.* 2012; Rodriguez, DeJesus and Cheng, 2014; Temel *et al.* 2010), the recommendation to stop can sometimes be emotionally challenging for an oncologist to make. In Bob's case, the experienced medical chaplain was able to ask an informed question, easing the pain of this recommendation for both the patient and the oncologist.

Chaplain Hogg's work demonstrates the importance of continuity for our patients and is an excellent reminder of this longitudinal care often lacking in both the inpatient and outpatient setting. It further demonstrates the added value of occasionally seeing patients together with our interdisciplinary colleagues to support the patient with our different skills, and to support and learn from each other in the challenges of doing this work. In Hogg's case, the chaplain is able to support Glen in private sessions and in a group setting by participating in his care conference. The chaplain is also able to advocate for Glen to speak for himself in this conference and use his own words to describe his goals of care. Wirpsa's work with Bob is also a testament to her long-standing relationship with the patient and his family and the luxury of time in each of her clinical encounters. Joint visits with the medical staff are also invaluable, as discussed above.

Faith, or questioning of one's faith, is central to narrative construction, and patients have demonstrated that they want their spiritual needs attended to, especially at the end of life (Steinhauser *et al.* 2000). Though there is growing interest in incorporating spirituality into medical education (Fortin and Barnett 2004), medical school and residency do not always train us well in these domains. As such, this important aspect of our patients' lives can be a source of discomfort (or sometimes direct conflict) for the medical team. Respecting the role faith plays in medical decision-making is often key to trust building between patients and their care providers. In this way, as in so many others, the medical chaplain becomes an integral part of our team. No matter our faith backgrounds, if we, as doctors, can embrace a patient's spiritual concerns, it strengthens our understanding of our patient's perspective and aids us in supporting their decision-making.

Conclusion

This case series illustrates the role of narrative in medical decision-making, and the unique place of the medical chaplain. It should be required reading for our interdisciplinary teams. Palliative Care has embraced the concepts of narrative competence, negative capability, and open-ended, patient-centered interviewing perhaps more than other fields in medicine, but each member of the interdisciplinary care team brings a unique perspective and skillset to the clinical encounter. Of significance is the longitudinal role of the chaplain, their interview skillset, and their prioritization of the patient narrative and spiritual needs. Their presence, skill, and support facilitate important medical decision-making at many stages of illness. These cases also highlight the importance of self-awareness in the provider–patient relationship. In each, the chaplains pay attention to their own grief and self-care as well as acknowledging their own identities in their co-creation of story with the patients. This collection is a welcome addition to training in Palliative Care, medical education and interdisciplinary teamwork.

References

CAPC (Center to Advance Palliative Care) (2018) *What is Palliative Care?* Available at www.capc.org/about/palliative-care

Charon, R. (2001) 'The patient–physician relationship. Narrative medicine: A model for empathy, reflection, profession, and trust.' *JAMA 286*, 15, 1897–1902.

Charon, R. (2004) 'Narrative and medicine.' *New England Journal of Medicine 350*, 9, 862–864.

Charon, R., DasGupta, S., Hermann, N., Irvine, C., *et al.* (2017) *The Principles and Practice of Narrative Medicine.* New York: Oxford University Press.

Coulehan, J. and Clary, P. (2005) 'Healing the healer: Poetry in palliative care.' *Journal of Palliative Medicine 8*, 2, 382–389.

Fortin, A.H. and Barnett, K.G. (2004) 'STUDENTJAMA. Medical school curricula in spirituality and medicine.' *JAMA 291*, 23, 2883.

Frank, A.W. (2014) 'Narrative ethics as dialogical story-telling.' *Hastings Center Report, 44*, s1, S16–S20.

Garro, L. and Mattingly, C. (2000) 'Narrative as Construct and Construction.' In L. Garro and C. Mattingly (eds) *Narrative and the Cultural Construction of Illness and Healing* (pp.1–50). Berkeley, CA: University of California Press.

Greer, J.A., Pirl, W.F., Jackson, V.A., Muzikansky, A., *et al.* (2012) 'Effect of early palliative care on chemotherapy use and end-of-life care in patients with metastatic non-small-cell lung cancer.' *Journal of Clinical Oncology 30*, 4, 394–400.

Icahn School of Medicine at Mount Sinai (2018) 'Early Assurance Programs.' Available at https://icahn.mssm.edu/education/medical/md-program/flexmed

Rodriguez, M.A, DeJesus, A.Y. and Cheng, L. (2014) 'Use of chemotherapy within the last 14 days of life in patients treated at a comprehensive cancer center.' *JAMA Internal Medicine 174*, 6, 989–991.

Segar, N. (2013) 'Bedside.' *Hastings Center Report 43*, 5, 8–9.

Segar, N. (2016) 'The moonlighter's list.' *Journal of Palliative Medicine 19*, 1, 114–115.

Smith, S., Brick, A., O'Hara, S. and Norman, C. (2014) 'Evidence of the cost and cost-effectiveness of palliative care: A literature review.' *Palliative Medicine 28*, 2, 130–150.

Steinhauser, K.E., Christakis, N.A., Clipp, E.C., McNeilly, M., McIntyre, L. and Tulsky, J.A. (2000) 'Factors considered important at the end of life by patients, family, physicians, and other care providers.' *JAMA 284*, 19, 2476–2482.

Temel, J.S., Greer, J.A., Muzikansky, A., Gallagher, E.R., *et al.* (2010) 'Early palliative care for patients with metastatic non-small-cell lung cancer.' *New England Journal of Medicine 363*, 8, 733–742.

VandeCreek, L. and Lucas, A. (2001) *The Discipline for Pastoral Care Giving: Foundations for Outcome Oriented Chaplaincy.* Binghampton, NY: Haworth Press.

Wright, A.A. and Katz, I.T. (2018) 'Beyond burnout – Redesigning care to restore meaning and sanity for physicians.' *New England Journal of Medicine 378*, 4, 309–311.

Yale School of Medicine (2018) 'The Workshop.' Residency Training Programs. Available at https://medicine.yale.edu/intmed/residency/crossprograminfo/writershop

PART II

EMOTIONS AND FAMILY DYNAMICS THAT IMPACT MEDICAL DECISION-MAKING

KAREN PUGLIESE AND M. JEANNE WIRPSA

W HAT happens in childhood matters. Psalm 139 assures us we are wondrously made, mysteriously and wondrously formed in secret, knit together in the liminal space of the womb (Jones 2000, p.801) But what happens next in those early years of childhood as our psyche or soul is formed and shaped? We are incredibly vulnerable, and those who long to protect and prepare us for life's hazardous journey are ultimately powerless to do so. Over time, roles reverse; illness, disease, and tragedy strike.

The first family drama we inhabit, biological or not, is the social setting in which we begin the process of individuation, of *becoming*. No matter the cast of characters or roles they are assigned, the collective characters constellate into "family"—an extended metaphor with spoken and unspoken beliefs, values, themes, and rules, as well as implicit and explicit biases. Simply stated, we then begin a process of psychological differentiation that lasts a lifetime. Its aim is the development of the individual personality and ultimately, psychological wholeness (Kerr and Bowen 1988). Existential or spiritual well-being relates to individuals' capacity to engage the inner life and mobilize their inner resources to meet the challenges of living authentically and ultimately address the problem of dying well. "The spiritual distress they may feel may not be expressed in language traditionally associated with religion or faith; however, spiritual struggle or distress is always revealed as a change or loss of meaning and sometimes, trying to reconstruct what is purposeful" (ACPE *et al.* 2018, p.6). Thomas Merton describes this process as restoring the "hidden wholeness that remains beneath the broken surface of our lives and the lives of those we serve" (quoted in Palmer 2004, p.4).

This process affects the choices and decisions we make throughout our lifetime: "Our subjective experience of life and our behaviors are governed by literally thousands of beliefs (ideas) that compose the map used for interpreting the events of our life (including our own mental events)" (Viorst 2002, p.227). Well-differentiated people retain relative autonomy in times of stress and are more flexible, adaptable, and independent of the emotionality about them. But, as Parker Palmer (2004, p.21) advises, "Living integral lives as adults is far more daunting than recovering our childhood capacity to commute between two worlds. As adults, we must achieve a complex integration that spans the contradictions between inner and outer reality that supports both personal integrity and the common good."

In the following cases, Chaplains Goheen, Swofford, and Vilagros creatively and effectively provide ministry to patients and families caught in the web of intense emotionality and strained family dynamics impacting medical decision-making. In each case, they assist the patient and family in the "complex integration" Palmer (2004) describes as they bring a working knowledge of how religious beliefs and practices are embedded in family systems and intertwined with emotional responses to illness, loss, and anticipated death. In each case, they integrate critical thinking with contemplative reflection on their own emotions and reactions, resulting in compassionate action. We will briefly introduce their ministry using the framework of four "pastoral tasks" particularly applicable to these cases: accompanying, linking, discerning, and ritualizing (Accardi 1990).

In her response to these three cases, Dr Mukherjee lifts up the theme of *accompanying*—articulating the ways in which each author serves as a companion and guide. Chaplains' education and formation equips them to serve as "wilderness guides"—venturing on the unfamiliar, unpredictable, and frightening terrain of uncertainty, grief, and loss. Chaplains recognize landmarks and help "travelers" to keep moving on their journey without feeling so lost and alone. Compassionate, contemplative listening and empathic, reflective response, along with cultural competence, enables chaplains to gauge patient and family needs and abilities, and provide appropriate assistance and solidarity on the difficult trails they traverse.

Chaplains must also be skilled story weavers, *linking* together patient, family, and medical team narratives to form a meaningful tapestry of their individual and collective experience. Intricately embedded in the weaving are sacred texts, scriptural stories, myths, and traditions—stories of reconciliation, healing, and hope. Goheen demonstrates the task of *linking* through his in-depth, lived understanding of the profile of the community he serves; through his insight into the role of "matriarch," including the impact of diminishment of his patient Rita's familial authority and role responsibilities; and through his proficiency in addressing ethical issues and authentic respect for the family's religious worldview. Goheen learns family values, roles, and history, and links the family story through his application of Bowen's family systems theories, profiles of differentiation, and the mutigenerational transmission process (Kerr and Bowen 1988). He gains family trust through his recognition of their ingrained religious value systems and his ability to link these values to others central to their faith tradition. Finally, he creatively interprets both the family and the medical team's narratives, facilitating a healthy inter-system relationship.

Swofford's ministry rests on a unique *linking* of people and pastoral strategies. She creatively enables her non-verbal patient, Mark, to give voice to his emotions, frustrations, and end-of-life concerns. Mark had always identified as a "self-made man," independent and hard working. Now, intubated and unable to communicate, he writes, "I'm a lab rat." Irate, threatening (and grieving), his daughter Karen threatens lawsuits and makes it more difficult for the medical team to hear and honor Mark's wishes. Joseph Featherstone, writing about "Family Matters," observes that he was "struck again and again by the mysterious capacity of people to give and withhold themselves on their own terms" (quoted in Viorst 2002, p.233). Swofford advocates for Mark by connecting him with his medical team and patiently developing a relationship with his daughter. Ultimately, working insightfully with their dynamics of resistance and defense, she restores the hidden wholeness beneath the broken relationship between father and daughter.

The task of *discernment* implies acknowledging and affirming hopes and dreams, lived experience, purpose and significance of life, and meaning and legacy leaving in death. Chaplains are equipped for this task with theological reflection skills, crucial conversation and confrontation expertise, and spiritual direction skills. Vilagos mobilizes her pastoral gifts and embarks on the task of *discerning* a pathway of hope through the ambiguous and paradoxical feelings enmeshed in her patient Aaron's family system. As tensions shift around Aaron, his wife Belinda, and their daughter Trina, Vilagos' care plan lays a foundation for post-traumatic growth and hope, based in part on her astute assessment of motivations, belief systems and theological perspectives, family dynamics, and emotions.

Vilagos also employs two intentional occurrences of the fourth pastoral task, *ritualizing*, "to elicit hope and ease the guilt and uncertainty that sometimes surrounds medical decision-making." Rituals are a key component of pastoral skill and authority. They acknowledge patients as *people*, with unique identities and stories. Rituals enhance spoken and unspoken communication, and in the midst of stressful, fearful, life-changing events, create sacred space in which to hold paradoxical feelings of confidence and hope in the midst of powerlessness and despair. Vilagos engages Belinda, Trina, *and* Aaron in creating handprints while encouraging story-telling throughout the print-making. She employs a second extended family ritual honoring Aaron's wish for the family to "come together," creating a restorative bond, and healing past hurts and divisions.

However *family* is defined or configured, it is important to recognize the patient and family, as well as the medical team, as an emotional unit with complex emotional reactions, responses, and interactions. In the literature about what non-chaplains perceive to be the role and responsibilities of the professional healthcare chaplain, care for the family and emotional support for both patient and family are commonly cited (in addition to the obvious provision of spiritual and religious care). What is missing in this literature, however, and even unrecognized by some chaplains themselves, is the way both emotions and family directly influence and sometimes impede the process of medical decision-making. The three chaplains featured in this section grasp the complex interrelation between emotion, family, spirituality and religion, and the trajectory of illness. At times they attend to one thread in isolation from the others; at other times, they deftly hold the warp and woof of the intricate tapestry, seeking wholeness and healing.

The following case studies recognize an equally important reality: the medical team itself functions as a "family system." Like the families in its care, its proscribed and stable roles and expectations are threatened with disruption by illness and loss. The medical team, including the chaplain, may become part of the family system for which they are caring as hopes and fears are displaced (through mechanisms of transference) onto them. Attention by the chaplain to the shifting roles and expectations, complex emotional reactions, responses and interactions of not only the patient's family but also of the medical team itself reduces tensions and conflict that can impede communication and thwart the medical decision-making process.

Chaplains possess the flexibility and expertise that allows for the establishment of deeply therapeutic relationships within the patient, family, and healthcare team systems. When families appear unable or unwilling to engage in a process of medical decision-making and teams are frustrated and disengaged, chaplains are skilled interpreters and healers of emotional, existential, and spiritual distress. Relational and emotional dynamics matter, and chaplains are adept at helping to ensure patient-centered medical decision-making and optimizing the health and well-being of patient and family systems and healthcare teams.

References

Accardi, R.F. (1990) 'Rehabilitation: Dreams Lost, Dreams Found.' In H. Hayes and C.J. van der Poel (eds) *Health Care Ministry: A Handbook for Chaplains* (pp.88–92). New York: Paulist Press.

ACPE: The Standard for Spiritual Care & Education, Association of Professional Chaplains, Canadian Association for Spiritual Care/Association canadienne de soins spirituels, National Association of Catholic Chaplains and Neshama: Association of Jewish Chaplains (2018) *The Impact of Professional Spiritual Care*. A joint publication. Available at www.spirit-filled.org/documents/APC18_Report.pdf

Jones, A. (ed.) (2000) *The Jerusalem Bible: Reader's Edition*. New York: Doubleday & Company, Inc.

Kerr, M.E. and Bowen, M. (1988) *Family Evaluation: An Approach Based on Bowen Theory*. New York: W.W. Norton & Company.

Palmer, P.J. (2004) *A Hidden Wholeness: The Journey Toward an Undivided Life*. San Francisco, CA: Jossey-Bass.

Viorst, J. (2002) *Necessary Losses: The Loves, Illusions, Dependencies, and Impossible Expectations that All of Us Have to Give Up in Order to Grow*. New York: The Free Press.

Chapter 6

RITA'S STORY

"Aren't we supposed to honor our mother and father?"—
Ray, grandson of the family matriarch, Rita

KEITH W. GOHEEN

Introduction

This case study illustrates the additive value of chaplaincy care in the often-complex process of establishing values-centered goals of care in the clinical setting. The study examines what happens to one family when their matriarch becomes critically ill, leaving the family in spiritual crisis.

Rita was an 84-year-old European-American woman with a history of multiple hospital admissions. She was the family matriarch, presiding over a clan whose roots sank deep into the local farmland. The family system was held together by religiously informed roles and social values that were modeled, mediated, and sustained by Rita. A devastating illness brought a new and difficult test to the family system and to their partnership in medical decision-making with the medical team. As dementia drained Rita's vibrant independence, her family fashioned a web of caring support but became divided when faced with end-of-life decisions. As the Palliative Care chaplain entrusted with their care, I served as mediator between family members and Rita's medical team, interpreting and harmonizing their value systems across the divide.

I am a board-certified chaplain and member of the Association of Professional Chaplains (APC). I received a Master of Divinity degree from the Andover Newton Theological School, where I was introduced to Family Systems Theory, and I went on to be ordained by the small, family-centered First Universalist Church in Orange, MA.

The hospital where I serve is a 101-year-old, community-owned, 200-bed institution located in a growing ocean-side retirement area surrounded by rural towns supporting family farming businesses. For the past 12 years, I have provided spiritual and religious care to patients and staff. Among my responsibilities, I serve on the growing Palliative Care team.

I was brought up in a small town nestled in the river hills in south central Pennsylvania, where the economy was based on family farming and manufacturing, and the dominant religious groups were socially conservative, evangelical Christians. As a result, I have an insider's understanding of the socially conservative, semi-rural character of native southern Delaware. Having lived in major East Coast metropolitan areas, I can also connect with the medical professionals and retirees moving into our service area from the more religiously diverse arc of surrounding cities. Personally and professionally, I strive to work from the place of the "radical middle," seeking to find the good amid a mutually caring common ground. As a son, spouse, father, and grandfather, I am growing in my appreciation of the multi-generational family and the necessity of social interdependence for genuine health.

The names and personally identifying information of the people involved in the following case have been altered to provide anonymity, as I was unable to obtain permission from the participants.

Case

I had met Rita and her family through a referral during an earlier admission. At the time, her dementia was still in an early stage and her personality was largely intact. She had been admitted for treatment of a chronic, rather than life-threatening, disease. Her first request at that time was simple, a prayer, because she said: "We all need to pray." With family gathered around the bedside, I discerned that her words were simultaneously a request and a teaching. Rita was exercising familial authority and role responsibility in this simple religious act. I agreed to lead prayer in recognition of Rita's authority and her invitation to serve in a pastoral role within her wider family circle.

Over the following visits, spanning several admissions, I observed the consistent use of religious language and metaphor in the family's routine conversations. The familial usage communicated emotional bonding and "membership" in the family system's most intimate circles more than interest in the theology. In our time together, conversations rarely strayed from Rita's stories about family, interspersed with praise for God. She saw the hand of God in every family success. Though seldom stated plainly, suffering was understood as a falling from God's favor. In Rita's moral canon, suffering would end when "things were set right." Through listening and careful affirmation, I demonstrated an understanding of the family's values, learned family roles and history, and gained their trust through respect for their religious worldview.

Rita experienced a dramatic decline in her health during the last few months of her life. The loss of her ability to swallow proved especially devastating for her loved ones. I sat with her family as they agonized with the decision about whether or not to provide Rita artificial nutrition through a G-tube (gastrointestinal tube).

According to the family's recounting of the meetings with physicians, the conversation with the attending hospitalist had been limited almost entirely to the clinical issues. Given the diagnosis of dysphagia, the doctor informed the family that the standard treatment would be the placement of a feeding tube. A referral was made to a surgeon, who assured the family that the procedure was routine. Physically, Rita was a good candidate. Not offered to the family was ethical guidance and education drawing from a growing body of clinical evidence recommending against placing this medical device in patients with advanced dementia. The necessity of discerning the procedure's value in terms of desirability was left entirely to the family. Having only received expert technical information, the family felt adrift without expert ethical guidance.

They agreed that the once perpetually industrious Rita would not have wanted to be kept alive this way, but no one was willing to stop feeding her. Son-in-law Bobby spoke for the group: "She has fed all of us. How can we not feed her?" The family system was absent its matriarch, who should be making these difficult decisions. They were emotionally powerless and conflicted as they faced the larger threat of losing her. I remained in the pastoral role. Following Rita's teaching, we gathered together, seeking guidance in prayer. A G-tube was subsequently placed.

Within two months, Rita was hospitalized again. The tube site was not healing. Even in her dementia, Rita's hand would find the intrusive device and pull at it. Repairs were attempted and more protective bandaging was devised. Within weeks, however, Rita was back with a still unhealed and ugly-looking wound. The doctors asked for permission to remove it. In a rare show of disharmony, the family became acrimonious. Under heaven, things needed to be set right.

As Rita's mental capacities had waned, the primary weight of day-to-day care fell to Rita's daughter-in-law Jean and Jean's daughter Missy. Long married to Mike, Rita's oldest son, Jean enjoyed daughter status in the family. Semi-retired and living in a home with an extra bedroom, Jean and Missy, who attended the local community college, had agreed to move Rita into their home when it had first become clear that Rita was no longer able to live alone. Other family would drop in or "spell" (give a break to) the primary caregivers, and everyone kept close tabs on her progress. Home healthcare staff visited regularly after the surgery. The family followed instructions and continued to lavish attention on Rita. It wasn't supposed to go this way.

Now, Rita's restlessness in the bed was difficult to interpret. Was it the dementia? Was it physical pain? Was she expressing disapproval of the whole mess? Speculation filled the room. Although the family placed no blame on Jean, it was clear that she was feeling guilt. Each time a physician or wound care nurse came into the room, Jean would review her care regimen.

"What else could I do?" Jean asked in a plaintive voice. It was day four of the most recent admission, and once again, the hospitalist reassured her that nothing else could be done. "Sometimes," she added, "these things just happen." Jean continued to ruminate: "I couldn't keep her hands tied?" "No," agreed the doctor, "that would have been unkind to her." "Is there something I did wrong?" continued Jean. "From all that I have heard, you gave great care," assured the physician. Mike, wishing the cycle of questioning to end, spoke summarily: "You did fine. Like the doctor said, these things happen. Nobody's blaming you." Mike's words quieted the conversation, but did not address the underlying family belief; things don't just happen, everything happens for a reason.

In a religious world where God is in ultimate control of even the most mundane of details, there is no room for random misfortunes. Rita was suffering, the family was suffering, and everyone in the family understood that suffering was inflicted as a means of correcting behavior. Jean's ruminations had a soul-searching quality about them.

Evangelical Christianity places a high importance on individual moral accountability. It would be important to the family, and to Rita's well-being, that any moral failing be addressed so that familial harmony could be restored. Jean's self-questioning was a demonstration of her loving commitment to Rita and to the family's piety. Her introspection was mirrored in the family's collective efforts to find resolution.

Mike attempted to move the religious examination outside of the family's immediate responsibility. "Did something go wrong in surgery? Could all of this have been prevented?" he asked, holding the hospitalist's gaze and leaning forward in his chair. Ending an uncomfortable moment of silence, the hospitalist began: "I reviewed the surgeon's report in the chart and didn't see anything unusual noted." Mike's eyes closed, but his body remained alert. The doctor continued: "There is always a risk with any procedure, especially with patients who are elderly and have her condition." Mike flopped back in his chair and turned his face toward the window as if he had been slapped on the cheek. The other family members diverted their gazes. Conversation stopped. The physician finished her examination of the patient and quietly slipped from the room after assuring them that Wound Care would also be visiting today.

In the language of the family's religion, the source of the suffering was now made manifest. Once the physician had left the room, Mike named it for everyone: "We should have never agreed to this." Deborah, Mike's sister and Rita's heir apparent within the family system, spoke in the family's defense: "We thought she could get stronger. She has always bounced back before." Other heads nodded in agreement. "We had to try," offered Missy in a meek voice from a corner of the room. I noticed that the language had changed. The feeding therapy was now being discussed in the past tense.

The family was coming together again. The "sin" was in having chosen poorly. Having made the choice collectively, the family was now willing to hold the guilt for Rita's suffering collectively. In this way, the otherwise unbearable weight of the suffering was held systemically. It was a painful harmonic, but also honest, loving, and hopeful. Loving, because the family entered willingly into it, choosing suffering over abandonment. Hopeful, because their religion teaches that the shame of suffering can lead to the glory of redemption. Human confession and divine grace were needed for the journey. I invited the family into prayer.

The suffering was not limited to Rita and her family. The medical team struggled with the ethical dimensions of their work and with the emotional burden that came with the knowledge that they were contributing to Rita's discomfort.

Privately, the nurses counseled with each other. Confiding in me to one side of the nursing station, one of the nurses captured the team's growing alarm: "I feel like we are torturing her." A second nurse expressed frustration with the doctors who had been ineffective in persuading the family to change the plan of care. She wondered aloud about how much of her perspective she should share with family: "Why can't they see that she is not going to get better? I know they care about her, but somebody has to make them understand where all this is going." An aide noted that the overnight nurse had tried to talk to "the oldest daughter" the evening before, and added, "She wouldn't listen." In an effort to reconcile the seemingly vast gap between the nurses' ethical imperative, comfort in the course of dying, and the family's desire to "do everything," they tried to diagnose an as-yet undisclosed motivation that might still be unaddressed and thus hindering the transition to more appropriate forms of care.

The doctors carried misgivings, too. Beside the big window next to the dictation room, the hospitalist and I looked out across the town below us. "These cases are always hard," she said, half-sighing. "The family doesn't seem to hear what we are trying to tell them. I know they want her to get better and not be in pain. If she were my mother, I would want that too, and I know that they don't want her to die. Our options are really limited here."

An Intensive Care Unit (ICU) physician with whom I had worked for many years would begin difficult family consultations with this observation: "Families have hope, doctors have experience." The quote has become a spiritual metric for me, a way to assess the balance and flow of spiritual energy within the person, the family, and amid the relationships that form and reform in the course of treatment. In the most spiritually healthy relationships between families and staff, there must be a balance between hope and experience.

Across the board, the medical team had come to a clear, experience-based consensus. Rita was moving toward death, and it was likely to be a painful end. The moral stress was evident on their faces and in their conversations. Significantly, the stress had not risen to a level of spiritual crisis, requiring a focused intervention. The team was coping. Good care was being provided, and interdisciplinary collaboration continued. Helping them to find safe venues to name their hurts and explore their feelings without judgment was meeting their needs in the moment.

Having no experience with this kind of a situation, Rita's family had been putting all their spiritual eggs in the basket of hope; specifically, the hope that they might have their beloved matriarch with them for a while longer, and that she would flourish, as best as she was able, in their care. The collapse of this expectation had left the family in spiritual distress. They had lost hope. The spiritual exercise of inward examination and confession had led them to a form of forgiveness, in that they accepted the responsibility for their decision to place the G-tube. Forgiveness allowed them let go of the burden of the past. The exercise did not, however, produce an acceptable way forward.

The family could have humbly bowed to the medical team's expertise and accepted the recommendation. While solving the immediate problem, it would have also caused moral damage to the family system. They could not simply surrender their matriarch to the will and care of others. They needed to remain invested in her life, actively loving her, because it was what family was intended to do. The understanding of a solution to the family's crisis began in my mind as a question: "From where will a new hope come?" As with all spiritually resilient systems, the answer would need to come from within the family.

The final decision about removing the G-tube remained unaddressed. The Palliative Care team was asked to intervene. We joined all of Rita's children and several of their spouses around a hospital conference room table. Other relatives were linked by speakerphone. The solemnity of the meeting made it a sacred, values-centered, clan gathering. They were deciding their common course as they decided Rita's fate.

Agony grew as the team retold the now familiar medical story, with its options and risks. Deborah withdrew from the conversation, saying she couldn't decide. The resulting power vacuum left everyone adrift. The conversation became confused. Finally, Ray, a grandson, asked the religious question: "Aren't we supposed to honor our mother and our father? How can starving Mom-Mom be honoring our mother and father?" Ray's appeal to a religiously derived family value crystalized the struggle. The medical team leaned back in their chairs. Family heads drooped or turned upward toward the blue sky just outside the meeting room window. The speakerphone poured out silence.

Exercising the pastoral role given to me by the family and risking the trust I had cultivated by openly shifting my social alignment to the medical team, I hoped to be the bridge reconnecting the two sides and rebalancing the hope–experience equation. With a carefully measured tone, I began: "You ask a very good religious question, Ray." Turning my gaze to the Palliative Care team, I stated: "As the resident religious professional, I think it is my responsibility to provide an answer. I hope you can hear what is on my heart."

Turning my attention back to the family members present in the room, who were now wide-eyed and focused on my face, I continued:

> I think I can speak for all the hospital staff at this table, I certainly know it for myself, that you and your family love Rita dearly, that she is important to you, and that more than anything else, you want to do right by her. From the beginning, your desire and your care have been nothing but honorable. Things have not turned out for the best, but it has not been from your lack of trying. I think she would be proud to know how hard everyone has worked to do the right thing.

A softly-spoken, "I agree," came from the Palliative Care physician leading the meeting. Other members of the team nodded in solemn agreement. I read relief and grateful recognition in the family's faces. Jean dabbed at tears forming in her eyes.

Absolved of wrongdoing, the family could release the collective sense of guilt and shame. The possibility of moving forward could now re-emerge, but the family was not re-empowered to take over her care. I continued, this time addressing the medical team's dilemma. "From what I understand, the medical staff is saying that there is nothing more they can do to make Rita better. Her body isn't responding to treatment, and no medical care can help if the body isn't able to do its part." There were nods of affirmation from the medical team. The family began to glance at one another. The idea that there might be a limit to treatment seemed to generate some surprise. I continued: "Rita's body is telling us something important. We need to honor this message." A few heads nodded in agreement, but most of the group sat quietly. No one was looking away. The mood of the room felt pensive.

Focusing on the speakerphone, I spoke directly:

Ray, when I turn to the scriptures, I see time and again where Jesus offered mercy to those who were suffering. We can continue trying medical treatments to keep your Mom-Mom with us, but we will never make her better than she is right now. I think that the best way your family can honor this person you all love dearly is to offer her mercy. What do you feel would be most merciful?

There was a long silence. The family began to re-establish eye contact. Faces softened. Once tense shoulders now slumped forward. I spoke to Ray. "Do my thoughts make sense to you?" Ray's voice, cracking with emotion, answered: "Yeah. I don't like it, but I get it. I just don't want to see her die." It was now safe to talk about Rita's dying. Relief replaced despair. Grief was no longer postponed.

Bobby pulled back in his chair and looked to the ceiling: "Lord, she has been through so much." Deborah and Jean locked eyes across the table. A rapid series of emotions flashed across their faces. Deborah began weeping openly. Her daughter rose to comfort her. "I'm sorry, Deb," said Jean, tears adorning her cheeks. Deborah lay her head on the table. After a few minutes, Deborah drew herself upright in the chair. Looking to the Palliative Care physician, she asked: "So what's next?" Deborah's leadership re-centered the family, bringing them out of their private sorrows and back into the work at hand. The family system showed its resilience and found a way through the crisis. A new hope, grounded in a shared religious and ethical value, redeemed the strained relationship between the medical team and the family.

The conversation soon moved to hospice care, and the family rallied to the new task. Things were set right, to use Rita's life-defining metaphor. They would find redemption by loving her out of this world as much as they had loved her in it.

Analysis

Religious values inform decision-making processes and can be used by families as they seek to determine the appropriate goals of care for a loved one. Sometimes, the religious orientation is explicit. More often, it is so deeply embedded within the family structure and culture that it operates outside of conscious awareness. Detecting and engaging engrained religious value systems requires expertise.

Few clinicians have significant training in religious values systems or the emotional dynamics of families. Misinterpretations of religious language and the failure to recognize differing values systems can lead to a communications breakdown and a corresponding loss of collaboration between families and the care team. When working to heal the wounds of distrust between medical teams and families, especially during times when emotions are running high and the potential outcomes bear great weight, I find it helpful to employ Murray Bowen's Family Systems Theory (1978) as an analytical tool, regarding this situation as a care-centered relational system under duress.

Family systems operate within a commonly held narrative from which family members derive roles that are functional and meaningful. The religious component of the family narrative is the animating story through which the family's spirituality is expressed in interpersonal behaviors. In order to address the spiritual dimension, I select and overlay a symbolic religious motif that captures the spiritual tone and theme of the family system. The combination of system and motif yields an evidence-based, diagnostic model, providing an orienting religious narrative that highlights the spiritual qualities of the participants' experiences.

Similarly, medical teams operate within a commonly held narrative that incorporates an animating ethical worldview. These ethics will be expressed openly at times but are more likely to be operating outside of conscious awareness. The team's "family system" incorporates an ethical story within the team's larger narrative. Skilled in interpretation of both the medical team's narrative and the family's narrative, the chaplain can be well positioned to facilitate a healthy inter-system relationship.

By the time we had all reached the family conference, there were high levels of anxiety on both sides. The clinical picture for a positive outcome by means of aggressive treatment, the one in which Rita might be healed and returned to her previous life, had become unrealistic. The medical team saw further aggressive interventions as providing no meaningful benefit, and feared that continuing treatment would only prolong her suffering. From within their meaning-making system, causing suffering without expectation of a greater good violated their ethical code. The recommendation was to transition fully to comfort care. When Rita's family requested continued curative treatment, the medical team felt their assessment of Rita's condition and prognosis was not being factored in the family's decision-making process. How could this family completely disregard the "evidence" and their expertise? The medical team felt challenged in their professional identities as providers of ethical and humane care.

For their part, Rita's family embraced a religious meaning-making system that required them to care for her by every means possible. "Bearing the Cross" of suffering and hardship, a well known and beloved religious motif referring to the Passion of Christ narrative, encouraged generations of Rita's family to forgo personal ease. The shared sacrifices of time and resources to support Rita along the trajectory of her lengthy disease process had become a source of emotional bonding rather than burden. It contributed to the family's sense of intimacy and purpose, even as they experienced conflict in regard to specific end-of-life decisions.

The combined knowledge of the family's system and their religious framework led to my assessment that stopping curative treatment would cause the family to risk losing the spiritually rich and emotionally familiar common cause that was uniting them. They saw themselves as suffering alongside Rita. Suffering, both Rita's and their own, had a positive moral value which was not shared by the medical team. Within their religious value system, they were fulfilling their call to imitate the passion of Christ. If the family followed the recommendation of the medical team to focus on comfort, the organizing principle that gave them a sense of purpose and bound them together would be lost. Symbolically, they would be abandoning the Cross, a central religious motif. Stopping life-prolonging treatment, therefore, would mean being unfaithful to both their matriarch and faith.

Also active in the relational dynamics of the larger caregiving system is the relative importance of the loss that will be experienced by each sub-group. The loss of a patient is significant to a medical team, but it does not carry the spiritual, emotional, and social impact that will come with the death of one of the family's central figures. With Rita's death the medical team would continue, perhaps more experienced, but functionally unchanged. Rita's family, on the other hand, would undergo a systemic reorganization and would never function within the same constellation of family roles again.

The transformation had already begun as family members realigned themselves to accommodate the absence of Rita's leadership, but Rita's death would leave a vacuum that they feared would never be filled. How they would know themselves as a family would forever be changed.

Family Systems Theory (Bowen 1978; Miller and Winstead-Fry 1982) teaches us that the energy fueling the family's resistance is a symptom of the inevitability of change. Conversations that disrupt the equilibrium reduce the family's ability to absorb the clinical information offered by the medical staff. The family's limited capacity to cope with threatening external information diminished their ability to integrate the reality of Rita's medical condition. There was too much at stake for the family system in its immediate configuration.

Ironically, the point of greatest contention was also the point of greatest opportunity for common ground: caring for Rita. We needed to shift the family's emotional and cognitive resources away from their presenting priorities, resisting anticipatory grief and the impending restructuring of the family system onto the direct care of Rita. The locus for that shift was created when Ray, a family member further from the role of decisional leadership, asked a poignant question that reflected the family's shared religious sensibilities. Ray's invocation of the commandment to honor thy father and mother was likely intended as an argument to proceed with feeding, reinforced by the negative imagery of starvation. The non-verbal expressions and silence by family members suggest that they heard it in this way.

Amid the leadership crisis within Rita's family, I assumed a prophetic, future-oriented role, helping the family find cohesiveness through a different interpretation of the religious value to honor your mother and father. I sought to find a place of common understanding by linking the concepts of religious honor and medical beneficence, and building a bridge between the family and the medical team. The shift of the dominant religious motif of mercy liberated the family from the bonding value of suffering. I facilitated their shift by relocating my religious authority, joining Ray in Rita's vacated religious leadership role. I intentionally used a collaborative and consensus leadership style. This left Rita's role as matriarch respectfully unfilled, allowing the family emotional space to collectively assume the decision-maker role.

Viewed through Murray Bowen's (1978) Family Systems Theory's Profiles of Differentiation, the family was functioning at a Moderate

Level of Differentiation. They were unable to process the intellectual information because the emotional content was dominant in the family system (Miller and Winstead-Fry 1982). The vacancy of Rita's long-held social and emotional position as the oldest generation female complicated the emotional dynamics within the family system. According to Murray's theory, Rita's role as matriarch required her to be the most self-differentiated member in the system (Miller and Winstead-Fry 1982). With Rita emotionally absent, the system became less differentiated. Without a regulating leader or person with the authority to interpret the meaning of family events, they became emotionally mired in the present.

The next generation struggled to re-establish emotional authority. According to Bowen's theory, in the Multigenerational Transmission Process (Miller and Winstead-Fry 1982) families "inherit" and "bequeath" their emotional systems in patterns stretching back three to four generations. The individuals within each generation may behave differently, but the system tends to preserve the overall pattern. Rita's adult children entered this stage of the process with charged emotions.

Because the family's religious system closely resembled its internal relational system, I was able to assume a role paralleling the emotional role of the church pastor. The pastor frequently functions as a tertiary member of the extended family, offering advice and support but not possessing direct authority within the family system. Within the network of relational triangles in Bowen's theory, the family members may form a triangulated relationship with the pastor for therapeutic purposes, utilizing the triangle to resolve relational tensions (Miller and Winstead-Fry 1982). In this case, I was able to establish a therapeutic triangle with the medical team and the family. My positive relationship with both opened a channel of communication that built the trust necessary for shared decision-making. I lifted up the mutually held value of "care for Rita" that spoke to values central to the family and the medical team, mercy and beneficence.

Rita went home and died peacefully, surrounded by family. As pastoral care would be provided by others, likely a shared caring between the hospice chaplain and their own pastor, my relationship with Rita and her family ended. I have wondered about the impact her death may have had on this particular family system. I suspect that the family was able to re-establish the multigenerational emotional system, though with some potentially novel adaptations. Rita and her ancestral ways will likely remain revered among the family, perhaps for several generations. It is unlikely that another matriarch will emerge with the same authority, because the resources necessary to support this role are no longer available in the way they were in Rita's generation. And maybe, just maybe, the emerging family system will place a higher value on mercy. The medical system was undoubtedly impacted by their interface with Rita and her family in ways that remain to be discovered. One thing is for certain: Rita's legacy as teacher and matriarch lives on.

References

Bowen, M. (1978) *Family Therapy in Clinical Practice*. Lanham, MD: Rowan & Littlefield Publishers, Inc.

Miller, S.R. and Winstead-Fry, P. (1982) *Family Systems Theory in Nursing Practice*. Reston, VA: Reston Publishing.

Further reading

Kerr, M. and Bowen, M. (1988) *Family Evaluation: An Approach Based on Bowen Theory*. New York: W.W. Norton & Company.

Rosenblatt, P.C. (1994) *Metaphors of Family Systems Theory: Toward New Constructions*. New York: Guilford Press.

Chapter 7

MARK'S STORY

"Take this trach out; I don't want to live this way"—Mark,
a middle-aged man with acute respiratory disease

MELANIE SWOFFORD

Introduction

This is a case highlighting how healthcare chaplains ensure the patient's voice is heard and medical preferences honored even when these conflict with the wishes of family members or the healthcare team. By addressing family dynamics, emotions of guilt and grief, and complex theological stances about faith and healing, the chaplain plays a pivotal role in helping the patient and family reach consensus and find peace. This is a real case with names and some details changed in order to protect the identities of those involved.

The patient, Mark, was a 70-something-old man with a history of chronic heart failure (CHF) and chronic obstructive pulmonary disease (COPD). He lived with his daughter in a rural town where she worked for a well-known and well-feared judge. The patient had a history of smoking and was known to spend a lot of time outdoors doing yard work before his CHF and COPD had developed so far as to cause him to give that up. Before he was admitted to the hospital, Mark had been mostly able to care for himself physically, with minimal help from his daughter. He valued independence and was described as a "self-made man," owning his own business and working hard his whole life. Mark was admitted to hospital in respiratory distress. He was sedated and on ventilator support; after a few days, his daughter decided on a tracheostomy (trach) as it appeared that his need for respiratory support would not be short-lived.

The medical team assumed Karen was the sole legal substitute decision-maker because she gave the team "Power of Attorney" (POA) documents. When Mark awoke, he was upset at having the trach and was constantly trying to pull it out. He wrote notes about not wanting to live this way. Mark refused treatments, but his daughter would insist upon those treatments. Karen would repeatedly call every doctor who had seen her father until they would do what she wanted, whether indicated or not, to appease this grieving and irate family member. The daughter threatened lawsuits and raised her voice to the nurses, making it even more difficult for the medical team to hear and honor the patient's wishes. Karen's connections further added to the pressure on the medical team.

I am a board-certified chaplain with over 10 years of chaplaincy experience. I've been at this hospital for seven of those years. I am an ordained United Methodist Elder in full connection and have served at various United Methodist churches. I am endorsed with the United Methodist Endorsing Agency to serve in the capacity of hospital chaplain. I met Mark and his family shortly after he was admitted to the hospital. The hospital is a teaching hospital that is part of a larger regional health system. It is the main hospital, with over 700 beds and the busiest Emergency Department in the state. We are located along two of the busiest highways in the state and serve a community of military veterans, active duty military, and their families. The hospital serves 75 percent Medicare and Medicaid patients, who come from several counties. These consist of rural communities with farmers and those who work on farms. We are in the "Bible Belt" of Southeastern US, so the primary religion of the area is Christian, with a majority in the Pentecostal denomination.

I am the primary clinical staff chaplain located in this hospital. The Pastoral Care Department is made up of a director and myself as the primary chaplains at this main hospital, with a half-time chaplain at one of our other smaller hospitals. We have a clinical pastoral education (CPE) program whose students help cover visitation on the floors and on-call for the hospital. We have a force of volunteer chaplains who fill in on-call for the nights that students are not able to cover. The director, the half-time chaplain, and I cover on-call for all the other hospitals in the system. I am the Critical Care and Medical Service Lines chaplain as well as the Palliative Care chaplain. One of my primary roles is to speak with surrogate decision-makers in the

Intensive Care Units (ICUs) to help them work through situations such as this one and come to terms with the decisions being made. I work as a translator between the medical team and the decision-maker as well as between the surrogate decision-maker and patient as needed.

Case

I was asked to visit Mark after he had received aggressive care in the ICU for nearly a month because, as the nurse said, "the patient seems depressed." I'd heard from some of the team that Mark consistently communicated that he did not want the trach, ventilator, or other life-prolonging interventions. When I met him, he expressed his desires in writing about not wanting this treatment.

Chaplain: "Mark, I am Chaplain Swofford. I am on rounds in the unit and wanted to stop in to say hi. [I don't usually open with the nurse recommendation to encourage a greater sense of trust with a patient.] Tell me, how are you today?"

Mark: [Mark tried to mouth something, but I was having trouble understanding him. He made the motion for writing.]

Chaplain: "Let me find a clipboard and some paper. I'll be right back."

Mark: [When I got back, he wrote] "I am Mark [last name]. The date is [the correct date]. I am at [the teaching] hospital. I do not want this tube in my throat."

Chaplain: "Sir, do you understand that without that tube you wouldn't be able to breathe? Your daughter made that choice to help keep you alive."

Mark: [Writing] "I don't want to be a lab rat."

Chaplain: "I understand. Have you ever talked to your daughter about this?"

Mark: [Mark shook his head no.]

Chaplain: "What do you think she'd do if she heard you say that?"

Mark: [Writing] "Really upset."

Chaplain: "So she would get upset so it's hard to tell her? [Mark nodded his head.] Well, have you told the doctors any of this?"

Mark: [Writing] "Never ask."

Chaplain: "So the doctors never ask." [Mark nodded his head.]

Mark: [Writing] "Dr talk over me. I'm a lab rat."

Chaplain: "Let me make sure I understand. You are saying your daughter would get really upset so you haven't shared with her? [Mark nodded.] Now you just shared that the doctors don't talk to you and only talk to each other to make decisions. [Mark nodded.] This makes you feel like a lab rat? [Mark nodded.] Wow! That would make me feel depressed. How are you with this?"

Mark: [Writing] "I don't want to have this tube. I'm tired. This is not living."

Chaplain: "What is living?"

Mark: [Writing] "Seeing sun, walking on grass, humming a tune, talking to people and not breathing out of a tube."

Chaplain: "What if you showed these notes to Karen? Would she start to understand? [Mark shook his head no.] Are you afraid that she'll be upset because she'll be alone? [Mark nodded his head.] If you want, I can come in and be with you when you show them to her. [He pointed at me and mouthed 'talk.'] You want me to talk to her? [Mark nodded his head.] I will talk to her, but only you can really share this conversation in a way that will help her understand. I'll tell you what. I'll try to talk to her and find out how she is coping. You seem very worried about that. I'll see what I can offer her in terms of support. We'll start there. Does that sound good?"

Mark: [Writing] "Yes."

Chaplain: "Okay, but keep the clipboard and paper. This way you can also talk to the doctor and the nurses to let them know what you need and want. It might help."

Following this initial visit, I knew I needed to find a way to make a case for Mark's medical preferences to be respected. As there was some question about whether Mark had the capacity to decide about his own medical care, I asked the primary doctor to order a psychiatric consult. The psychiatrist's report clearly indicated that Mark understood his condition, the decisions before him, the consequences of deciding to forgo life-prolonging medical care, and the alternative of continuing aggressive treatment. Psychiatry instructed the medical team to speak to the patient, not the daughter, about treatment options. Despite the report, the attending physician continued the course of treatment that the daughter had requested.

I decided another possible avenue for advocating for the patient might be found by reviewing the "POA paperwork" that had been placed in Mark's chart. I hoped to find guidance for his surrogate indicating that quality of life mattered more to him than length of life, or something to that effect. I believed this would aid in conversations between the daughter and patient. At that time, I discovered that the documents were POA documents giving the daughter permission to handle the patient's finances, not his medical decisions. Much to my surprise, I uncovered evidence that Mark also had a son. I relayed both pieces of information to the attending physician. Despite this information, the attending physician decided to continue with his course of aggressive treatment per the daughter's request.

Knowing the daughter needed support, the nurse decided (against our protocol) to ask Karen if she would like to meet with me. Her first response was anger. She expressed suspicion that the only reason I was called in was that it was time for her father to die. Karen insisted that her father was improving; she refused to speak with me. I continued to see Mark, however, as I was clear he had the right to spiritual guidance and support for himself. At the conclusion of our initial visit, he had made it clear to me that he wanted follow-up visits on a regular basis.

When I finally wound up connecting with Karen, it happened in the most happenstance way and unusual place. I was at an educational booth teaching those who came by about advance directives. Karen stopped, curious to find out what the booth was all about. When she realized who was staffing the booth (the chaplain she had refused to see), I could tell she was reluctant to engage. However, after a few minutes of more casual conversation, Karen began to open up about her fears and concerns for her father.

She explained how she was the sole caregiver. Karen talked about the toll it was taking on her, emotionally and physically. She also related that she felt pressure from the medical team to limit life-sustaining treatment for her father. Karen voiced her fear that she would be failing her father if she made the decisions to change his code status to a Do Not Resuscitate (DNR) and to make her father "comfort care." Karen described how lonely she felt in everything. She was not married; her world was primarily made up of going to work and taking care of her father. (She did not mention the patient's son, so I decided to refrain from bringing him up in order to build trust at this critical juncture in our relationship.)

Over the next few months, I spoke with Karen on multiple occasions. In fact, there were many times when she refused to speak with other medical team members and would insist on only talking to me. In the course of these conversations, I learned that Karen came from a faith tradition that held that if she let her father die, it was a sign that her faith wasn't sufficiently strong. God's miraculous intervention was conditional upon her unwavering belief that God would provide Mark with a complete health and total healing. One day she and I talked a great deal about this aspect of her faith.

Karen: "I must be strong. I must remember that God works miracles. People have come out of this before."

Chaplain: "Why do you need to be so strong?"

Karen: "Someone must believe that a miracle will work. Someone must have enough faith."

Chaplain: "So that person is you? What happens if your faith isn't enough?"

Karen: "I can't think about that. I don't want him to give up."

Chaplain: "It seems to me that you are putting a whole lot of pressure on yourself."

Karen: "But I must take care of him."

Chaplain: "You are."

Karen: "No, I mean he needs a miracle."

Chaplain: "Yes. And what is a miracle?"

Karen: "My dad gets better and isn't sick."

Chaplain: "Wouldn't that be lovely?"

Karen: "And then he could come home with me."

Chaplain: "What happens if a miracle healing doesn't bring him home with you?"

Karen: "What do you mean?"

Chaplain: "Karen, I know from our conversations that you are a Christian and believe strongly in God. And yes, God does some amazing miracles. Tell me more about your faith."

Karen: "Well, I believe Jesus died on a cross and gives us salvation. That if we believe in him, one day we will live in eternity with Jesus."

Chaplain: "So one day after this life we will live with Jesus?"

Karen: "Yeah, in Heaven."

Chaplain: "What's Heaven like?"

Karen: "It is supposed to be a beautiful, happy place where there is no more sickness or disease or pain."

Chaplain: "Sounds like a great place. Sounds like a place that is easier than living on earth."

Karen: "Yeah [smiling], it makes me happy to think about it."

Chaplain: "And we get to live there if we believe in Jesus?"

Karen: "Yes."

Chaplain: "That's miraculous!"

Karen: "What do you mean?"

Chaplain: "Well, we are not perfect people and God is perfect. We are sinful and God is not, right?"

Karen: "Yes."

Chaplain: "Well, if that's the case, then, isn't it a miracle that we can be with Jesus in Heaven?"

Karen: "I guess you are right."

Chaplain: "What if there are two miracles? Just as a thought. There is the miraculous on earth where we are healed and continue to live with people here. Then there is the greater miracle that we will be healed and be with Jesus."

Karen: "I never thought of it that way."

Chaplain: "Think about it. Your faith is not weak because someone dies. There is strength in listening for God to tell you which miracle He wants to do."

Karen: "I guess I'll need to think about that. I just don't want my father to die."

Chaplain: "I know, and my prayer if it were my father would be to keep him around because I'd miss him. It would be very difficult for me if my own dad died, so I can only imagine what you are going through."

Karen: "Yeah, I'd miss my dad. Yet I do wonder about whether he is in pain sometimes. Is it selfish to want him to stay here?"

Chaplain: "If you didn't I'd be surprised. You love him and without him there would be a big hole in your life. It's not about you deciding if that helps. It's about what decision God wants to make and what your father wants to have happen. If you listen, I believe you'll know in your heart."

I knew from my interactions in private with Mark that he did not share this belief system. He believed a life well lived was most important. Living in the hospital any longer was incongruent with his definition of quality of life. His faith told him that something better was ahead for him—that's where he'd get his miracle and quality of life! What I found extremely frustrating, however, was that Mark was hesitant to share this with his daughter. At first, when the three of us were together, even with my nudging and providing ample opening and prompts, Mark would not disclose to his daughter the depth of his distress over the situation.

So, I began my mediation between father and daughter by talking to each separately. I validated Mark's voice. I encouraged him to communicate his wishes to Karen. I explored the nature of his relationship with Karen, learning from Mark (and later from Karen privately) that theirs was a complicated one. The clipboard I had given Mark had been taken away several times, so I made sure he had another clipboard to work with. My thinking was that maybe it would be easier for him to communicate through this mechanism. I invited him to write down exactly what he wanted to say to his daughter. Mark wrote that he loved Karen and wanted her to be okay. In fragmented sentences, but as clearly as he possibly could, he also wrote that he didn't want any of these aggressive treatments.

When I then met with Karen separately, she focused on not wanting to fail her father as his caregiver. She named feelings of guilt and loneliness. She began to open up about how she felt she failed as a wife when her husband left her. At one point, she mentioned watching her father; she wondered aloud if he might be in pain. Her concern for him opened the door for me to encourage her to ask Mark directly about his experience, especially about his possible suffering. Karen confessed that she was afraid that if she broached this topic with Mark she would be the one to make her father give up on life.

When I sat down with Mark and his daughter together, with Mark's permission I showed the notes he had written to his daughter. Karen cried. She then courageously asked whether he was suffering. Through the conversation, they both discovered that each one of them was afraid to disappoint the other. They were both trying to put on "happy" faces to protect and sustain the other. Mark became more vulnerable, opening up about the sadness he felt that he would never see the outside world again. Karen shared her deep fear of being alone. At the end of this conversation, Mark and Karen together consented to a DNR order. Shortly thereafter, at the end of a long five months in the ICU, Mark passed away with Karen by his side. He could no longer communicate, but he had found his voice. Mark's protectiveness and love for his daughter had been expressed, as had his preference to put a limit on life-prolonging medical interventions.

Analysis

At the point I stepped in to request a psychiatric consult, communication between all involved had stalled. Karen's insistence that all aggressive measures be employed to save her father's life conflicted with what the medical team were hearing from Mark directly and what they were witnessing when he attempted to pull out the many tubes keeping him alive. I encouraged the doctor to utilize a psychiatric consult to demonstrate to the daughter that the patient could still make his own decisions. Despite the psychiatric assessment, the attending physician was not convinced that the patient fully understood his choices. Without certainty that Mark completely understood the irreversible consequence of removing the trach, the doctor felt morally obligated to defer to the daughter who was clearly fully coherent and knew full well the consequences of continuing or withdrawing respiratory support.

I sought out further advice from Patient Relations and Risk Management to find out what options I had to aid the patient. It was my opinion that the patient's voice was being silenced by the medical team due to fear of the daughter's threats of legal action. I spoke directly to the attending physician to advocate for Mark's role as his own decision-maker. When that approach failed to change the course of treatment, I found that my best approach was to support Mark in bringing his wishes up directly with his daughter.

Hope for a miracle—denial, grief, or faithfulness?

It is understood and seen by most chaplains that surrogate decision-makers are often asked to make decisions they may or may not understand and may or may not be ready for. A research study through Case Western Reserve University and the University of South of Florida looked at the struggles that decision-makers find (Hickman *et al.* 2016). Participants in this study expressed shock and uncertainty in the face of the decline of their loved one. They talked about feelings of guilt and powerlessness in making decisions, often not understanding what is being asked of them or understanding fully the importance of the decisions (Hickman *et al.* 2016). In this case study, the patient, Mark, came in with respiratory distress and unable to speak for himself. So his daughter, Karen, was asked to step in as decision-maker. She made decisions for her father's care from a place of compassion and love, but perhaps not from a place of full understanding. When her father became more aware and could express himself, Karen, as decision-maker, found herself in an impossible situation. She had been doing the best she could to make decisions for her father. Now, in the face of hearing her father's wishes, she found herself full of guilt and possible confusion. Out of this feeling, it is likely that she was more direct and forceful with the medical team. She was likely to demand even more treatments the medical team deemed "futile." In the face of this forcefulness, the medical team made decisions to follow her directives over the wishes of the patient.

In the face of this type of guilt and feelings of uncertainty, many decision-makers would turn to their spiritual leaders for help (Sulmasy 2007). Karen had a very strong faith that she said impacts her decision-making. However, Karen did not have a church or a spiritual leader in the community. She mentioned that she felt guilty for not going to church and thought that God might be upset with her because of this. With no spiritual leader in the community, Karen was inclined to believe that with God upset at her, her father's condition was punishment for her actions. A common theological concept of Christians in this area of the country is that if one has enough faith and has led a good, sinless life, they or the one they are praying for will be completely healed. Often Christians will reference Hezekiah from the Bible as proof that this is the case. Hezekiah was told he was going to die, but turned to the wall and cried out to God to save him. It was said that because of his faith he was given 15 more years to live (2 Kings 20:1–11). Karen referenced this scripture as proof that miracles happen. She said that despite her past failings she was determined to continue in faith. The more her father talked about wanting to stop aggressive treatment, the more she clung to the belief that her faith could save her father.

Compounding this belief was the fact that caring for her father and work were her only two activities. Research has shown that two of the things that hinder decision-making for surrogates are lack of support and lack of positive coping strategies (Vig *et al.* 2007). It is possible that her coping mechanism was to demand what the team referred to as "futile treatments." Thinking about the loneliness and isolation she might face upon his death might have also been a significant factor in Karen's decision-making. Using the language of miracles might be self-preservation. Karen was facing the potential loss of her father. She was experiencing anticipatory grief (Nugent 2013). This type of grief, seen as a person grows closer to an undesirable outcome, can be both confusing and painful. Self-preservation could be done through a spoken belief in miracles. This way, she would not have to face the pain and worry associated with her father's death. She could continue to think of him as someone who would leave the hospital healthy.

Denial can also be part of this complexity of emotions and reactions. Using miracles as denial and as self-preservation appear at first to be the same sides of the coin. However, using miracles as self-preservation involves knowing somewhere deep within that there is no hope for healing. Denial is a stronger emotion. Denial is the inability to accept the reality of the situation. It is completely avoiding any talk about the illness of the patient. When in this stage, often a family will come at times when the physician is not there to avoid what they may say. Someone who is speaking out of self-preservation tends to understand that the answer to their prayers might be "no." Someone in denial will refuse to accept "no" as an answer (Sulmasy 2007). Whether it is out of self-preservation or denial, the belief can hinder the decision-making process and lead to continued aggressive treatment when there is no possibility of a cure.

The question with Karen as well as many other caregivers is whether they are holding on to a miracle as true faithfulness, self-preservation, or denial. It could be that there is a mixture of all three, or pressure from outside forces. Karen appeared to be acting out of self-preservation. She avoided the medical personnel and used the language of miracles almost like a wall, saying that no "negative" talk should happen around her father. Karen struggled to accept her father's deterioration. She struggled to imagine that waiting on a miracle in the sense that she wanted might mean further pain rather than a cure. As with most surrogate decision-makers, she didn't fully understand the difference between aggressive treatment with a hope for a miracle and comfort care with a hope for a miracle. Mark, on his end, was afraid to tell his daughter what he wanted because he didn't want to cause her more pain. He was not in denial about his condition; he was afraid to cause any further pain for his daughter who would be left alone and grieving. In the end, it was helping Karen see that miracles can look different in different contexts that helped her begin conversations with her father. Those conversations then led to a resolution that allowed her father to die in comfort.

References

Hickman, R.L., Daly, B.J., Clochesy, J.M., O'Brien, J. and Leuchtag, M. (2016) 'Leveraging the lived experience of surrogate decision makers of the seriously ill to develop a decision support intervention.' *Applied Nursing Research, May,* 67–69.

Nugent, P. (2013) 'Anticipatory Grief.' PsychologyDictionary.org. Available at https://psychologydictionary.org/anticipatory-grief

Sulmasy, D. (2007) 'Distinguishing denial from authentic faith in miracles: A clinical-pastoral approach.' *Southern Medical Journal* 100, 12, 1268–1272.

Vig, E.K., Starks, H., Taylor, J.S., Hopley, E.K. and Fryer-Edwards, K. (2007) 'Surviving surrogate decision-making: What helps and hampers the experience of making medical decisions for others.' *Society of General Internal Medicine* 22, 9, 1274–1279.

Further reading

Anandarajah, G. and Hight, E. (2001) 'Spirituality and medical practice: Using the HOPE questions as a practical tool for spiritual assessment.' *American Family Physician* 63, 1, 81–89.

Azoulay, E., Chaize, M. and Kentish-Barnes, N. (2014) 'Involvement of ICU families in decisions: Fine-tuning the partnership.' *Annals of Intensive Care* 4, 1, 37.

Clarke, S. (2013) 'When they believe in miracles.' *Journal of Medical Ethics* 39, 9, 582–583.

Connors, R.B. and Smith, M.L. (1996) 'Religious insistence on medical treatment. Christian theology and re-imagination.' *Hastings Center Report* 26, 4, 23–30.

Crippen, D. and Hawryluck, L. (2004) 'Pro/con clinical debate: Life support should have a special status among therapies, and patients or their families should have a right to insist on this treatment even if it will not improve outcome.' *Critical Care* 8, 4, 231.

Danis, M. and Pollack, J.M. (2014) 'The valuable contribution of spiritual care to end-of-life care in the ICU*.' *Critical Care Medicine* 42, 9, 2131–2132.

Dugan, D.O. (1995) 'Praying for miracles: Practical responses to requests for medically futile treatments in the ICU setting.' *HEC Forum* 7, 4, 228–242.

Gutierrez, K.M. (2012) 'Experiences and needs of families regarding prognostic communication in an intensive care unit: Supporting families at the end of life.' *Critical Care Nursing Quarterly* 35, 3, 299–313.

Kalemkerian, G.P. (2005) 'Commentary on "unrealistic expectations".' *Journal of Clinical Oncology* 23, 18, 4233–4234.

Nelson, J.E., Walker, A.S., Luhrs, C.A., Cortez, T.B. and Pronovost, P.J. (2009) 'Family meetings made simpler: A toolkit for the intensive care unit.' *Journal of Critical Care* 24, 4, 626.

Puchalski, C.M. (2001) 'The role of spirituality in health care.' *Proceedings (Baylor University Medical Center)* 14, 4, 352–357.

Puchalski, C.M., Ferrell, B., Virani, R., Otis-Green, S., *et al.* (2009) 'Improving the quality of spiritual care as a dimension of palliative care: The report of the Consensus Conference.' *Journal of Palliative Medicine* 12, 10, 885–904.

Siddiqui, S., Sheikh, F. and Kamal, R. (2011) 'What families want – An assessment of family expectations in the ICU.' *International Archives of Medicine* 4, 1, 21.

Wall, R.J., Engelberg, R.A., Gries, C.J., Glavan, B.J. and Curtis, J.R. (2007) 'Spiritual care of families in the intensive care unit.' *Critical Care Medicine* 35, 4, 1084–1090.

Widera, E., Rosenfeld, K.E., Fromme, E.K., Sulmasy, D.P. and Arnold, R.M. (2011) 'Approaching patients and family members who hope for a miracle.' *Journal of Pain and Symptom Management 42*, 1, 119–125.

Wiegand, D.L., Grant, M., Cheon, J. and Gergis, M.A. (2013) 'Family-centered end-of-life care in the ICU.' *Journal of Gerontological Nursing 39*, 8, 60–68.

Willemse, S., Smeets, W., van Leeuwen, E., Janssen, L. and Foudraine, N.A. (2018) 'Spiritual care in the ICU: Perspectives of Dutch intensivists, ICU nurses, and spiritual caregivers.' *Journal of Religion & Health 57*, 2, 583–595.

Chapter 8

AARON'S STORY

"I don't want to give up on him, but I don't want to hurt him either"—Aaron's family as they struggle to do right by this 45-year-old who suffered a sudden life-threatening injury

TERESAMARIE T. VILAGOS

Introduction

This case study seeks to demonstrate how the use of story and ritual in acute situations addresses complex emotions that impact medical decision-making and help foster post-traumatic growth (PTG) for families of patients. Trauma is broadly understood as any life-altering event (Kashdan and Kane 2011) and is not limited to physical loss, illness, injury, or death. Traumatic events can impact the emotional and spiritual aspects of personhood as well as family dynamics and roles. Research on PTG over the past two decades shows that people affected by traumatic events, with support, have the potential for greater life appreciation, stronger personal relationships, and an enhanced sense of self and spiritual development (Kashdan and Kane 2011).

I am an Association of Professional Chaplains (APC) board-certified chaplain, endorsed Elder in good standing and appointed as Emergency Department chaplain by the United Methodist Church to this Level One Trauma Center in Southeastern US. My responsibility is to provide spiritual care for this department and the entire facility, which also includes a Level Two Trauma Children's Hospital.

Aaron is a 45-year-old African American male who suffered a life-threatening cardiovascular condition associated with untreated hyperthyroidism, known colloquially in medicine as a "thyroid storm." He was transferred to the Medical Intensive Care Unit (MICU) from an affiliated facility. His initial admitting diagnosis was shortness of breath. He and his spouse, Belinda, have a 15-year-old daughter, Trina; they live and work in a large metropolitan city. They are not active in a faith community, but Belinda occasionally attends a large non-denominational church. She described Aaron as a "believer."

Three chaplains assessed Belinda prior to my visit. They noted in the electronic medical record her desire for "deeper connection to transcendence," that she was "tearful," and their interventions included "encouragement" and "prayer." I met Belinda and Trina in the waiting room following Aaron's transfer from the outside hospital, and served as their chaplain until Aaron's death a few weeks later.

I made three attempts to contact Aaron's widow for permission to present this case study. Initially, a written letter was sent. It was followed up with an email and finally a telephone call. Belinda did not respond to any of my attempts. I sought advice from the executive director of the Spiritual Care and Education Department who also chairs the Ethics Committee about how to move forward. He reviewed the manuscript and made recommendations to preserve patient and family privacy within the document by eliminating identifying characteristics and using pseudonyms for all involved parties. I have made these changes. Even though the family may not recognize themselves in this case study, I remain indebted to them for allowing me to become part of their story.

Case

Day 1

The medical team shared with me that Aaron was in a critical condition and that death was imminent. In my initial meeting with the family, I learned that Belinda's spiritual practices include reading Psalms and prayer. I noticed Trina's flat affect and attributed it to possible stress and fear. My thoughts were confirmed through our conversation about her school, friends, likes and dislikes, when she revealed that her prominent thought was "death" and that she associated it with "fear."

I engaged Belinda through general conversation when she acknowledged the severity of Aaron's condition but importantly noted that she was "leaving room for a miracle." She was hesitant about having Trina in Aaron's room. Recalling my earlier conversation with Trina, I concluded that it would be beneficial for her to spend time with her father to help her cope with her fears, and cope in the face of her father's a death. To do this, I suggested that they create family handprints to make meaning and foster positive memory.

Day 3

Aaron's condition stabilized, though his prognosis was poor. Belinda discussed with me her plan to honor her husband's wishes, while trying to address her fears that she "didn't do enough." She shared complicated and conflicting concerns: "I don't want to give up on him but I don't want to hurt him either." Her sister-in-law, Darlene, was present during the conversation and appeared supportive and equally conflicted. They shared the story of a recent family gathering when Aaron wished that his family would "come together." They remembered him describing a gathering where the entire family would be together, laughing and enjoying each other's company. He hoped for a time that would be free from conflicts and past hurts.

I offered a silent presence as they laughed, cried, and replayed the event in the context of the present situation. I affirmed their use of story to cope by encouraging them to recall even the smallest of details and conversations. Through the use of story, the women reached the conclusion that Aaron would not want significant life-prolonging interventions. I also validated their reliance on faith by not discounting their stated hope for miraculous healing. I chose a relevant Psalm and prayed with them.

Days 4–6

Belinda began to express feelings of clarity and direction. She attributed these feelings to her sense of "answered prayer" which gave her feelings of "joy." She shared feeling "relieved," derived from a felt presence of the Holy.

A family member gave her a prophetic prayer for healing which she began reciting daily to Aaron. She also asked me to join in the recitation on one occasion. The content of the prayer focused on the power of God for miraculous healing, and the importance of faith and belief in God's power for this life and the life to come. Although I understand that healing can take all forms of relief from suffering,

I knew in this context Belinda was encouraged to pray for physical healing by her family member. The challenge of walking in these two realities can be overwhelming for both families and myself. It is a delicate balance that can only be met with kindness and compassion.

Day 8

Despite a poor prognosis, significant medical interventions were put in place to keep Aaron stable until Belinda and the family could come to terms with what was happening. Aaron's large extended family arrived, including the patriarch, who was also a clergyperson. He was open to my support as we gathered family to Aaron's bedside with permission from nursing staff. There was spontaneous singing and extemporaneous prayers mixed with laughter and tears. The family continued the ritual for an hour. The mood was joyful and the family noted a sense of "answered prayer" because they believed that Aaron had improved, evidenced by his eyes opening and some spontaneous movement. Darlene related the ritual back to her earlier conversation regarding Aaron's wish for the family to "come together."

Day 9

Unfortunately, Aaron's clinical condition and prognosis remained unchanged, and his aggressive treatment plan was modified. Aaron's father-in-law, Robert, expressed frustration with the changed care plan. He used a personal story of faith during adversity to relate to the situation. He shared with me that he came to the US alone on a refugee visa. Although well educated in his home country, he accepted menial jobs, working himself up to a position as a professor at a prestigious university. I listened empathically as I came to an understanding that for him, all things were possible with the help of God, so giving up on Aaron would be giving up on a God who had transformed his own life. I offered him affirmation and validation by confirming my thoughts and interpretation of his faith experience and beliefs to build on our relationship.

Day 13

Consults for Palliative Care and Ethics were initiated regarding the determination of Medical Futility.[1] The family wanted to transfer Aaron to an outside hospital for a second opinion. Three outside hospitals declined. Palliative Care notes indicated that Belinda stated feelings of "betrayal" by the medical staff and "guilt" for not being more insistent. There was reference to Belinda's confusion about perceived improvement.

I met with the ethicist following their consultation with Belinda and Robert. He noted that the family was at an "impasse" and wanted my insights. I described their deep spiritual reliance on God's power of transcendence to bring healing despite the medical circumstances.

I met with Belinda following her consultations and she appeared distraught.

Chaplain: "Hi Belinda, how are you feeling?"

Belinda: "I just don't know, I guess I'm feeling upset."

Chaplain: "Would you mind sharing your feelings with me?"

Belinda: "Well, my father and I met with one of your chaplains, I think he is an ethicist? There were others there, too, it got to be confusing because so many people were talking."

Chaplain: "I was aware of the Ethics consult initiated by the medical team, so I guess in addition to the chaplain ethicist there was someone else from Palliative Care as well as the medical team."

Belinda: "Yes, and I think some residents or students, too. I only recognized a few faces."

Chaplain: "I can see how that might be overwhelming."

Belinda: "Very!"

Chaplain: "You said your father was present as well. Do you have any insights into his feeling about the meeting?"

---

1   If treatment is medically futile and offers no benefit whatsoever, there is no obligation to offer to initiate, or to offer to continue, the treatment. Note, however, that it is extremely important that the provider communicate with the patient or the patient's representative(s) regarding the treatment plan and recognizes that "futile" is often a value judgment.

Belinda: "That was hard too, because you know my father is a deeply spiritual man and he told me he felt like the team was dismissing his faith and belief that he could be healed."

Chaplain: "Hmmm, would you say your father might have felt invalidated?"

Belinda: "Yes! And me too. He's come in all the way from the Midwest to support me and help out and now I feel like they don't even want to consider his beliefs."

Chaplain: "I can see how that would hurt."

Belinda: "Yes!"

Chaplain: "Did you make any headway with Aaron's care plan?"

Belinda: "No, not really. There aren't any hospitals that will accept him as a patient, so I guess we're stuck here. Don't get me wrong, the nursing staff has been nice, but I'm not sure the doctors hear me. They want me to consider a DNR [Do Not Resuscitate]."

Chaplain: "Have you and Aaron ever discussed that?"

Belinda: "No, we didn't think we'd need to."

Chaplain: "I can understand, you're both so young."

Belinda: [Smiling] "Thanks, but now I wish we did."

Chaplain: "I know you can't go back in time, but what do you think Aaron might say to you in this situation?"

Belinda: "I don't know, I just don't know. I want to give him every chance, but the doctors imply the more they do, the more likelihood that it might be hurting him. I just don't know. Is it wrong to still hope for a miracle?"

Chaplain: "I can understand it's hard, but maybe if we looked back to the earlier conversation we had with his sister... You ladies shared that Aaron had a wish for the family to come together. Do you think it's possible that miracles are not always getting what we ask for but the privilege of witnessing God's movement in our lives?"

Belinda: "He did say that at Thanksgiving. He wanted everyone around having a good time and putting the past behind."

Chaplain: "Do you think Aaron got his wish? Maybe we even witnessed God's movement when his family came to visit."

Belinda: "Yeah, he did. I just didn't think it would be like this." [She struggles to hold back tears.]

Chaplain: "I'm sure he had something else in mind, but you made his wish happen and it was a great celebration with singing and prayers. Some might say a miracle."

Belinda: "Yes, maybe. He would have liked it."

Chaplain: "I'm sure he did."

Belinda: "You're right, I know he did."

Chaplain: "Do you want to talk more about the meeting?"

Belinda: "No, I think I really need to pray about it."

Chaplain: "That sound like a good plan. Do you mind if I pray for you both?"

Belinda: "No, please do."

Chaplain: "Blessed Father God, thank you for being the healer you are, hear us now as we come before you with heavy hearts facing decisions that are difficult to consider, let alone make. I ask that you breathe your breath on Belinda and fill her with your Spirit so that you can impart wisdom and peace as she moves forward as her beloved's advocate. Bless her and her family. Bless our team and fill them with wisdom, knowledge, and compassion so they are agents of your healing. We ask this in your Holy name. Amen."

Belinda: "Thank you." [She hugs me, as she has on many occasions.]

Chaplain: [Warmly receiving the hug] "You're welcome. I'll stop by tomorrow."

Goodbyes were exchanged as she walked back to Aaron's room. She appeared to relate to my efforts and be comforted by them.

Day 14

Belinda shared that she was in a "better place today." She stated that she was "making plans" at the family's suggestion but "not giving up." I affirmed her apparent conflicting feelings offering consolation, supportive presence, and prayer.

Aaron's condition continued to destabilize and decline. At some point during the week Belinda changed his code status to DNR. Although I wasn't directly involved in that conversation, I feel that my ministry with Belinda and our conversations around "not giving up" and "not hurting him" helped her reach her decision.

Aaron died with Belinda, Trina, and Robert at his bedside. The mood was appropriately sad as the family grieved through tears and silence. I offered a final prayer at the bedside.

Analysis

PTG theory suggests that intentional review and reflection will benefit individuals as they move along the spiritual and emotional healing continuum (Tedeschi and Calhoun 1996). As the primary pastoral presence, I enlisted a posture of compassion. My goal was to lay the groundwork to foster PTG and hope. In the initial stages of the crisis, I assessed that it was important that Belinda have a strong sense of being cared for because her support system was not present. Studies show that intentional interventions and aftercare make PTG possible and can strengthen resilience to future adversity (Prati and Pietrantoni 2009). My initial spiritual assessment included her motivations, belief system, autonomy, and nature of coping (Saylor 2014). I concluded that Belinda was in an "individuative-reflective"[2] faith stage (Project Gutenburg Self-Publishing Press 2018). She acknowledged the difficulties in her role as primary healthcare decision-maker, advocate, and spouse. Belinda shared on multiple occasions the struggle between not doing enough and doing too much. It was evident that it was difficult for her to balance the family's certainty for miraculous physical healing and the inevitability of death as presented by the medical team's determination of medical futility.

---

2   A stage of *angst* and struggle. The individual takes personal responsibility for their beliefs and feelings. As one can reflect on their own beliefs, there is an openness to a new complexity of faith, but this also increases the awareness of conflicts in one's belief.

She reflected on her own beliefs and sought out spiritual direction from others, including me. During our visits, she shared that her primary fear was not death, but in making the "right" decision for her husband, and relied fully on her felt presence of the Holy to manage the complexity and conflicts.

The skillset I used to promote PTG also empowered Belinda over the two-week period in her role. She and I developed a mutual trust that grew from my non-anxious presence in the face of her suffering and created an openness to share her fears. Deep listening helped me hear Belinda and her family's story. I reflected on that story so I could help them to make meaning in the face of adversity. I worked with the nursing staff to create safe, comfortable spaces to further enhance the rituals used to share story in the hope of creating legacy (Pennel 2009). Participating in family rituals helped me better understand the family's spiritual and cultural resources for dealing with adversity and stress (Roberts 2012). In addition, religious and spiritual coping mechanisms offered a positive adjustment to stress (Prati and Pietrantoni 2009).

There were two occurrences of ritual that added another layer to the healing story. The intentional interventions were employed to elicit hope that can ease the guilt and uncertainty that sometimes surrounds medical decision-making. The first ritual was creating ink handprints with Belinda, Trina, and Aaron. I intentionally laid out the handprints with interlocking thumbs so that it appeared as a heart in the middle of the page. Trina was encouraged to choose her favorite colors and to remember special times with her dad. Although she did not verbalize her memory, I concluded she was feeling positive by her smile. Belinda also chose to make her own print with Aaron and a family print as well. I was purposeful in making this a ritualistic event by encouraging story-telling as well as talking to Aaron as I explained the process, and lovingly cleaned the ink from his hands with a warmed cloth, to ensure that Belinda and Trina felt he was very much a part of the project.

The second ritual emerged as a result of my spiritual assessment that had revealed common themes and metaphors embedded in Aaron's Thanksgiving Day wish for the family to "come together." It was clear to me that my role was not to provide medical or theological answers but to help them navigate and reframe their existential questions to prevent gridlock and promote healing (Friedman 1999).

The question of purpose and meaning—what good could come from Aaron's death—was answered as the family gathered together at Aaron's bedside, putting away past hurts and divisions.

Conclusion

At the time of Aaron's death, Belinda seemed to have reconciled her conflicting feelings; she consented to change his code status to DNR and to focus on comfort as the primary goal. She utilized prayer, scripture, reflection, and a felt presence of the Holy to reach that decision. My role as a chaplain was to facilitate her coping skills and to be a resource to her through active listening, advocacy, prayer, and presence. I intentionally sought to build trust so that she could navigate the unknown as it related to Aaron's condition. The use of open communication helped ease her feelings of guilt (Saylor 2014).

Trusting a stranger is unnatural. People are inherently skeptical. However, this isn't always the case with medical care because people place a great deal of trust in physicians and nurses, valuing their training, knowledge, and expertise. It is important that this trust not be breached, because it can lead to a breakdown in communication and alienation at a time when families and medical care teams need to be on the same page. I intentionally engaged the interdisciplinary team by conferring with Aaron's nurse and reviewing the patient's medical record before each visit. I also conveyed Belinda's spiritual and emotional state to the team. Despite my efforts, a breach of trust occurred between Belinda and the medical team regarding Aaron's level of care and interventions. Belinda wanted Aaron transferred to another facility. The medical team wanted to evoke the Futility Policy, which she perceived as "giving up." Understandably, I reasoned that Belinda was experiencing the dynamics of grief when she witnessed Aaron's eye movements and believed he was improving.

Belinda needed to develop trust in herself. She voiced divided feelings on several occasions, "not giving up versus not hurting" Aaron. She was also conflicted in embracing the reality of medical limitations for healing versus embracing her faith and hope for miraculous healing. I sought to overcome these dichotomies through intentional reframing. I encouraged her to consider the possibility that miracles are not always getting what we ask for but the privilege of witnessing God's movement in our lives. I suggested the possibility that we witnessed God's movement when his family came to visit and all gathered together in prayer. Ultimately, my relating the story of Aaron's desire to "gather family" enabled Belinda to see that her husband's hope for family unity had been fulfilled; this proved to be the healing balm needed by all.

References

Friedman, E. (1999) *A Failure of Nerve: Leadership in the Era of the Quick Fix.* New York: Church Publishing.

Kashdan, T.B. and Kane, J.Q. (2011) 'Posttraumatic distress and the presence of posttraumatic growth and meaning in life: Experiential avoidance as a moderator.' *Personality and Individual Differences 50,* 1, 84–89.

Pennel, J.J. (2009) *The Gift of Presence: A Guide to Helping Those Who Suffer.* Nashville, TN: Abingdon Press.

Prati, G. and Pietrantoni, L. (2009) 'Optimism, social support, and coping strategies as factors contributing to posttraumatic growth: A meta-analysis.' *Journal of Loss and Trauma 14,* 5, 364–366.

Project Gutenburg Self-Publishing Press (2018) *Fowler's Stages of Faith Development.* Available at http://self.gutenberg.org/articles/eng/Fowler%27s_stages_of_faith_development

Roberts, S.B. (ed.) (2012) *Professional Spiritual and Pastoral Care: A Practical Clergy and Chaplain's Handbook.* Woodstock, VT: SkyLight Paths Publishing.

Saylor, D. (2014) 'The chaplain's role in bio-ethical decision making.' *Care Giver 3,* 1, 111–114.

Tedeschi, R.G. and Calhoun, L.G. (1996) 'Posttraumatic growth inventory: Measuring the positive legacy of trauma.' *Journal of Traumatic Stress 9,* 3, 455–471.

Further reading

Becknell, J.S. (2017) 'Building blocks: A multi-theoretical preventative model to promote post-traumatic growth.' *Wisdom in Education 7,* 2, 1–11.

Cadell, S., Regehr, C. and Hemsworth, D. (2003) 'Factors contributing to posttraumatic growth: A proposed structural equation model.' *American Journal of Orthopsychiatry 73,* 3, 279–287.

Calhoun, L.G., Cann, A., Tedeschi, R.G. and McMillan, J. (2000) 'A correlational test of the relationship between posttraumatic growth, religion and cognitive processing.' *Journal of Traumatic Stress 13,* 3, 521–527.

Cisney, J.S. and Ellers, K.L. (2009). *The First 48 Hours: Spiritual Caregivers as First Responders.* Nashville, TN: Abingdon Press.

Fitchett, G. and Nolan, S. (2015) *Spiritual Care in Practice: Case Studies in Healthcare Chaplaincy.* London: Jessica Kingsley Publishers.

Frank, A. (2002) *At the Will of the Body: Reflections on Illness.* New York: Houghton Mifflin Company.

Handzo, G. and Wintz, S. (2006) 'We speak the language.' *Healing Spirit 1,* 2, 21–23.

Hefferon, K., Grealy, M. and Mutrie, N. (2009) 'Post-traumatic growth and life-threatening physical illness: A systematic review of the qualitative literature.' *British Journal of Health Psychology 14*, Pt 2, 343–378.

Holden, K.B., Hernandez, N.D., Wrenn, G.L. and Belton, A.S. (2016) 'Resilience: Protective factors for depression and post traumatic stress disorder among African American women?' *Health Culture and Society 9*, 8, 12–29.

King, S.D. (2011) 'Touched by an angel: A chaplain's response to the case study's key interventions, styles and themes/outcomes.' *Journal of Healthcare Chaplaincy 17*, 1–2, 38–45.

McCormick, S.C. and Hildebrand, A.A. (2015) 'A qualitative study of patient and family perceptions of chaplain presence during post-trauma care.' *Journal of Health Care Chaplaincy 21*, 2, 60–75.

Savage, J. (1996) *Listening and Caring Skills: A Guide for Groups and Leaders.* Nashville, TN: Abingdon Press.

Taku, K., Calhoun, L.G. and Tedeschi, R.G. (2008) 'The factor structure of the Posttraumatic Growth Inventory: A comparison of five models using confirmatory factor analysis.' *Journal of Traumatic Stress 21*, 2, 158–164.

Tedeschi, R.G. and Calhoun, L.G. (2004) 'Posttraumatic growth: Conceptual foundations and empirical evidence.' *Psychological Inquiry 15*, 1, 1–18.

VanderWeele, T. (2017) 'On the promotion of human flourishing.' *Perspective 114*, 31, 8148–8156.

Chapter 9

CRITICAL RESPONSE TO EMOTIONS AND FAMILY DYNAMICS CASE STUDIES

A Chaplain's Perspective

LINDA F. PIOTROWSKI

Introduction

The chaplain's involvement with a patient and family nearing the end of life and facing difficult decisions is rarely adequately appreciated. Not only is a board-certified chaplain the expert on the medical team in matters related to spirituality and religious beliefs, they are trained to recognize and attend to the psychosocial aspects of a patient's care. The three cases contained in this section demonstrate the difference it makes when chaplains bring their specific training in whole person care to the medical decision-making process.

Chaplains possess an understanding of theological concepts, religious traditions, ethical frameworks, spiritual practices, and rituals. This training positions them to respond with sensitivity and respect to people from diverse cultures, religious faiths, and spiritual traditions— and to those with no spiritual or religious tradition. Chaplains are competent in assessing how specific beliefs impact health, illness, wellness, hope (or the lack of it), and medical decisions. Chaplains are skilled in performing transformative rituals that integrate religious belief with the affective dimension of human experience. Additionally, they are trained in behavioral sciences, including human and faith development, family systems, socioeconomic, and cultural theory. Of note, most chaplains receive extensive training in negotiating the complex dynamic of families; many are certified as marriage and family counselors. Skill in counseling techniques such as motivational interviewing equips chaplains to follow the lead of their patients and patients. Reflective listening, another counseling technique, enables chaplains to read body language, unspoken messages, motivations, and underlying emotions hidden beneath spoken words.

Other members of the multidisciplinary or interdisciplinary team often do not possess the unique constellation of skills provided by the holistic nature of chaplaincy training. While physicians now receive training in delivering bad news and recognizing the psychosocial needs of their patients, few possess the knowledge or have comfort in attending to religious or spiritual needs. Many physicians recognize and can acknowledge patient emotions such as grief, anger, or guilt, though most do not possess the knowledge, skills, and ability needed to assist patients and families to unravel the complexity of emotions that impact medical decision-making.

While social workers and psychologists receive extensive training in Family Systems Theory as well as the emotional aspects of the impact of critical and life-threatening illness on patients and family, few can untangle how religious beliefs and systems intersect with family dynamics. More importantly, members of these disciplines do not possess the spiritual authority to intervene when religious beliefs embedded in family systems impact medical decision-making.

The cases offered by Chaplains Goheen, Swofford, and Vilagos highlight how illness and loss impact family systems, and how the chaplain's knowledge of both family systems and religious frameworks position them to support medical decision-making. In Goheen's case, the multigenerational family system faces the loss of their matriarch and spiritual leader. In Swofford's case, father and daughter are separated by disparate religious beliefs about death and dying and the inability to communicate about the anticipated disruption to their dyad. In Vilagos' case, the close-knit nuclear family of Aaron, Belinda, and Trina is torn apart by a sudden traumatic injury. In each instance, the chaplain intervenes to promote transformational healing of the family system in the face of loss.

Goheen's case study

There is growing evidence that religious beliefs and family preferences influence medical decisions. The *Journal of Clinical Oncology* published a survey of 100 patients with advanced lung disease, their caregivers, and 257 medical oncologists. Investigators asked participants to rank the importance of factors that might influence chemotherapy decisions: oncologists' recommendation, faith in God, ability of treatment to cure the disease, side effects, family doctor's recommendation, spouse's recommendations, and children's recommendations. The results indicated that health professionals underestimate the role played by both religious beliefs and family values in the choices patients make about their medical care (Silvestri *et al.* 2003).

Goheen's description of the care team meeting suggests that the medical staff were at a complete loss when questions of a spiritual and religious nature arose, and needed someone with expertise in this area to intervene. Goheen not only understood the evangelical religious beliefs of Rita and her family, but he possessed an insider's knowledge of the family-centered First Universalist Church. It is clear from his case that one cannot be understood in isolation from the other due to the sacralizing of the multigenerational family system within the evangelical tradition.

Goheen draws upon his training in family systems as he describes this family as a "care-centered relational system under duress." He skillfully integrates his theoretical knowledge with his acquired knowledge of the family's religious framework, regarding suffering and the obligation to honor one's elders as he adopts a prophetic, future-oriented role. His assumes a leadership role that fits with the family's framework, where the pastor is granted honorary status as a tertiary member of the family.

Goheen is therefore able to negotiate the complex family dynamics informed by evangelical Christian beliefs about sin, suffering, and redemption that are impacting the family's decision about removing the feeding tube from Rita, the family matriarch. As described by classic Family Systems Theory, he observes when Deborah, the "heir apparent" of the family or the matriarch in waiting, "disengaged" from the family unit (Bowen 1993). He observed a power vacuum when a grandson voiced the pivotal question: "Aren't we supposed to honor our mother and father? How can starving Mom-Mom be honoring our mother and father?" Attending to shifting family roles as well as to the feelings of guilt and shame, Goheen used his pastoral authority to nudge the family forward, toward a new equilibrium.

In the evangelical tradition, members of a family have assigned roles and relational rules to which they must adhere. By using a virtue central to the faith—mercy—he broadened their self-understanding and expanded the possibilities of who they could now be within this family structure.

Swofford's case study

The intense bond between father and daughter depicted in Swofford's case is threatened by the degree of stress placed on the family system by his advanced chronic heart failure (CHF) and chronic obstructive pulmonary disease (COPD). Swofford's training in Family Systems Theory provides a lens for her to see what is at play for both family members. The degree of resistance expressed by the daughter Karen to accepting her father's (Mark) prognosis, her manipulation and need for control, and her initial avoidance of the chaplain indicate she is deeply threatened by this potential loss. As she is threatened, she in turn threatens a lawsuit if the medical team obeys the patient's wishes rather than hers.

Likewise, Mark's inability to communicate his wishes directly to his daughter suggest a protective, father role that he was unable to relinquish in spite of his desire to die and be at peace.

Swofford clearly observes the power reversal in the relationship when Mark is unable to speak for himself. The daughter has become the protector or one in control; the father the dependent "child." By attending to this patient's non-verbal body language as well as asking appropriate clarifying questions with great patience and perseverance, she helps Mark experience some satisfaction in knowing that his feelings are being "heard." Ultimately, this act of attending to his emotions ensures the care plan aligned with his deepest wishes and needs. This time-consuming, yet extremely valuable, one-to-one time with the patient provides Swofford with leadership and legitimacy when she speaks to the medical team about the patient. She again advocates for him by requesting his primary doctor order a psychiatric consult in order to assure the other team members that the patient has the capacity to make decisions about his own treatment. Deftly, Swofford is also trying to honor the former role of father and daughter so it can be grieved before it is forever changed by Mark's death.

Swofford is attuned to the daughter's resistance to engage around the difficult choices faced by the patient. She is careful in her approach, refraining from direct engagement until the daughter is ready to speak about her fears and concerns. It is important to note that in spite of the daughter's initial rejection, Swofford remains open to interaction and support for her. This is what ultimately enables the patient's daughter to engage in substantive discussions regarding strongly held beliefs about miracles and her hope that her father might yet "come home."

Swofford is adept at recognizing the shared grief father and daughter are individually experiencing but failing to express to each other. The suffering she witnesses is multidimensional: "Suffering is a concept closely related to spirituality... It can exist in all four domains of quality of life: physical, psychological, social, and spiritual" (Ferrell and Thrane 2011, p.11). With continued ministry to both the patient and daughter, Swofford creates a sacred space where they can hear one another. Through written notes and spoken words they are able to broach their love and concern for each other. They speak of the fears and the losses each is anticipating. Their suffering is ameliorated and they are able to come to a consensus about the goals of care.

Key to this movement is Swofford's recognition that though authentic on one level, the daughter's belief in a miraculous healing functions to reinforce her denial. When she senses that the daughter is emotionally ready, she invites her to reframe her understanding of miraculous healing rather than challenge it directly. Swofford thereby facilitates respect for the conflicting belief systems of father and daughter. More importantly, she ensures the patient's deepest needs to be released from his suffering and know his daughter would be okay are met. After five long months in the Intensive Care Unit (ICU), the patient dies peacefully with his daughter at his side.

Chaplains must be knowledgeable about the factors that hinder decision-making for patients and family members who are surrogates. Anticipatory grief, the mechanism of denial, and fear of the unknown lead families to engage in differing avoidance techniques such as not visiting when they know physicians will be present, avoiding family meetings, and only focusing on the "good news" offered in medical updates. Swofford recognizes the burden the patient's daughter is experiencing, and offers guidance in navigating the complex emotions of loss, guilt, and fear of abandonment. Swofford demonstrates sensitivity, constancy, compassion, and openness to the patient and his daughter. She advocates for them both by listening carefully to the complex intersection of faith, emotions, and familial roles at play. Her non-judging presence and constant compassionate faithfulness models for the patient and his daughter a God who will not abandon either one of them.

Vilagos' case study

In this case, we see a creative use of ritual and story-telling to address family dynamics and promote spiritual growth and healing. Vilagos uses the ritual of making ink handprints with the patient, his wife, and daughter to allow each to hear and honor the stories, hopes, and fears of the others. Later, she uses the ritual of family prayer to fulfill the need for forgiveness and coming together as a family.

Vilagos names post-traumatic growth (PTG) as the primary theoretical framework that informs her spiritual assessment and leads her to select story-telling combined with ritual as interventions to assist the family in processing their feelings of guilt, responsibility, and grief. Rituals, whether secular or explicitly religious, have the power to move people from one space to another. The language of ritual is affective, touching the spiritual, emotional, and cognitive dimensions of human experience and longing. Ritual is forward-looking even as it acknowledges where people are in the present (and sometimes in the past).

PTG theory deals primarily with the after-effects of trauma and stress, including illness and bereavement. It recognizes that both on an individual level and as a family system, disruption occurs. PTG theory posits that illness and loss need not only cause distress and rupture; they may also be the catalyst for personal and familial role development. Movement toward wholeness is possible; attention to meaning-making, spirituality, and community are key to healing and growth. Vilagos lays a firm foundation for the family to experience growth after the patient dies. She uses active compassionate listening to encourage story-telling; the story-telling in turn invites ritualizing of memories and relationships that might serve as places of reimaging "family" in the absence of one of its members.

There is always the danger that a family member is not ready to move from their current stance of doubt, grief, guilt, or disbelief regarding a patient's condition. Chaplains walk a fine line in honoring a family member's beliefs and feelings while holding the door open for movement in their decision-making process. There is always the danger of alienating the very person we are attempting to serve. Hospitality means, primarily, the creation of free space. Vilagos practices true hospitality in creating safe and sacred space for each family member to be him or herself. She is able to compassionately listen to each person, affirm their memories and beliefs, all the while encouraging their understanding and acceptance of the current reality.

It would not occur to all chaplains (with the exception possibly of those who work in pediatrics or baby loss) to use art as ritual as Vilagos does in this case. Clearly, she selects the handprinting ritual based upon her assessment of the depth of loss and abandonment each family member is experiencing. In a similar way, she crafts the final ritual to honor the patient's desire for family unity even as she makes room for the family's continued need to give voice to the depth and substance of their grief. Having been heard and valued, the family is able to reconcile their conflicting beliefs and come together to honor the patient's life and wishes.

Conclusion

These three cases demonstrate how family dynamics and complex emotions complicate medical decision-making. Each chaplain uses a unique approach to spiritual care to enable decision-making that ultimately aligns with the patient's wishes. By attending to the spoken and unspoken needs and desires of each member of the family and to the dynamics of the family system itself, each chaplain tailors a care plan based upon a psychosocial theory and/or framework suitable to each case. Were it not for the multifaceted training and skillset of these chaplains that allowed each to pay attention to the many threads of meaning, belief, roles, and emotions, the process of making high-stakes medical decisions with and for a loved one might have resulted in an unraveling rather than a strengthening of the family system.

References

Bowen, M. (1993) *Family Therapy in Clinical Practice.* Lanham, MD: Rowman & Littlefield Publishers.

Ferrell, B. and Thrane, S. (2011) 'Spirituality, religion, and end of life care.' In K. Doka and A. Tucci (eds) *Living with Grief: Spirituality and End-of-Life Care* (Chapter One). Washington, DC: Hospice Foundation of America.
Silvestri, G.A., Knittig, S., Zoller, J.S. and Nietert, P.J. (2003) 'Importance of faith on medical decisions regarding cancer care.' *Journal of Clinical Oncology 21*, 7, 1379–1382.

Further reading

Kidd, R. (2012) 'Foundational Listening and Responding Skills.' In S.B. Roberts (ed.) *Professional Spiritual and Pastoral Care: A Practical Clergy and Chaplain's Handbook* (pp.92–105). Woodstock, VT: SkyLights Paths Publishing.
Koenig, H.G. (2004) 'Religion, spirituality, and medicine: Research findings and implications for clinical practice.' *Southern Medical Journal 97*, 12, 1194–1200.
Koenig, H.G. and Handzo, G. (2004) 'Spiritual care: Whose job is it anyway?' *Southern Medical Journal 97*, 12, 1242–1244.
Piotrowski, L.F. (2017) 'The chaplain's role as catalyst for "good death."' *Health Progress November–December*, 61–64.
Shannon, S.E. and Tatum, P. (2002) 'Spirituality and end of life care.' *Missouri Medicine 99*, 10, 571–576.
Tedeschi, R.G. and Calhoun, L.G. (2004) 'Posttraumatic growth: Conceptual foundations and empirical evidence.' *Psychological Inquiry 15*, 1, 1–18.

Chapter 10

CRITICAL RESPONSE TO EMOTIONS AND FAMILY DYNAMICS CASE STUDIES

A Psychologist's Perspective

DEBJANI MUKHERJEE

When a loved one is hospitalized and critical medical decisions need to be made, the decision-making process can be impacted by strong emotions and long-standing family dynamics. As a licensed clinical psychologist and clinical ethicist working primarily in physical medicine and rehabilitation, the fundamental role of the family in medical decision-making is deeply familiar. While we think about medical decisions in terms of individual respect for autonomy and choices, in reality, patients with and without capacity to make their own decisions rely on their families to guide, support, advise, and sometimes make decisions on their behalf. Family dynamics, both healthy and unhealthy, are therefore part of many medical decisions, healthcare providers have a necessarily limited window into the dynamics and their impact, and communication can become muddled and conflict-laden. The role of the chaplain in medical decision-making can be critical in increasing understanding, improving communication, and accompanying individual patients, families, and healthcare providers through very stressful situations. In this set of case studies, some key themes emerged that illustrate the complexity of the short- and long-term family responses and dynamics in this context. I will briefly focus on two larger themes: (1) negotiation and effective use of emotion and (2) therapeutic presence. Both of these themes underscore the process rather than the specific content of how chaplains address heightened emotions in complex medical decision-making.

Negotiation and effective use of emotion

The first theme is the need to negotiate and effectively use emotion, particularly in interactions between patients and surrogates, medical teams and families, and within families. This involves facilitating communication, reframing, attending to emotion, and negotiating potential conflict. As Fisher and Shapiro (2005) point out in their book, *Beyond Reason: Using Emotions as You Negotiate*, negative and positive emotions impact the process of negotiating in complex ways. Simple examples include the fact that negative emotions can lead to "a tense relationship filled with distrust, communication that is limited and confrontational" or getting stuck in your position (Fisher and Shapiro 2005, p.9). On the other hand, positive emotions can lead to a "cooperative working relationship, open, easy, two-way conversation, and listening and learning about each other's concerns and wants" (Fisher and Shapiro 2005, p.9). Medical decision-making, by its very context, often involves intense emotion and potentially negative emotions such as guilt, anger, fear, worry, and sadness. A negotiation that attends to emotion will address negative emotion and foster positive emotions such as gratitude, hope, and serenity. It is also important to note that every human being involved in the medical setting—the patient, family members, friends, and medical team members, including chaplains—is experiencing emotions. An awareness of this complex reality and some space to allow emotions to emerge but not override discussions and decisions can be beneficial in the negotiation process. Chaplains who are trained in counseling and listening skills can help create these metaphorical spaces to process and work through decisions.

Fisher and Shapiro (2005) also identify five core concerns in negotiation: appreciation, affiliation, autonomy, status, and role. Briefly, "core concerns are human wants that are important to almost everyone in virtually every negotiation. They are often unspoken..." (Fisher and Shapiro 2005, p.15). Each of these core concerns, when addressed effectively, can ease emotionally challenging situations. In fact, Fisher and Shapiro recommend, "Rather than trying to deal directly with scores of changing emotions affecting you and others, you can turn your attention to the five core concerns" (2005, p.21). Of particular note in these three cases is the chaplains' use of appreciation. Expressing appreciation is "to understand each other's point of view; to find merit in what each of us thinks, feels or does; and to communicate our understanding through words and actions" (Fisher and Shapiro 2005, p.28). Feeling appreciated leads to positive emotions, and even if you disagree, the process can be smoother and more amicable. Fisher and Shapiro (2005) discuss three obstacles to feeling appreciated:

> First, each of us may *fail to understand* the other side's point of view... Second, if we disagree with what the other person is saying, we may *criticize the merit* in whatever they say or do... Third, each of us may *fail to communicate* any merit we see in the other side's thoughts, feelings or actions. (2005, p.29; emphasis added)

This failure to understand, recognize, and communicate the merit in others' arguments can lead to an erosion of trust and open communication, avoidance, and negative feelings. In the illustrative case examples, communication has broken down or participants are at an impasse. When a chaplain is involved in conflicts around medical decision-making and reacting to potentially entrenched positions, expressing appreciation for diverse viewpoints, finding merit and value, communicating clearly, and attending to non-verbal signals can ease the conflict.

In addition to expressing appreciation, all three authors describe examples of attuning to and using emotion effectively, often reframing the conflict and uncovering or discovering ways to move forward. For example, Chaplain Swofford describes the different views that her patient Mark and his daughter Karen have about his hospitalization, quality of life, and wishes about continuing medical treatment. "He believed a life well lived was most important. Living in the hospital any longer was incongruent with his definition of quality of life. His faith told him that something better was ahead for him—that's where he'd get his miracle and quality of life!" His daughter, on the other hand, is waiting for a different kind of miracle, one where her father's medical condition changes. Mark is distressed and unable to communicate with his daughter. Karen is guilty and fearful. Their relationship had been complicated and in this extremely stressful situation, communication broke down. "In the end, helping Karen see that miracles can look different in different contexts empowered her to begin meaningful and authentic conversations with her father." Swofford helps uncover underlying interests and concerns, attends to emotion, improves communication, and gently brings father and daughter closer to understanding each other.

Chaplain Vilagos also expresses appreciation and gains understanding of conflicting emotions. She describes her patient's wife struggling:

> ...between not doing enough and doing too much. Clearly it was difficult for her to balance the family's certainty for miraculous physical healing and the inevitability of death as presented by the medical team's determination of Medical Futility... During our visits she shared that her primary fear was not death, but making the "right" decision for her husband.

This tension of not doing enough versus doing too much is clarified and the underlying fear of making a wrong decision emerges. Vilagos also uses stories and rituals to communicate, bringing cohesion and a sense of meaning. For example, she includes the patient in storytelling and ritual as she "lovingly cleaned the ink from his hands with a warmed cloth" to underscore to his wife and daughter that he is a part of the ritual.

Chaplain Goheen employs the therapeutic technique of reframing after appreciating the diverse perspectives of family members and the medical team. This family struggles with the decision about placing and removing a feeding tube. Comments such as, "She has fed all of us. How can we not feed her" and "Aren't we supposed to honor our mother and our father? How can starving Mom-Mom be honoring our mother and father?" arise in the course of discussions. Goheen appreciates the family's perspective, understands its merit, underscores the current situation, and reframes honor to include mercy, "focusing on mercy as the religious answer to suffering." Goheen also appreciates the differing perspectives of the medical team and the patient's family. "The medical team saw further aggressive interventions as providing no meaningful benefit and feared that continuing treatment would only prolong her suffering." In each of these case studies, the authors delve into an understanding of varying perspectives, acknowledge and accompany strong emotions, validate the merit of conflicting views, and address concerns. They do not avoid negative emotions and facilitate the emergence of more positive emotions.

Therapeutic presence

The second theme that illustrates the complexity of the short- and long-term family responses and dynamics and the effective intervention by the chaplain is accompanying, empathizing, and being a therapeutic presence. In *Therapeutic Presence: A Mindful Approach to Effective Therapy*, Geller and Greenberg (2012) offer a comprehensive account of this concept. They define therapeutic presence as:

> ...the state of having one's whole self in the encounter with a client by being completely in the moment on a multiplicity of levels—physically, emotionally, cognitively, and spiritually. Therapeutic presence involves being in contact with one's integrated and healthy self, while being open and receptive to what is poignant in the moment and immersed in it, with a larger sense of spaciousness and expansion of awareness and perception. (2012, p.7)

I am using a less formal definition of the term to describe accompanying, supporting, and being with patients and families in the moments when they make difficult medical decisions. Each of the authors may very well have embodied the concept of therapeutic presence that Geller and Greenberg describe above; however, because their commentaries do not reflect on this aspect of their own experience, we are unable to know the degree to which they intentionally brought their "whole selves" to the encounter.

Swofford describes a process of accompanying both her patient Mark and his daughter Karen on their journey. She blends cognitive assessment, emotional attunement, and spiritual understanding in this description:

> My assessment of Karen's reaction to her father's condition led me to question whether she was holding on to the hope for a miracle as true faithfulness, desperate self-preservation or strong denial. Karen appeared to me to be acting out of self-preservation. She avoided the medical personnel and used the language of miracles almost like a wall of protection, demanding that no "negative" talk should be spoken around her father.

Vilagos describes how therapeutic presence is key to her effective engagement with Belinda:

> She and I developed a mutual trust that grew from my non-anxious presence in the face of her suffering and resulted in an openness to share her fears. Deep listening helped me hear Belinda and her family's story. I reflected on that story with them so I could help to make meaning in the face of adversity.

Goheen describes a similar phenomenon: "Through listening and careful affirmation, I demonstrated an understanding of the family's values, learned family role and history and gained their trust through respect for their religious worldview."

In "A qualitative study of patient and family perceptions of chaplain presence during post-trauma care," McCormick and Hildebrand (2015, p.60) identify three key themes of chaplaincy care—the "attributes valued in the chaplain's presence, the elements necessary to form relationship with the chaplain, and the role of the chaplain in helping patients to discover and expressing meaning in their experiences." While they don't use the term "therapeutic presence," the examples they describe from their interviews are analogous. For example, a comment about positive aspects of chaplaincy care was: "Sensing how much to say or not to say and how long to visit is important from the very start" (McCormick and Hildebrand 2015, p.66). As far as characteristics, respondents suggested that "the desired chaplain demeanor was one that is consistently calm, gentle, and respectful... Being respectful also meant not being too talkative or assertive, but rather to listen and follow the participant's lead" (McCormick and Hildebrand 2015, p.67). Participants also reported that chaplains must demonstrate compassion and empathy without any indication of judgment of the patient or family member. These qualities are related to a therapeutic presence and were behaviors and stances that the three case examples illustrate. Moreover, being present in the moment and attuned to cognitive, emotional, physical, and spiritual aspects of the patient, family members, and of the chaplains themselves can lead to the awareness that is described in the definition of therapeutic presence, and can help illuminate a clearer path through the dynamics. Therapeutic presence is also intrinsically linked to perceived support, compassion, and empathy. In a study of the "Perceptions of chaplains' value and impact within hospital care teams," Cunningham and colleagues (2017) gathered data from patients and healthcare providers to develop a rich picture of the contributions of hospital chaplains. In one query, patients were asked, "What was the most helpful or encouraging part of your interactions with chaplains?" The top five themes (based on 188 separate responses in patient interviews) included support (spiritual)—24 percent, availability and time spent—21 percent, compassion and empathy—19 percent, conversation (someone to talk to)—11 percent, and support (general)—9 percent (Cunningham *et al.* 2017, p.1242). While spiritual support was the most helpful part, simply spending time and accompanying patients with compassion and empathy were second and third. When navigating complex medical decisions, support from healthcare providers can be critical to decreasing distress and increasing ease.

However, non-chaplain healthcare providers in the Cunningham and colleagues (2017) study noted that "they feel uncomfortable broaching or discussing topics and questions associated with religion/spirituality themselves, and were thankful to know that chaplains were trained and available to assist patients and family members who might wish to discuss these topics" (2017, p.1241). The authors also note that the results of their study:

> ...clearly show that when integrated into healthcare teams, chaplains have an ability to connect with patients on a different level than other healthcare professionals and can provide pastoral and humanistic care and perspective to patients, a form of care and perspective that would not be expected from physicians or nurses. (Cunningham *et al.* 2017, p.1245)

In the case studies described by Goheen, Swofford, and Vilagos, their unique contributions to easing family dynamics and tensions while making difficult medical decisions underscore this point. It should also be noted that therapeutic presence includes being there physically, emotionally, cognitively, and *spiritually*. As chaplains with unique training on the healthcare team, the authors elucidate how they guide the families spiritually. While negotiating with an attention to emotion, and being fully present, the chaplains simultaneously use their subject matter expertise and training in attending to suffering. Perhaps one distinction is that emotional reactions are felt in the moment, while spiritual perspectives are often more consistent over time.

Swofford describes the fact that the patient's daughter "mentioned that she felt guilty not going to church, and thought that God might be upset with her because of this. With no spiritual leader in the community, Karen was also inclined to believe that if God was upset at her, then her father's condition could be punishment for her actions." Swofford recognizes and explores this belief in the context of a discussion about medical decision-making. Vilagos clarifies that her "role was not to provide medical or theological answers but to help the family navigate and reframe their existential questions to prevent gridlock and promote healing." This focus on preventing gridlock while working with spiritual perspectives exemplifies the focus on process and outcomes rather than specific spiritual content. Vilagos also meets with the ethicist and describes the family's deep spiritual reliance on God's power of transcendence to bring healing despite the medical circumstances. She "sought to find a place of common understanding between the concept of religious honor and medical beneficence, thereby building a bridge between the family and the medical team."

Negotiating with emotion and therapeutic presence are two key approaches to deal with intense, fluctuating, and complex emotional scenarios. Of note is that all three chaplains describe a process that unfolds over time and involves gaining the trust of the various stakeholders. They describe listening, gathering information, wading through competing perspectives, and using their spiritual, clinical, and interpersonal knowledge to ease the tensions. They also describe their own grounding in the settings in which they work, and presumably through their own journey as chaplains are able to put forward an "integrated and healthy self" that could foster the healing process. Healthcare chaplains are often thrust in the middle of complex family dynamics, swirling emotions, and variable interpretations of information. Using their skills of emotional engagement and discernment, appreciating and validating core human concerns, and being fully present, their efforts can be instrumental and uniquely contribute to facilitating complex medical decision-making.

References

Cunningham, C.J.L., Panda, M., Lambert, J., Daniels, G. and DeMars, K. (2017) 'Perceptions of chaplains' value and impact within hospital care teams.' *Journal of Religion and Health* 56, 4, 1231–1247.

Fisher, R. and Shapiro, D. (2005) *Beyond Reason: Using Emotions as You Negotiate.* New York: Penguin Books.

Geller, S.M. and Greenberg, L.S. (2012) *Therapeutic Presence: A Mindful Approach to Effective Therapy.* Washington, DC: American Psychological Association.

McCormick, S.C. and Hildebrand, A.A. (2015) 'A qualitative study of patient and family perceptions of presence during post-trauma care.' *Journal of Health Care Chaplaincy 21,* 2, 60–75.

PART III

NEGOTIATING RELIGIOUS AND CULTURAL DIFFERENCES

M. JEANNE WIRPSA

WHY are healthcare chaplains able to serve as religious and cultural interpreters, negotiators, and brokers in the process of medical decision-making? How do chaplains straddle the world of medicine and the world(s) inhabited by the patients and families they serve without losing their grounding? How do chaplains notice, acknowledge, and bracket (to greater or lesser degrees) their interpretative lens, formed and informed by their unique life experience, education and training, and religious and cultural location?

The concept or practice of "cultural humility" offers insight into how Chaplains Axelrud, Kirby, and Rosencrans—and those they represent in the profession more generally—effectively cross the boundaries of diverse cultures and religions, including their own. Cultural humility might best be thought of as a virtue, a stance, or a way of being. It transcends knowledge about and respect for diverse worldviews. It is a life-long process rather than a competency that can be demonstrated at any one point in time. Moreover, cultural humility recognizes that culture is not "a static characteristic that can be studied and mastered; rather, culture seems to be fluid, subjective, and as multifaceted as the individuals within it" (Derrington, Paquette and Johnson 2018, p.S189).

In a recent concept analysis of "cultural humility," Foronda and colleagues (2016) uncover the following five attributes: openness, self-awareness, egolessness, supportive interaction, and self-reflection and critique. A person is culturally humble if they have an open mind, are willing to explore new ideas, and are aware of their own strengths, limitations, and values. They engage in an ongoing process of critically reflecting on and refining their own thoughts, feelings, and actions. A culturally humble individual is modest, down-to-earth, and approaches others as equals. Interactions with an individual who is culturally humble result in positive human exchanges that are supportive, engaging, and mutually accountable (Foronda *et al.* 2016). Cultural humility also includes a commitment to "redressing power imbalances in the physician–patient dynamic, and to developing mutually beneficial and non-paternalistic partnerships with communities on behalf of individuals and defined populations," as Tervalon and Murray-Garcia (1998, p.123) contend in a separate analysis of the concept. In the medical system, Stone (2017) adds, a key feature of or companion to cultural humility is "epistemic humility"—the acceptance that clinical diagnoses and prognoses are always fallible and should be subject to ongoing evaluation and revision. Epistemic humility includes respecting not only what health conditions means for patients' lives but also people's wisdom about their medical condition.

Chaplaincy training has as one of its core aims the cultivation of self-awareness and epistemic humility. Even as the profession of chaplaincy has embraced evidence-based practice and the development of skill-based competencies, formation of the chaplain's character and self-critical lens remains central. Historically, this has taken place through the use of verbatims; case studies might be considered an extension of that literary and pedagogical genre. Board-certified professional healthcare chaplains must demonstrate that they are self-reflective and able to "identify one's professional strengths and limitation in the provision of care" (BCCI 2017, PIC1). Chaplains are required to "articulate ways in which one's feelings, attitudes, values, and assumptions affect professional practice" (BCCI 2017, PIC2). Additionally, chaplains must show that they "function in a manner that respects the physical, emotional, cultural and spiritual boundaries of others" (BCCI 2017, PIC4). Other qualifications for certification require that chaplains provide care that appreciates and respects diversity, attend to developmental and life stage differences of patients and family members, and provide religious resources to people from all traditions. Cultural knowledge, sensitivity, and awareness are cultivated through didactic presentations—on marginalized populations, the impact of disability, gender, or sexual orientation on health and healthcare needs, and on diverse religious beliefs and practices. However, it is the additional focus on self-awareness and epistemic humility through group learning processes, critical reflection on verbatims, and the formative exchange with a clinical pastoral education (CPE) supervisor that promotes the virtue of "cultural humility" within chaplaincy as a profession.

Cultural humility as embodied and exercised by chaplains curtails and corrects the conscious or unconscious reliance on stereotypes by other members of the healthcare team, as seen in the case studies presented by Chaplains Rosencrans and Axelrud. It also acts as a check on the epistemic authority of medicine itself, as we see in Chaplain Kirby's case study. As each of these cases reveal, the culture chaplains frequently unveil is that of medicine itself. Core assumptions of this unique culture include: a biophysical ontology of illness and healing, an approach to decision-making grounded in rationality, and an anthropology that is individualistic rather than communal.

In their interactions with families and with the healthcare team, each of these chaplains demonstrates key attributes or facets of cultural humility cited in the research literature on this concept. Let me lift up just a few key moments. Kirby demonstrates both openness and self-awareness when she asks Alma's family to "say more" about their explanation for her illness: "She's got a broken heart." In unpacking the threads of the story, she locates their rage in the context of the history of racism in US healthcare, even as she leverages her experience within the LGBTQ community to better appreciate their level of distrust. Rosencrans demonstrates the attribute "egolessness" as she patiently surrenders herself to the historical and political narrative of Mohammed, the Palestinian Muslim husband of her patient. Like Kirby, Rosencrans positions herself as an advocate for the family's wisdom when she helps the medical team grasp the significance of the religious meaning of pain and suffering. Axelrud confesses how he struggled to bracket his own family experience when interacting with Sarah's family, demonstrating the attribute "self-awareness and critique." He practices "interprofessional cultural humility" as he accepts as valid the multiple interpretations of Sarah's healing voiced by various members of the medical team.

Shared decision-making in cross-cultural encounters requires "flexibility and taking extreme care when eliciting the contextual characteristics that are relevant to a particular patient or family" (Derrington *et al.* 2018, p.S191). Chaplains in the cases that follow bring cultural humility to their interactions with families in their care, enabling them to elicit the unique, nuanced interpretation of the cause of illness and healing. Their cultural humility enables them to recognize not only when unfamiliar beliefs and practices impact the medical decision-making process, but also when the family's model of decision-making itself differs from the approach of the medical team. Finally, cultural humility empowers chaplains to acknowledge, negotiate, and redress the power imbalances inherent in medical decision-making. The integration of professional healthcare chaplains into shared decision-making is essential when cultural and religious differences exist between clinicians and patients and families in their care. If we concede that every interaction in healthcare is "cross-cultural"—because medicine is its own unique culture foreign to most patients and families—then integrating chaplains into all teams where complex, high-stakes decisions are faced will help ensure those decisions are truly patient-centered.

References

BCCI (Board of Chaplaincy Certification, Inc.) (2017) *Common Qualifications and Competencies for Professional Chaplains.* Available at www.professionalchaplains. org/files/2017%20Common%20Qualifications%20and%20Competencies%20 for%20Professional%20Chaplains.pdf

Derrington, S.F., Paquette, E. and Johnson, K.A. (2018) 'Cross-cultural interactions and shared decision-making.' *Pediatrics 142*, Suppl. 3, S187–S192.

Foronda, C., Baptiste, D.L., Reinholdt, M.M. and Ousman, K. (2016) 'Cultural humility: A concept analysis.' *Journal of Transcultural Nursing 27*, 3, 210–217.

Stone, J.R. (2017) 'Cultivating humility and diagnostic openness in clinical judgment.' *AMA Journal of Ethics 19*, 10, 970–977.

Tervalon, M. and Murray-Garcia, J. (1998) 'Cultural humility versus cultural competence: A critical distinction in defining physician training outcomes in multicultural education.' *Journal of Health Care for the Poor and Underserved 9*, 2, 117–125.

Chapter 11

SARAH'S STORY

"If G-d feels Sarah should experience a recovery, it will be a great gift. However, if G-d doesn't, my belief system will never change"—Leah, an Orthodox Jew, speaking about G-d's role in her daughter's devastating illness

ABRAHAM AXELRUD

Introduction

The patient, Sarah, is Leah and Benjamin's newly pregnant 25-year-old daughter. Benjamin is a vascular surgeon and Leah is a respected female religious leader in her community. They are active members in their community of Orthodox Jews where Leah is both an instructor and leads a prayer group for women. The year I met them, the family left as usual for their annual summer vacation on Eastern Long Island. The second evening away, Sarah collapsed in her mother's arms and was rushed to a local hospital. In transit, Sarah lost the baby.

After an initial exam and tests, Sarah was rushed to the hospital where I serve. She suffered a massive brain bleed and had to be intubated immediately. She was unresponsive and after a short time a tracheostomy was ordered. Sarah's prognosis was poor and it was likely she would remain in a vegetative state, or worse, decompensate further and die from neurological causes (brain death).

Sarah's family requested a chaplain who was a rabbi even though she was not on my unit of coverage. As a result, I had the privilege of caring for Sarah, Benjamin, and Leah for over five months. The family agreed to this publication if their anonymity was respected. The names, ages, places, and identifying characteristics have been changed. I am grateful to Sarah and her family for allowing me to hold and tell their story.

I am a board-certified chaplain with 20 years' experience. I was ordained as an Orthodox rabbi but currently practice in the Conservative tradition, leaning towards Orthodoxy. The hospital serves patients who are the most diverse in the US. Only a small percentage of staff and patients are of the Jewish faith. The staff make every effort to understand as much as they can about the backgrounds, traditions, practices, and beliefs of their diverse patient population. Chaplains meet with patients of all faiths and traditions.

Case

When asked to see Sarah's family, I thoughtfully considered what pastoral approach I would adopt as I approached this challenging situation. As a result of my previous experience with parents whose child suffered a devastating injury, I speculated that Benjamin and Leah might be praying for G-d to overturn nature and perform a miracle. I decided if they brought up miraculous healing, I would provide the full range of opinions on miracles and the complex understanding presented in the tradition. I would remind the family of the traditional prayers that present healing in a holistic way.

In the end, I was mistaken about how they were facing the tragic situation of their daughter. Their understanding of healing, prayer, and divine power was complex, nuanced, and rooted deeply in the Orthodox Jewish set of beliefs rather than born of a desperate wish to have their daughter with them. My visits became intense explorations of Jewish beliefs and texts about the power of prayer and how the good deeds of others might influence whether divine intervention was in Sarah's future. Benjamin was less optimistic than his wife. He understood that, medically, she was nearly brain dead, and there was no reason for hope. Nonetheless, his Orthodox faith was strong and he did not lose hope.

I also realized immediately that putting up the proverbial emotional wall between patient and healthcare provider would be difficult for me. I have three daughters who are close in age to Sarah. One of my first thoughts was, how could I handle this kind of tragedy? How could I ever help my family go through this and how could I maintain a belief in G-d? I felt I might just be too close. I decided to work through these feelings rather than remove myself from the situation. I hoped my closeness might serve to raise my sensitivity and empathy and engage honestly and openly with these grieving parents. In retrospect, my proximity at times made it hard to bracket my emotional responses and pastoral fears born of seeing other parents pray in desperation for a miracle for their child.

I visited Sarah and her family daily. On my first visit, I found them deep in prayer so I asked if I might join them. In Judaism, there are specific prayers for people who are ill. For example, there is a prayer recited in the synagogue for the sick on Monday, Thursday, and Saturday when the Torah (the scroll containing the five books of Moses) is read. The prayer calls for a healing of body and spirit. I offered these prayers out of respect for their traditional approach to Jewish observances.

I asked open-ended questions in order to facilitate conversation about their feelings, hopes, and wishes. Once shared, I validated their experience and feelings, always offering support. This was followed by engaging them in their view of the concepts of healing drawn from Orthodox Jewish tradition. Out of my suspicion that they might be harboring hopes of a miraculous divine intervention, I used daily prayers to lift up the miracles that happen every day and are part of our life. The rooster crows every morning at sunrise, we have clothes to wear, we wake up, and so on. (Although Jews believe that G-d can intervene in nature, I, along with many Jews, hold that this is a rare occurrence and probably unlikely in this case.)

On my second visit, I encountered Leah praying and speaking to Sarah. It was Friday so I brought electric candles and grape juice to the family. Candles, challah bread, and grape juice (wine, if not in the hospital) are needed to begin the celebration of the Sabbath. This simple gesture served as a respectful entrée into the room even though they actually had their own resources for the Sabbath. It was also a good excuse to visit and reflect spiritually with them on the situation.

Emunah and bitachon

My visit began with what would become the usual Friday visit from then on.

Chaplain: "I brought Sabbath candles—electric, of course—grape juice, wine, and challah."

Leah: "Thank you. You have a *mitzvah* [a good deed that follows a commandment]."

Chaplain: "How is Sarah?"

Leah: "No change, but with G-d's help she will continue to fight."

Chaplain: "How are you doing?"

Leah: "I am as good as I can be and my *tephilot* [prayers] as always are for her."

Chaplain: "It is wonderful that you're by your daughter's side. I have to commend you on your devotion to her and G-d. I notice that you are steeped in prayer and very connected to your daughter at the same time. *Baynenu u'vain atzmeinu* [Hebrew saying, implying 'between us as Jews'], how do you find your strength? You don't appear to ever break down."

Leah: "I do. I find my strength in my *emunah* and *bitachon*, in G-d along with the support of my family and community."

These two concepts are pillars of faith in Jewish tradition. Conventional definitions are provided here:

Emunah: Maimonides explains "The creator blessed be He, created and orchestrates all activities and He alone did, does and will do all actions" (Maimonides 1386). "There is no such thing as happenstance. There is no random occurrence. G-d is intricately involved in the running of the world" (Rabbi Ben Tzion Shafier explaining Maimonides, 2017).

Bitachon: *Bitachon* means trust. Rabbis define *bitachon* as "relying on G-d and trusting G-d to watch over and protect those who have faith."

The two words are bandied about by Jews of faith, but their meanings are often not explored in the context of the life experience and situation at hand. In our rich conversations, I was able to elicit and affirm their rich meanings with this family.

I asked Leah how she thought G-d would watch over Sarah. It was then that she finally brought up the idea of a miracle explicitly. She told me that she hoped G-d would consider a miracle, but if not, G-d would make the correct decision about Sarah's future. She and her family would accept G-d's decision. I asked Leah what *emunah* and *bitachon* meant to her and how these pillars of faith help her and Benjamin deal with their daughter's situation.

Leah: "G-d can do anything. It means nothing to Him to cure my daughter or anyone else. We pray for a complete recovery and know that G-d can heal, and hope that this is His will. Whether He chooses to heal her or not we TRUST (*bitachon*) that G-d loves us and everything is ultimately for the good. Since at the moment of crisis and even now there is pain and suffering, it is hard to feel that it is good. But as we know this is a short-lived world leading to a world of eternity. In the whole picture of eternity, we trust that whatever Hashem (G-d) chooses for us is for our ultimate good and G-d loves us. The goal is to remember that, to feel it, and to live with the trust in Hashem's loving kindness even when we are in so much pain."

Given the nature of Leah's faith, I was relieved that we could finally talk openly about the power of prayer itself. I had long been asking myself the following: I am a parent and share her understanding of these aspects of Jewish belief, but how could a parent not pray and ask for help by miraculous intervention? Was Leah fooling herself? Was she intellectualizing her beliefs and wishes, or were they really as developed and complex as she presented them to be? I knew that family members who hope for a miracle when they are told by physicians that their loved one has no hope of survival experience more complicated grief responses (Zier *et al.* 2009). As a parent and as a chaplain, I was concerned for Sarah's parents in spite of what I had witnessed of their faith and inner strength.

Leah's answer showed me the depth of her relationship with G-d. With deep composure and trust, she responded.

Leah: "G-d knows that we want a miracle. Of course, I believe that G-d has the power to change the world. I firmly believe we are part of a greater plan of G-d's creation. If G-d feels Sarah should experience a recovery, it will be a great gift. However, if G-d forbid, G-d doesn't, my belief system will never change. Understand, that in our hearts that's exactly what we want."

The end game

It should be noted that by this time in the course of Sarah's illness, she was exhibiting some ability to track; the medical assessment, however, was that this did not represent a significant improvement in her condition. Various scans read by experts at our hospital and at outside locations had confirmed Sarah's poor prognosis for cognitive recovery.

One of the rabbis in Leah's community suggested that she go to the graves of great rabbis and pray for her daughter's recovery. This is an ancient practice that is not often done, but Leah agreed. She went with a group of women led by the rabbi who made the suggestion. Benjamin remained at Sarah's bedside. While he was sitting quietly beside her, Sarah woke up, spoke to her father, and asked for her mother.

Immediately, Benjamin telephoned Leah at the cemetery. He said, "Someone wants to talk to you." It was reported that upon hearing her daughter's voice, Leah collapsed on the ground and had to be held up by those around her. Whether or not this was the case, she rushed back to the hospital where she carried on a normal conversation with her daughter.

Analysis

What may not be immediately apparent in the above narrative is my awareness that I became a "bridge of understanding" between the family and the medical team. Some of the staff felt uncomfortable entering Sarah's room even to examine her; they wanted to avoid having to speak about anything that had to do with her future. Some were Sarah's age with young children at home. However, there was a great deal of compassion for a mother who had to go through being at her daughter's bedside in the face of such a poor prognosis. Although the team had been in this position before, the fact that they would see Leah praying, in what seemed to be desperation to save her child, had a significant emotional impact on them.

I spoke individually, privately, and informally to each staff member who cared for Sarah, providing emotional support for their struggles and acknowledging their proximity to the situation when relevant. I used these conversations as an opportunity to build a bridge of compassion and understanding. Central to our conversations was the topic of "prayer." I used a reframing technique to help staff who thought Leah's actions were simply those of a desperate mother. I explained that the word "prayer" has its origins in Old French and is defined as a kind of "begging or pleading." In Judaism, praying is a way to reflect on G-d and G-d's place in the world. The verb "to pray" in Hebrew is *L'hitpallel*, the reflexive of *tephila* (to communicate with G-d), which is to reflect on one's relationship with G-d. Prayer or *tephila* is intended to strengthen one's relationship with G-d, acknowledging what G-d has done for the individual.

The medical center where I work has a very diverse population and staff. For many years, the population and staff were mostly of the Jewish faith. As time went on, the surrounding area changed demographically, as did the staff. Now the staff have little understanding of how Jewish Orthodox religious beliefs impact the healthcare decisions being made by families. In this case, because of my relationship with the family and my role as a rabbi, I assessed that I needed to lay the groundwork for decisions that might arise if Sarah's condition worsened. I came to this conclusion because the staff would ask questions about the family's religious and cultural practices, and as time went on, about Jewish medical decision-making.

I explained Sabbath observances and answered their questions about why Leah always had a hair covering. I tried to offer insight into why the family brought food from home, even when our hospital offered kosher food. Giving the staff a deeper appreciation for Jewish Orthodox practices and observances helped open the door for discussion of other important concepts impacting medical decision-making by Sarah's parents. The nature of the questions progressed over time: "Will the family have a problem if she needs a blood transfusion in the same way a Jehovah Witness patient would?"

I provided them with insights into how and when life support might be removed under Jewish law based on a definition of death. In the Orthodox belief system, death is a cessation of both respiration and heartbeat, I explained in layperson's terms. Patients are to be kept alive at all costs. Sarah, therefore, could not be extubated even though she might be declared "brain dead" under the Western medical understanding of death. When these kinds of decisions have to be made, I informed the staff, an expert in Jewish law and medicine must be consulted, as there are many nuances in interpretation and application of the law to an individual situation.

Bedside staff were clearly distressed as they asked: "If the neurologists determined that Sarah were brain dead, but the family insist on her remaining in the hospital, what would happen?" "What would it be like to care for a patient [they] thought was dead?" "Was it fair to other patients to keep Sarah on a ventilator?" "What would [they] say to the family?" Although I had no easy answers for the staff, I did my best to explain what was potentially at stake religiously for this family. I provided emotional support to the staff for what I anticipated would be a case of extreme moral distress. Increasing understanding and empathy, I believe, kept the staff from prematurely pressuring the parents to engage in end-of-life decision-making that would have created a chasm between family and the medical team.

An equally important outcome was that when the staff digested these concepts, they were more comfortable entering the room and having a light exchange with Leah or other members of the family. They no longer hesitated to discuss Sarah's condition. They engaged Leah in routine medical decisions about medications and tests and in Sarah's care more generally. They felt freer to talk openly about the medical plan for the day and even for the future. Rather than see Leah as someone to be pitied as a grieving mother, they related to her as part of the healing team. In fact, they began to see her as a strong and spiritual person. Interchanges became longer; the relationship between the medical team and Sarah's family was strengthened.

When I first met Sarah's parents, it was clear they were doing everything within their power to keep Sarah alive in spite of the grim prognosis. While honoring their perspective, I was prepared to consider the alternative—Sarah might get worse instead of better. I anticipated that if Sarah were to decompensate further, there would be *halachic* issues in Jewish law that would impact how decisions were made and what were permissible end-of-life choices.

As mentioned previously, Orthodox Jewish patients and their families will usually rely on their personal rabbi to serve as a *posek* (a legal decision-maker on matters of Jewish law) or will contact a rabbi who is a *posek* on the issues at hand (Loike *et al.* 2010). In our conversations, Leah told me that her rabbi was a *posek* and was familiar with Sarah's case. Leah remained in contact with her own rabbi throughout Sarah's lengthy stay in the hospital, even though in the end he did not need to issue a *halachic* ruling about the complexity of when death occurs and under what circumstances it is permissible to remove life support.

With Sarah's family, I was prepared to discuss the recommendations of their rabbi should the situation arise. In my experience with other Orthodox families, it was not unusual for them to need this additional resource to process the grief, hope, and other emotions that would be at play when faced with a decision regarding withholding or withdrawing life-sustaining treatment. Attention to medical decision-making would be integral to the provision of spiritual care I provided. Yet, the boundaries were clear: I would serve as a chaplain and their rabbi would be the *posek* if and when this were needed. I continued giving the family support and spending time with Leah, having long conversations about Judaism and belief. I felt that having these interchanges would help Leah focus on her understanding of G-d's role in the world. This would give her strength for the rest of her journey with Sarah. It would also put her in a position to guide her family, both in terms of their hopes and fears for Sarah and also as they continued to live their normal lives.

People in the Orthodox community had become aware of the situation, given Leah's role as a leader and due to the ongoing involvement of her rabbi. "What was the hospital's policy on care for the Orthodox Jewish patient?" they asked me. "Would the ethical-legal rulings of Judaism regarding determination of death be honored?" In turn, the hospital administration also began to express concern: if we were not sensitive to this Orthodox patient and family, would it cause the institution to lose future patients? I served as a liaison between these two communities, attempting to hear and honor the positions of both. In the end, the ultimate end-of-life conflict never actualized, but I helped lay a groundwork of understanding and mutual respect for the concerns of each party.

Conclusion

When Sarah woke up, I happened to be on the unit and was ushered into her room. As I entered, I thought she had died. To my surprise, I saw her lying down and talking to her mother on the phone. I began to cry. Is this a miracle, I thought? When the family was out of earshot, I asked one of the Orthodox doctors whether there had been an error. Did the radiologist who read the scans make a mistake? They responded by telling me that the scans were sent to two other major hospitals, with all radiologists having the same opinion. I asked another doctor how this could be. She just pointed to heaven.

Team members voiced their own opinions about what had occurred. Some said, "Things like these do, in fact, happen." Non-believers acknowledged that medicine cannot yet fully explain all that occurs in the human body and in the healing process. Other members of the team referred to their own religion, saying, "Jesus took care of her." I shared Leah's beliefs throughout our journey together, agreeing with the concept that "G-d can do everything," even as I did not expect to be a witness to a real miracle.

References

Loike, J., Gillick, M., Mayer, S., Prager, K., et al. (2010) 'The critical role of religion: Caring for the dying patient from an Orthodox Jewish perspective.' *Journal of Palliative Medicine 13*, 10, 1267–1271.

Maimonides, M. (1386) *Mishneh Torah: Division Zemanim.*

Shafier, B.T. (2017) 'Faith.' Orthodox Union.

Zier, L.S., Burak, J.H., Micco, G., Chipman, A.K., Frank, J.A. and White, D.B. (2009) 'Surrogate decision makers' responses to physicians' predictions of medical futility.' *Chest 136*, 1, 110–117.

Further reading

Hirsch, E.G. (1906) 'God.' In I. Singer *et al.* (eds) *The Jewish Encyclopedia*. New York: Funk and Wagnalls. Available at www.jewishencyclopedia.com/articles/6725-god

Kohler, K. (1906) 'Miracle.' In I. Singer, I. *et al.* (eds) *The Jewish Encyclopedia*. New York: Funk and Wagnalls. Available at www.jewishencyclopedia.com/articles/10869-miracle

Puchalski, C.M. (2006) 'Spirituality and medicine: Curricula in medical education.' *Journal of Cancer Education 21*, 1, 14–18.

Puchalski, C.M., Lunsford, B., Harris, M.H. and Miller, R.T. (2006) 'Interdisciplinary spiritual care for seriously ill and dying patients: A collaborative model.' *The Cancer Journal 12*, 5, 398–416.

Widera, E.W., Rosenfeld, K.E., Fromme, E.K., Sulmasy, D.P. and Arnold, R.M. (2011) 'Approaching patients and family members who hope for a miracle.' *Journal of Pain and Symptom Management 42*, 1, 199–125.

Chapter 12

ALMA'S STORY

*"She's dying from a broken heart"—Mary telling
the story of her sister Alma's death*

MICHELLE KIRBY

Introduction

The patient, fictitiously named "Alma," was an African American woman in her late seventies, living in a historically African American neighborhood, near an urban center. She was the matriarch of her family, many of whom live in the metropolitan area of the hospital. She has a large family, several children, and grandchildren. The patient was unknown to me prior to this ministry event. She had been admitted to the Intensive Care Unit (ICU) after being rushed to the hospital on a stroke alert. She had suffered a catastrophic stroke, which was impairing her breathing.

I chose this story for this book because it exemplifies the importance of listening with cultural sensitivity in a crisis when there are difficult decisions to be made. As this event happened over nine years ago and I had no ongoing relationship with the family and do not have access to their contact information, I was not able to seek permission to publish "Alma's story." In keeping with guidelines for case study research, I therefore changed all identifying features (names, particular descriptors such as age, location of care) in order to protect the privacy of those involved. As this case features cultural conflicts, I retained only general references to racial, ethnic, and religious characteristics of the family and staff. My sincere hope is to honor this family's story and their grief by bringing it to others for education.

I am a European American, lesbian-identified, female chaplain, endorsed by the Metropolitan Community Church. I had been serving this non-profit community hospital, which I'll call "St Thomas," for approximately five years. St Thomas serves a highly diverse population, from the very wealthy to those who are homeless, representing the diversity of the surrounding neighborhoods. The primary cultures served by St Thomas include: European/White Americans, including a significant minority of Russian patients, first-generation Chinese and Vietnamese immigrants, and African Americans. St Thomas utilized a hospitalist company that staffed the hospital on nights and weekends, often with young doctors, freshly graduated from medical residency programs.

Prior to this event, I was an active member of the Palliative Care team and the Ethics Committee at St Thomas. I was on-call, paged by an ICU nurse to "be with the family."

Case

When I arrived to the ICU area, I initially observed a group of 12–15 predominately African American people milling anxiously around the waiting room and hallway. The privacy doors had been closed, keeping the family out of the ICU. From experience, I knew that this was only done during shift change and high stress times, such as codes. Not recognizing anyone in the family, I entered the ICU to learn more about the clinical situation. I immediately observed several nurses and doctors engaged in the all-too-familiar dance of stabilizing a critical patient. I assessed what was happening and scanned the area to see who was the least busy. Seeing no one idle, I approached the area and a young woman in a white coat labeled "Dr L," who quickly and breathlessly said, "Oh Chaplain, I'm so glad you're here!"

I remember that I did not recall ever meeting Dr L before, though many of the nurses were known to me. She was the on-call hospitalist, and I realized that she looked just a few years my junior. Then in my mid-thirties, I still found it a little unnerving that a fully licensed physician could be younger than me.

"The family doesn't understand. I've tried to explain!" She spoke rapidly, busy with the patient. I asked about the patient's medical condition. "She has a brain bleed. It's getting worse, and they want us to do everything." She had work to do, and I made my way back to the family. I had been called to countless codes over the past five years, and knew that the team trusted me as a chaplain. In my previous experience in the ICU, the staff had witnessed me negotiate complex spiritual, cultural, and relational conflicts before. This case was one of many where I had demonstrated that I was an advocate for patients, families, and the staff in heated moments of crisis.

As I exited the ICU, several family members turned to me. I assumed this was because I was wearing a lab coat, which was the uniform expectation at St Thomas. I imagined that they saw me as a member of staff, someone who could potentially offer an update. I identified myself as a chaplain, and said that the staff were working very hard. There were multiple people present, some who were sitting down, watching TV, texting, or occupied with children. A woman who appeared to be in her late fifties introduced herself as Alma's "baby sister," Mary. I asked about who was present, and she introduced me to the various family members and relations. Among others, she introduced a daughter-in-law, Jasmine, as a nurse. Amidst introductions, she and others began to tell the story of the last couple of weeks. The following is a re-creation of the story I heard, told in waves over approximately 20 minutes.

"This is just like with Tyrell. They brought him to the hospital, and they couldn't save him. Dead on arrival... Now it's killing her too... She's got a broken heart." I encouraged them to say more, to try and sort out the threads. "She took care of that boy from the day he was born... She was too old for babies, but what could she do? She loved him with all that she had."

I asked questions like, "Who is Tyrell?" The more I asked and listened, the more they shared. "What happened?"

"He was shot! Right in front of her building! They brought him to the hospital, and couldn't save him... They said they did everything they could, but you wonder... Cops too. The system's just stacked." The grief was so strong, the anger so vivid. I could feel the energy rising. "When did he get shot?" I asked.

"Just two weeks ago." Heads shook, and grief was palpable.

Internally, my head swam with emotion. I thought about all I had read about the mistrust of American medical institutions by African American families. As a lesbian woman, I have experienced a similar mistrust from within LGBT communities, particularly among the generation who survived the initial waves of the AIDS epidemic. I have heard many friends express similar rage at the government, or Reagan more specifically. I understand this mistrust as a "healthy suspicion" of systems that have repeatedly failed minority communities (Lee *et al.* 2007). I feel righteous anger about studies I've read that have revealed actual abuses by the medical community of African American people and communities, such as Tuskegee and Henrietta Lacks (Skloot 2010). My training in clinical pastoral education (CPE) has also taught me that unprocessed complex grief can be triggered by any similar circumstances.

As I asked more about these past two weeks, I learned that Tyrell was only buried the day before. The family had been gathered at Alma's house after the funeral. Someone came to check on her today, and found her collapsed. In a lull in the family's story, I turned to Jasmine and asked if she thought the family understood the diagnosis. She had been detached from the story-telling, distracted by her phone. She seemed concerned, and appeared to be texting someone. She responded by saying, "Well, *I* understand," and conveyed some uncertainty about "the family." Her tone and her body language indicated that she didn't want to impose her opinions on her in-laws. She shrugged when I asked if she thought they needed to talk with the doctor again.

Having established a connection with the family, I decided to check in with the medical team. During the day, the Palliative Care coordinator would serve as an intermediary. At night, the on-call chaplain was seen as a representative of the Palliative Care team.

In my experience at St Thomas, I knew that the medical team would provide all aggressive measures unless someone was certain of a patient's wishes. Once the patient was stabilized, the team would review the patient's medical records, identify a family decision-maker, and establish goals of care. I had seen patients intubated against their wishes or the wishes of the family, and in futile medical circumstances, because the medical team had difficulty communicating with the family. Sometimes the medical team was unfamiliar with using interpreters, or used words the family couldn't understand. More often, it seemed that there was no one available to provide a bridge between the family and staff during critical moments of crisis, such as this one. Hence, patients might linger unnecessarily in the ICU for days or weeks until a decision was reached or a new crisis emerged.

Returning to the ICU, I asked Dr L if she would talk with the family again. She seemed exasperated and said, "I've talked to them three times! They keep saying there's something wrong with her heart, but her heart is strong! We could hook her up to a vent and she could live as a vegetable for a long time!" Finally, a light bulb went off in my head. I realized that she was taking Mary's statement that she was "dying of a broken heart" literally.

"I don't think that's what they mean," I replied. "Her grandson was shot two weeks ago, and the funeral was yesterday. They're saying she has a broken heart, because of her *grief.* They don't mean it literally." The young doctor looked up, stunned, and suddenly empathetic. With this new context, she seemed willing to try again. The patient was getting prepped for an EEG (electroencephalogram), and she said I could bring the family in.

I returned with Mary and Alma's oldest son, John. When Dr L explained that the patient was receiving a test to assess the extent of the brain damage, I asked them what they heard. Mary began to cry, saying that Alma's "heart was broken." When the doctor began to contradict her and explain Alma's exact medical condition, I interrupted. I asked Dr L if there were any treatment options the family needed to discuss. She cautiously and nervously explained ventilation, and that the patient might not ever regain consciousness. Again, I asked what the family understood. Mary very clearly conveyed that, "Alma would not want to be hooked up to some machine forever." The doctor asked if they knew what might happen if she were not ventilated, and Mary said, quite firmly, "She can go and take care of Tyrell." I restated these words in a way that both the family and the doctor could understand, saying, "So, you do not want the doctor to keep her alive using a breathing machine?" Mary affirmed these wishes, and her nephew nodded in agreement.

When we returned to the extended family, I asked Mary if she thought her family would like to pray. "Yes, chaplain!" was the strong reply. The entire family gathered in a circle and held hands, even those who'd previously been distracted by technology. I asked if I should begin, and I heard another, "Yes, chaplain!" I opened the prayer very simply: "God, we are gathered together to pray for Alma, we lift up these prayers that are on our hearts."

For at least 10 minutes, family members took turns praying aloud in a style that was familiar to me as a minister in a denomination founded by a defrocked Pentecostal preacher. I had attended and presided over many healing prayers in my years in ministry, and this prayer was at the least emotion-filled, and what my church would call Spirit-filled. There were prayers for miracles and God's will to be done. There were prayers for Alma and Tyrell, and for others I didn't know. Mary's prayer rose above the others: "God take Alma to be with you, so that she can look after Tyrell. We know that he is with you, and that you are calling her home so that she can be with him in paradise." This prayer was met with affirmations of "Amen" and "Yes, Jesus." When the words eventually ceased, I said a few words to close, and the family dispersed.

Sometime in the next hour or two, the results of the EEG revealed that Alma's brain activity was nearly nil. This was the second of two tests that showed a marked decline since the initial test. The patient's breathing was increasingly labored, and the family was allowed into the ICU to be with Alma. Mary kept repeating, "God is calling my sister to be with her grandson."

The family remained in the ICU until Alma breathed her last breath. She died peacefully, with her family gathered around her, saying prayers and singing hymns. Some of her family understood that she had died of an intracerebral hemorrhage. In my assessment, the family was at peace that she was in heaven with her beloved grandson.

Analysis

In her book, *The Spirit Catches and You Fall Down*, Anne Fadiman (2012) mentions "Eight Questions" to elicit a patient's "explanatory model" of their medical condition. "The Eight Questions" include "What do you call the problem?," "What do you think has caused the problem?," and "Why do you think it started when it did?" (Fadiman 2012). The family's grief about the patient was expressed through the lens of their grief about her grandson. Their interpretation of Alma's death was a spiritual interpretation, not a scientific or medical analysis. The physician, on the other hand, was speaking as a young doctor, recently vested with the full powers and credentials of Western medicine. Throughout her book, Fadiman highlights the culture and assumptions of modern medicine; for example, that physicians are trained to see disease through the lenses of data, facts, and diagnostic rubrics. The culture of modern medicine fails to recognize its own epistemic assumptions or to consider the source of truth of other cultures. Fadiman (2012) argues, to the contrary, that non-Western cultures and religions are profoundly shaped by emotions, subjectivity, and relationships.

As a best practice, chaplains act as cultural brokers between families and the medical staff when we perceive such breakdowns in communication. Doctors are trained to listen for data, detail, and facts, while chaplains are trained to listen for meta-stories, meaning, and values.

In this case, I perceived that the family had spiritually diagnosed a medical crisis due to their recent experience of traumatic grief (Wolfelt 2014). Multicultural theorists Derald Wing Sue and David Sue (2003) refer to these differences as *high* and *low context* communication. The physician was focused on the *low context* "fact" that the patient had an injury to the *brain*. Meanwhile, the family had decided that the patient was "dying of a broken heart." In the past, I had seen similar miscommunications lead to prolonged ICU stays, which, in turn, led to moral distress in both the families and staff.

Emotionally, I assessed the family's grief as primarily stemming from the recent death of Tyrell. I understood that they were conflating the two events, and I heard them connecting the deaths to one another as cause and effect. If the family had said anything about Tyrell to the staff, it was likely disregarded as an unrelated detail to the medical crisis at hand. Physicians are trained to diagnose by sorting through vast amounts of information and focusing on what is germane only to this medical event. This *low context* way of thinking ignored the impact of the family's grief on their decision-making.

As a chaplain, my experience is that African American patients see clergy as a preferred method of emotional support over therapists or other counselors. Wanda Lee *et al.* (2007, p.128) suggest that, "counselors might also consider the benefits of 'pastoral initiative,' the expectation that clergy will go to people and intervene on their own initiative and without specific invitation."

At St Thomas, I regularly experienced more openness to chaplaincy by African American patients and families than any other sub-group of people. Many patients sought counsel from chaplains before asking their doctor questions, about significant decisions or because of family conflicts. For these reasons, I concluded that this family may have first shared their grief with me as a chaplain because of their trust for the clergy, or simply due to the fact that I had time to listen.

I thus intervened first, by providing an outlet for the family to express their grief and anger about their beloved grandson, nephew, brother, and uncle. They needed someone on the staff to hear and hold their distrust for "the system." What I heard was that it was not the doctors who had killed Tyrell, but "the system." I knew that I represented "the system," so I wanted to be sure they knew that I was there to advocate for them.

One of the ways that I communicated my care for this family was by asking who was present and how the people were related. An important step in building relationships with African American patients is to ask, "Who is the family?" (Lee *et al.* 2007). This intervention began the story-telling process, which helped to develop rapport, and also helped me identify who was the key decision-maker. Once the conversation began to flow, I asked this question directly. This allowed me to identify who should talk with the physician, when and if the time came to decide.

I was also aware that I was navigating a complex, multicultural care team, headed by a young Asian American physician. In my experience, communication gaps between staff and patients were often as simple as pronunciation, eye contact, and vocabulary. Sometimes there was subtle cultural bias, or micro-aggression, on the side of the member of staff or the patient/family. In this case, I wondered if the family asked for "everything" to be done because they distrusted that the hospital would use all means possible to save Alma. I felt some irritation with the doctor's need to explain the disease process, and I wondered if the doctor assumed that the family couldn't understand due to their education or medical knowledge.

Despite all these influences, my goal was to set aside my own biases and listen, interpret, and facilitate communication. I empathized with both the doctor and the family and used the skills of active listening to build understanding. I sensed the shift in the physician when I spoke with her the second time. She looked surprised when I said, "They're saying she has a broken heart, because of her *grief*." When I brought the decision-makers to talk with the doctor, I did not need her to accept their interpretation that the patient was dying of a broken heart any more than I needed the family to understand or accept the doctor's diagnosis. I had learned through several years of experience that failure to listen to a family's *values* and ask the right questions at the right time could lead to prolonged, unnecessary ICU stays. My hope was to be the "Balm in Gilead" for this grieving family.[1]

The transformative role of prayer in medical decision-making is rarely acknowledged. The language of prayer is affective rather than rational. It has the power to touch participants on the level of emotions and worldview in a way that conversation or dialogue may not. As a form of ritual, prayers offered during a medical crisis can open a space for the sacred and create room for an acceptance of death as part of the religious life cycle. In a time of medical crisis, rituals can help people embrace death and make space for the sacred (Anderson 2001).

Rituals also have a long tradition of bringing people together. After Mary and John spoke with Dr L, I asked Mary if she thought the family would like to pray because I wasn't sure how many people would be open to prayer. The way that the family gathered into a circle, almost instantly, spoke volumes about the importance of faith in their life. Through her prayer, Mary offered her family her spiritual interpretation of the events in a culturally and spiritually appropriate manner. Through this ritual, she was both praying and teaching.

Through the call and response ritual of saying "Amen," the family communicated their assent and approval of Mary's interpretation. As a chaplain, I assessed that her words brought the family peace and hope during a difficult and painful experience. My pastoral initiative was to take leadership with the family in suggesting the ritual of prayer. I also trust in the divine, transcendent power of Spirit, and believe that the family experienced my prayer as genuine and heartfelt. My role was to listen, to facilitate communication with the family and the medical team, to interpret their story to the hospital staff, and to take leadership in making space for the sanctity of death.

References

Anderson, M. (2001) *Sacred Dying: Creating Rituals for Embracing the End of Life.* Roseville, CA: Prima Publishing.

Fadiman, A. (2012) *The Spirit Catches and You Fall Down: A Hmong Child, Her American Doctors, and the Collision of Two Cultures.* New York: Farrar, Strauss & Giroux.

---

1 Referring to Jeremiah 8:22, "Is there no balm in Gilead? Is there no physician there? Why then is there no healing for the wounds of my people?" which can be found in the spiritual by John Newton, "There is a Balm in Gilead."

Lee, W., Blando, J.A., Mizelle, N.D. and Orzoco, G.L. (eds) (2007) *Introduction to Multicultural Counseling for Helping Professionals.* New York: Routledge.

Skloot, R. (2010) *The Immortal Life of Henrietta Lacks.* New York: Random House.

Sue, D.W. and Sue, D. (2003) *Counseling the Culturally Diverse: Theory and Practice.* New York: Wiley & Sons.

Wolfelt, A. (2014) *Reframing PTSD as Traumatic Grief: How Caregivers Can Companion Traumatized Grievers through Catch-Up Mourning.* Fort Collins, CO: Companion Press.

Chapter 13

AYESAH'S STORY

"Allah will save her"—Mohammed
talking about his wife, Ayesah

EMILY DUNCAN ROSENCRANS

Introduction

This case study focuses on the chaplain's role as cultural broker between the medical team and a Palestinian Muslim family. This family held a set of Muslim beliefs that were particular to their own interpretation of Islam and intertwined with their deep grief and trauma over the loss of land, culture, and identity. In addition, they had a distrust of Western medicine due to their recent experience in another hospital.

The question this case addresses is, "How do we, as chaplains, help to lessen the distance between the religious and cultural beliefs of our patients and families and those embedded in the practice of medicine?"

The setting is the Intensive Care Unit (ICU) of a 100-bed community hospital that is predominantly Caucasian, Anglo-Saxon, and Protestant. The communities adjacent to this suburb are very diverse; the hospital staff is also diverse.

Ayesah is a 50-year-old Palestinian Muslim woman who has been married for 30 years. She has four children: a devoted daughter, Layla, the eldest, 25, and three sons ranging in age from 16 to 22. There are many extended members of the family as well: the patient's two brothers, two sisters, mother, and various other relatives and friends.

For about a year, Ayesah's family had taken her from doctor to doctor and hospital to hospital, trying to find out what was wrong with her. She was misdiagnosed at another large hospital in the area.

When they took her in for hernia repair surgery, they discovered she was filled with cancer. To hear the family tell the story, the doctors said there was nothing they could do, that Ayesah was dying, and discharged her. In shock, they brought her to our hospital looking for hope. For the second time within a couple of months, she had been admitted, only this time she was so sick she had to be intubated immediately. She had Stage IV cancer and was in kidney failure, liver failure, respiratory failure, and heart failure.

I am a Caucasian, middle-class woman with 30 years of ordained ministry in the Presbyterian Church (PCUSA), 12 years of which has been in professional chaplaincy. I am also a certified Marriage and Family Therapy chaplain and certified in Palliative Care chaplaincy. As the Manager of Spiritual Care, I occupy a seat on the Ethics Committee of the hospital.

I attempted to contact members of Ayesah's family to ask permission to share this story. Unfortunately, the contact information retained by the hospital was outdated. Therefore, in keeping with ethical practices for case study research, I have changed the names and identifying features of Ayesah and her family, while retaining key features of the narrative of care.

Case

An ICU physician called for an Ethics consult after the patient was on life support for three weeks because he no longer felt comfortable with the family's decision to continue treatment. The family refused any discussion of ending life support but, in the eyes of the medical team, the care was now "futile," or more appropriately, "non-beneficial" (Bosslet et al. 2015). Even when the intensivist explained that the patient was suffering and we were prolonging her suffering by continuing life support, the family was not moved. The suffering was not a reason to discontinue aggressive treatment. Keeping her alive was their goal. They were waiting for Allah to intervene with a miracle. Eventually, the patient's sister even asked if we could remove all pain medication.

Islamic music in Arabic and Islamic prayers were heard making a gentle hum from cell phones placed near the patient day and night. In keeping with their religious practice, the family had asked (and the hospital had granted their request) that only women nurses care for Ayesah. Family members camped out in the patient's room night and day, making it hard for staff to work with the patient. They constantly questioned everything being done. They were hostile and suspicious of the medical staff. The adolescent sons were angry, even raging at the staff with increasing intensity. At one point one of the tall, strong sons yelled at a very petite bedside nurse, "You are killing my mother!" She did not react and allowed him to rage. At another point, one of the sons yelled at the physician, "You have the cure for cancer and you are just withholding it!" Lack of respect or appreciation shown to the staff by the family created compassion fatigue. Eventually, security had to be posted outside the patient's door because the staff was feeling threatened.

First encounter

I entered the room. It smelled of decay. The air was stale. It was dark. I could hear the soft Muslim chanting of prayers on a cell phone placed near the patient. Ayesah's husband, Mohammed, was at the bedside. He appeared to be a proud, dignified man: well dressed, clean, and middle-aged. He spoke English well.

I told Mohammed I was the chaplain and asked if I might speak with him. I said gently, "I am so sorry for what you are going through, for what you are *all* going through."

When I asked how he was doing, he spoke at length of his distress, of his love for his wife, and his marriage of 30 years. He mentioned hoping and praying. I noted that he said *Inshallah* (God willing) many times. I therefore felt comfortable acknowledging and affirming the strength of his faith. He said yes, it was very important.

Mohammed then told me about his history as a Palestinian Muslim man.

Mohammed: "We owned land in Palestine for 900 years. Then the world said, 'Give Palestine to the Jews' after WWII, and we tried to stay, and co-exist, but our land was taken from us in the Six Day War. We tried to make ends meet, but it became harder and harder...so we came here. Terrible, the way the world just looks the other way, everyone is on the side of the Jews. No one thinks about Muslims who owned the land for centuries, who farmed there, lived there...no one cares... Our family was an important family. Like tribal chiefs—we rendered judgments in legal disputes. Highly respected. Then nothing. No land, No rights. Water taken from our land for their land. The world does nothing!"

To cross the chasm of distrust and trauma between us, I decided to mention the trip I took to Israel in 2007, the complexities of a land that is seen as holy to three major world religions. I also drew upon a book, *The Lemon Tree* (Tolan 2006), about a Jewish woman who grew up on land given to her family after the Holocaust being visited by the previous Muslim owners of the land, to extend understanding and empathy. I told the story of how the Muslim owners loved the land, the house, and the lemon tree on it. The Muslim family grieved the loss of their land and their lemon tree. The Jewish woman who was raised on that land, in turn, grieved that her presence there was because of what this other family lost. "Such a complicated history," I said.

Mohammed appeared to soften. He looked at me for the first time, a sideways glance. He added that most people do not know or do not care. "It's all about the Jews. What about us? No one cares about us. So we came here for the opportunity to build a better life. Now look at my wife...but I have faith. We believe there will be a miracle."

I affirmed his desire for a miracle and joined him in hoping for a miracle, but added that miracles are rare, especially in this advanced state of illness. I wanted to join in his hope but speak realistically as well, a fragile balance to sustain. I was using the AMEN approach of talking about the hope for a miracle—Affirm the hope, Meet people where they are, Educate, No matter what, we are here for you (Cooper *et al.* 2014).

I asked Mohammed to tell me about his wife. He teared up and could not talk. I indicated that his emotions told me how very precious she was to him. I let this holy moment stand by giving it silence and space.

I then asked what he had been told about Ayesah's condition. I have been trained to find out what people know, and what people acknowledge about what they have been told, especially when navigating end-of-life discussions (Vandekieft 2001).

Mohammed: "She has cancer. Very bad. She has been on this machine for two weeks now. They say she is worse."

I looked at her. Her mouth was open. I could see her teeth, but they were dry and dark. Her body was swollen. Her dark skin looked almost gray. She was so small.

Mohammed: "Everything is shutting down: kidneys, heart, lungs... *But Allah will save her.* We have four children. She must live. I don't know if they are doing everything they can for her. She is my wife, the mother of my children. And we lost precious time. Downtown at [previous hospital] she was misdiagnosed. They thought it was a hernia, then an obstruction, then, finally, they took her to surgery and said it was cancer. It was everywhere. Stage IV. Nothing to do, they said. We took her home. Then we brought her here. She was so sick. Why did it take so long to know? Six months of run around! Now...they say it is too late."

I acknowledged that he seemed to feel betrayed by the medical profession.

Mohammed: "They are supposed to be smart, they are supposed to see the signs. It is because we are not from here, they look down on us, we are not important."

I heard his anger, and I heard the hurt, pain and sadness underneath it. Mostly I saw a proud, determined man who wanted desperately to have power over this.

I named for him what I kept feeling throughout his story, because I have learned that what a patient's story stirs up in me is usually what they are experiencing, too. "It must be hard to feel *powerless* to make that happen. It is not easy to wait and watch and hope." Mohammed was nodding and crying. I said, "I pray you get your miracle. *Inshallah.*" With the acknowledgement of Mohammed's faith and powerlessness, I began to feel he was opening his soul to me and somehow benefiting from being heard and having his feelings named. This was my most significant intervention after assessing this family's powerlessness as the underlying force driving their emotions and interactions.

Subsequent encounters

The next day I had a conversation with the eldest daughter, Layla. I learned from the staff that she was at the bedside 95 percent of the time. Layla was slight and beautiful. I noticed how her hijab was coordinated with her clothes and shoes. I imagined she looked a great deal like her mother once looked. Layla appeared downcast, drawn, and exhausted.

I introduced myself and asked how her mother was doing. She shrugged and looked at me suspiciously. Layla said, "The doctors say there is nothing more they can do." She shrugged. "She cannot breathe on her own. She is in organ failure. But we are still hoping and praying."

I acknowledged her sadness and her fatigue. I asked if she was able to take time to care for herself. (I was concerned for her and wondered who in the world was caring about her now.) I then asked her to tell me about her mother. This is an aspect of Dignity Therapy and Life Review, that to tell and hear the story of the person who is ill acknowledges their impact and worth (Chochinov 2012). She told me that her mother had been the center, the soul of the family. She had been the force that held them together and gave them strength. Now she was dying. They had no time to prepare. They felt cheated and abandoned by the medical system that misdiagnosed her for six months.

I affirmed Layla's incredible strength and asked if that came from her mother. (I did this to help her see how her mother's strength was in her and probably helping her cope.) She wept as she affirmed that the woman dying in the bed before her was indeed the source of her strength. I decided to risk asking what she thought was going to happen, as I sensed a growing acceptance from her of the impending loss, her anticipatory grief.

Layla: "She is going to die."

Chaplain: "Yes." [I affirmed with sad resignation.]

During the conversation that ensued I was able to solicit the daughter's support for her brothers and father, whom she acknowledged were struggling much more than she to accept what was happening. She agreed to try to talk to them, to help them prepare for what was to come. I also helped her see the compassion of the staff, and encouraged her to speak to her family about thanking the nurses and doctors for their extraordinary care.

Final encounter

After many weeks, a test revealed that Ayesah was brain dead. The ICU intensivist on duty asked me how to tell the family. Knowing the distrust of this family, that they were smart and wanted to be treated with respect, and that they needed to learn and decide for themselves, I said, "Show them the tests, the X-rays, the scans. Teach them what brain death looks like. Let them see it for themselves."

Then we called a family conference. They asked to have their extended family at this meeting, and to have four doctors present. They said this was in the *Quran*, and we did as they asked to provide them the peace they deserved. (I have since been told this is not in the *Quran*.)

As a form of hospitality, our department developed a bereavement cart program to provide nourishment for families keeping vigil at the bedside of a loved one who is dying. I told them I was going to order a cart with refreshments for them and asked if they had dietary restrictions or preferences. They asked for no pork, and that it be vegetarian. I ordered a bereavement cart with hummus, pita, vegetables, juice, and water.

At the interdisciplinary meeting after the doctors explained the medical facts, I asked, "What do you think is happening with your mother?" One of the 14 family members present, whom I did not know, said, "She is with God." I nodded, "Yes, I believe she is." I looked around and inquired, "What about the rest of you?" One of the sons said, yet again, that we had the cure for cancer and we withheld it. Another wailed that we were letting her die. The youngest son interjected, "The nurse killed her." The brothers of the patient began to speak up and demonstrated themselves to be the real leaders in the family system. Though only one step removed from the rawness, they remained composed and measured in their words. They called the family to prayers of thanksgiving and release.

The medical staff explained that since she was brain dead, they wanted to know if we could withdraw life support. The family was not quite ready. I encouraged them to go home, think, and pray, and the next day we would meet again. As I left for the day, I saw all the older women in their burqas sitting in the family waiting room with the youngest of the sons, age 16, as he rocked to and fro on his knees, prayed, and cried. I felt deep compassion for this boy who was losing his mother. I thanked the women for being there for him.

The next day, as we began to meet again, Ayesah stopped breathing and her heart stopped. The family together cried out, "Allah took her." They accepted that she was gone. We prayed together. They left quietly and peacefully. As they left, I continued to pray that theywoul d find peace and healing in their close familial bonds and that their faith would give them strength.

Analysis

After my first meeting with Mohammed, it became clear to me that this family entered our system with very little trust. They came to this country about 10 years ago for a better life and better healthcare, and due to their struggle to maintain their identity, yet find belonging and community, they had long felt marginalized and disenfranchised. It is not unusual for immigrants to feel they are in a strange land with values and norms that are foreign. This time, their sense of marginalization was at the hands of the medical establishment.

I approached this family with genuine concern and curiosity. I listened. I observed. I respected their position and did not feel a need to change their minds or their decisions.

Theologically, I tried throughout my encounters with the family to embody and point them toward the God who sees them, El Roi, the name given to God by Hagar in Genesis 17:13. Perhaps they did understand, at some level, that we were seeing them and hearing them. They stayed. They engaged in dialogue. They even let me, and other members of our interdisciplinary team, provide them with information to help them understand the medical perspective.

Isaiah 45:3 says, "I will give you the treasures of darkness and wisdom stored in secret places..." It was my goal to acknowledge what was happening and lift it up as worthy of recognition and reflection. Even in the darkness and in the shadow of death, remembering a life with honor and gratitude can be a gift. Experiencing care and compassion in the midst of our grief can be a treasure.

Psychologically, this family was highly defended: they were guarded, suspicious, proud, determined, and demanding. They were separate from the dominant Western culture. They did not want to assimilate or adopt our ways of thinking or being. Any kind of injustice touched a nerve because they had experienced much that was demeaning, depersonalizing, objectifying, and unfair. They fought to survive and wanted a voice in what was happening. What I also observed and honored as I sought to build a bridge between "us and them" was their willingness to trust this patient (wife and mother) to our care. In my interactions I came to believe that they deeply desired understanding, support, and connection.

My empathy for this family was also strengthened by my understanding of Trauma Theory and Family Systems Theory (Bloom 1997; Bowlby 1978; Friedman 1985; Hollander-Goldfein, Isserman and Goldenberg 2003; Satir 1972). People are not at their best when they are overwhelmed and traumatized with a loss like this; therefore, some of their anger could be explained as reflecting their pain, hurt, and sadness as well as their fear of losing their rock, their anchor, and the greatest source of love, stability, and strength in their family system.

Sociologically, I learned this Muslim family was very religious and had strong ties to their immediate and extended family, as well as their Muslim community. They did not attend or have an affiliation with a mosque. It was unclear to me whether their beliefs were idiosyncratic or would have been supported by an imam. As in traditional Muslim families, the men were granted decision-making authority while the women quietly served, prayed, and provided care and emotional support (Al-Krenawi and Graham 2005).

To gain more insight into specific beliefs that might be impacting their perspective and medical decisions, I consulted cultural information available on our hospital website. I used the information provided only as a starting point, never an ending point, recognizing that there is great variation within every tradition and even greater diversity in how specific families appropriate and live out their traditions. I read that in general, Palestinian Muslims value life at all costs, and will often want aggressive measures to extend life. I also read that suffering often has a different connotation than it does for many people from Jewish or Christian backgrounds—or most secular Westerners—who want to avoid or alleviate suffering.

After I demonstrated respect for this family's history and culture in general, various members trusted me enough to reveal the reason they were refusing pain medications on Ayesah's behalf. They shared their firm belief that suffering was a way to atone for sin, the means by which Allah draws believers closer, and that a faithful believer will be rewarded with entrance to paradise.

I tried to help the medical team appreciate what was at stake for this patient and for this family, because the physicians were appalled when asked to stop giving pain medication to a suffering patient. I explained what I had learned from the family about their religious beliefs and cultural perspective on suffering and pain medication. Although the intensivist heard me, he also felt obligated to tell the family he could not ethically withhold pain medication. I agreed with his position. The physician explained to me and the Ethics Committee, and later to the family, that he had taken an oath never to do anything that he knew would cause great harm and suffering. He gave Ayesah's family the option of transferring her home or to another hospital if they did not like the way he was treating the patient and managing the pain. Instead, they chose to stay and allow the pain medication to continue. The daughter later confided in me that she was relieved, as she had heard her mother moaning and could not bear to think she was suffering.

When the medical team decided care was inappropriate, or not benefiting to the patient, I once again was in a position to be a cultural broker for this family. In a meeting held without the family present, the intensivist shared his considerable distress in continuing to provide medical interventions when nothing was helping, and he determined the treatments might be hurting her. Her skin was thin. She was weeping from extreme edema. She was in multi-organ failure. Although comatose at this point, he argued that we were torturing her, and it was torturing the medical staff to participate in this. There was discussion of the resources being allocated, and the irrationality, if not insanity, of the family.

I spoke up at that point, saying,

Let me tell you about this family. They are Muslims, from Palestine. They are scrappy because they have had to be, to survive. They came here for a better life...and now she is dying. She is everything to this family. She holds it together. And because she is dying, they are twisting in the wind. They are traumatized. And then they notice almost every single doctor is white, some are Jewish, and they tell her there is no hope...after six months of misdiagnosing her. They have no trust in medicine, no trust in anyone not of their faith perspective.

The Jewish doctor in the room said, "I get it."

I continued, "We often talk to people about not prolonging suffering, but to them her suffering is her atonement that will lead to a better after life. This time is not 'futile' in their eyes. It has meaning and value."

When the medical team suggested we should turn to the daughter for decision-making as she was "more reasonable," I helped them understand that in this culture and family system it was only the patient's husband (along with the other men in the family) who would make the decisions. They expressed that he was more intractable in his resistance to talking about treatments that were non-beneficial. I reminded them that it was trauma, lots and lots of traumatization, marginalization, and disenfranchisement, causing him to be stuck, unable to make decisions, unable to let her go.

I said, "Letting her go is tantamount to killing her. He can't. They can't. They can't handle that responsibility or the feeling that they might be contributing to her death by withdrawing life support. It isn't about quality of life but just LIFE...any life...they are holding on tenaciously to the only thing that is left." I continued, "We have to HONOR their reality. We can't push them. We have to 'let Allah decide' when and how she will die. Eventually she will declare herself. Until then, we have to support them."

In the end, I bore witness to a beautiful moment as a Jewish doctor from South America taught a Palestinian Muslim family about brain death. Although fear-based, pre-judging of the "other" had occurred, here they were children of Abraham, one and all, gathered around monitors, sharing, learning, asking questions, working together. Our compassion grew, and their trust grew. They became more a part of and less adversarial with the healthcare team. The family managed their feelings with more vulnerability toward the end.

I am proud that we supported this devout, traumatized, and grieving family, and that we attended to the moral distress of the staff. From my perspective, everyone saw this family with more understanding and compassion, even some of the staff who at times were terrified by the intensity of their anger and rage. As a hospital team, we grew through this experience.

In the end, we lessened the distance between us. The outcome was that the family left in peace. They accepted her death when it came. The staff felt their feelings were heard and their safety was important to the hospital, and they provided excellent care. My prayer is that we may we all find ways to continue to lessen the distance between us. *Inshallah.*

References

Al-Krenawi, A.B. and Graham, J.R. (2005) 'Marital therapy for Arab Muslim Palestinian couples in the context of reacculturation.' *The Family Journal 13*, 3, 300–310.

Bloom, S. (1997) *Creating Sanctuary: Toward the Evolution of Sane Societies.* New York: Routledge.

Bosslet, G.T., Pope, T., Rubenfeld, G.D., Lo, B., *et al.* (2015) 'An official ATS/AACN/ACCP/ESICM/SCCM policy statement: Responding to requests for potentially inappropriate treatments in Intensive Care Units.' *American Journal of Respiratory and Critical Care Medicine 191*, 11, 1318–1330.

Bowlby, J. (1978) 'Attachment theory and its therapeutic implications.' *Adolescent Psychiatry 6*, 5–33.

Chochinov, H. (2012) *Dignity Therapy: Final Words for Final Days.* Oxford: Oxford University Press.

Cooper, R., Ferguson, A., Bodurtha, J.N. and Smith, T.J. (2014) 'AMEN in challenging conversations: Bridging the gaps between faith, hope, and medicine.' *Journal of Oncology Practice 10*, 4, e191–e195.

Friedman, E. (1985) *Generation to Generation: Family Process in Church and Synagogue.* New York: The Guilford Press.

Hollander-Goldfein, B., Isserman, N. and Goldenberg, J. (2003) *Transcending Trauma: Survival, Resilience, and Clinical Implications in Survivor Families* (Psychological Stress Series). New York: Routledge.

Tolan, S. (2006) *The Lemon Tree.* New York: Bloomsbury.

Satir, V. (1972) *Peoplemaking.* Palo Alto, CA: Science and Behavior Books.

Vandekieft, G.K. (2001) 'Breaking bad news.' *American Family Physician 64*, 12, 1975–1979.

Further reading

Eid, P. (2003) 'The interplay between ethnicity, religion, and gender among second-generation Christian and Muslim Arabs in Montreal.' *Canadian Ethnic Studies Journal 35*, 2, 30–62.

Wirpsa, M.J., Johnson, R.E., Bieler, J., Boyken, L., *et al.* (2019) 'Interprofessional models for shared decision making: The role of the healthcare chaplain.' *Journal of Healthcare Chaplaincy 25*, 1, 20–44.

Chapter 14

CRITICAL RESPONSE TO NEGOTIATING RELIGIOUS AND CULTURAL DIFFERENCES CASES STUDIES

A Chaplain's Response

KAREN LIEBERMAN

Introduction

The cases in this section reflect an important reality that religious or cultural influences are often relevant, and sometimes central, to the goal-setting and medical decision-making processes. A familiar and obvious example is the situation of Jehovah's Witness patients who refuse blood transfusions on religious grounds. A less obvious example might involve a patient or family member who insists on aggressive treatment in the face of a tenuous prognosis. Is the patient in denial? Does the patient have a poor or incomplete understanding of the medical facts and realities? Or is the decision to pursue aggressive treatment an expression of religious or cultural values?

As the clinical team member with specific education and training to engage with patients, families, and staff around such influences, the professional healthcare chaplain plays an integral role in ensuring that religious and cultural values and priorities are identified, understood, honored, and integrated into the care plan. The cases in this section demonstrate at least three related ways in which the chaplains involved performed this valuable function: staff education, holding liminal space, and healing through humanizing.

Staff education

Some chaplains provide general educational support for staff about religious or cultural ideas and practices. By teaching staff about traditions with which they may be unfamiliar, the chaplain attempts to diminish staff discomfort and uncertainty around those traditions. In addition, chaplains strive to increase staff empathy by improving understanding about how patients and their families rely on these traditions to help them cope during a crisis. This appears to be the primary mode of intervention for Chaplain Axelrud, and it seems to be an approach that is generally comfortable for chaplains who are also ordained clergy and whose education, training, and experience includes teaching and preaching as a primary focus. This approach may be a more natural intervention when the chaplain and patient and family embrace a common religious background.

Holding liminal space

Most chaplains serve as bridge and translator between the medical staff and the patient and family. Often, the cultural divide is not necessarily between different religions or ethnicities, but rather between the medical culture and the non-medical culture. These cultures have different languages and are often grounded in very different assumptions. Chaplain Kirby intervenes in her case by using her specialized education and training to speak both the language of spirituality and the language of medicine. Her wearing a lab coat represents a physical manifestation of this liminality, a point to which I will return.

Healing through humanizing

Chaplains bring their extensive training in active listening, relationship and trust building, and cultural and religious competence into human-to-human connection with those they serve. In so doing, they focus not only on the specific problem that brought the patient and family into the healthcare system, but also on their inherent strengths and tools for coping and problem-solving. Chaplains work to ensure that the rest of the clinical care team embraces a holistic approach to the provision of care. Chaplain Rosencrans demonstrates this dimension of the chaplain's work by reorienting the care team to the very personal and complex way this family draws on their religious beliefs and cultural practices.

The chaplain as educator

The chaplain's educational role is multifaceted. In cases where chaplains are not central to medical decision-making, they may contribute indirectly by educating the staff about religious or cultural traditions that can influence this process. Axelrud's case study provides an example of such "meta" intervention. While he met regularly with the family for emotional support, his primary clinical intervention involves teaching the staff about principles and practices common to Orthodox Judaism. His approach can be seen in the interweaving within the case study itself of several detailed explications of various Jewish concepts, such as *emunah* and *bitachon*. Describing his approach, Axelrud explains, "the staff have little understanding of how Jewish Orthodox religious beliefs impact the healthcare decisions being made by families." He seeks to fill this gap in knowledge to enhance rapport between the team and the family, and to promote familiarity with and respect for religious ideas that may be relevant in a decision-making process.

In Rosencrans' case study, the chaplain's role in educating staff is more directly connected to an actual decision faced by the family and team. She first familiarizes herself generally with Islamic beliefs and practices, and then focuses on exploring how the family specifically understands their tradition and its impact on the decision at hand. Rosencrans writes, "I consulted cultural information available on our hospital website. I used the information provided only as a starting point, never an ending point, recognizing that there is great variation within every tradition and even greater diversity in how specific families appropriate and live out their traditions." Later in her analysis, Rosencrans describes how she elicits information from the family around pain management, revealing "their firm belief that suffering was a way to atone for sin." She then uses this information to educate staff. Although the medical staff held conflicting values that also needed to be heard, the chaplain's work in discerning and educating staff about religious and cultural influences on decision-making constructively advances the process.

Patients may also request educational support from the chaplain. When faced with an important decision, a patient or family member might ask what Catholicism (or Judaism, or Hinduism, etc.) teaches about a specific situation. This may occur when the patient does not have his or her own clergy to look to for guidance, or when the patient does not wish to involve clergy. The chaplain facilitates decision-making in these scenarios by providing information about the teachings of a particular religious or cultural tradition. A wise chaplain does so cautiously and with self-awareness about the possibility of projecting the chaplain's own understanding and interpretations onto the situation at hand.

Many patients rely on their own clergy to apply the tenets of their faith to medical decision-making. This does not mean that the chaplain has no role to play in such situations. On the contrary, the chaplain is adept at navigating an appropriate collaboration that honors different but congruent roles. With permission, the chaplain might contact family clergy to discuss the situation, provide accurate and up-to-date information, explain relevant hospital protocols and practices, and extend an invitation to participate in care conferences. Such partnerships are especially valuable in light of findings by Balboni and colleagues (2010) and Koss and colleagues (2018) that community clergy are more likely than hospital chaplains to recommend aggressive end-of-life care.

Notably, some patients who have the ability to make their own medical decisions actually cede that authority to someone else based on religious or cultural norms. For instance, as Axelrud explains, many Orthodox Jews turn to their own rabbi not only for assistance and guidance with decision-making, but to actually render an authoritative decision. And as Rosencrans describes, "in traditional Muslim families, the men were granted decision-making authority." Kirby, too, alludes to the importance of discerning who is the *de facto* decision-maker within a family system. This role clarification by the chaplain helps to avoid frustration and distress for patients and staff alike.

The chaplain in liminal space

Clinical chaplains bring a broad and varied skillset to the inter-disciplinary care team. Nevertheless, their role is often narrowly understood to be limited to the provision of strictly religious care.

This incomplete or narrow understanding can pose a formidable obstacle to chaplains' full integration into the care team generally and into the medical decision-making process specifically. As a result, chaplains are frequently overlooked in situations where their education, training, and experience could best enhance patient care.

Kirby's hospital requires that chaplains wear lab coats. While she does not elaborate on the origins of or reasons for this expectation, it seems plausible that the lab coat is intended to be a visual reminder that chaplains are members of the interdisciplinary clinical care team. This tangible representation of acceptance and "belonging" may significantly influence how the chaplain is perceived by other members of the team and, indeed, how chaplains view themselves and their role.

But what about the impact on patients and families? While the chaplain's perceived "otherness" may impede full integration with the care team, it may be the very quality that enables chaplains to enter into healing relationships with those they serve. Most patients are also experiencing a sense of estrangement and "otherness" in the healthcare system. Often, the very reason people open up to chaplains is that they perceive them as *not* being like everyone else on the care team (McCurdy 2012). The chaplain's ability to identify with the patient's experience may be the very foundation for a meaningful and trusting relationship.

The lab coat would seem to be symbolic of chaplains' intrinsic struggle to navigate this "foot-in-two-worlds" aspect of their role. For most chaplains, this grappling is not about choosing whether to dwell within the medical culture or outside it, but rather, how to occupy and bridge the space between the two.

There are a number of ways in which the professional healthcare chaplain serves as a bridge between the medical and non-medical cultures. For example, the medical environment often presents language barriers that impede communication which, in turn, affect decision-making. Sometimes this is literally because the patient speaks one language and the medical staff another (such as Spanish versus English). Frequently, the healthcare team also uses medical terminology not understood by patients and families. In contrast to the first situation, where the need for an interpreter is apparent, the language barrier in the latter situation may go completely undetected by the participants. Chaplains may be the first to recognize the issue.

I once saw a patient who had come to the Emergency Department with excruciating back pain. The patient, a truck driver, thought the pain was the result of strain from sitting behind the wheel for too many hours; however, evaluation revealed that he had end-stage cancer. Staff explained that there were no treatment options for him at this late stage. The diagnosis caught him completely off-guard, and he became emotionally volatile. Physicians in the Emergency Department repeatedly offered him palliative radiation, but the patient angrily and adamantly refused. He was transferred to the floor for pain management, where the hospitalist and I met with him. The patient continued to rage, and the physician, with exasperation in his voice, finally asked the patient how he could help. The patient implored, "Do something about this pain." The physician irritably pointed out that the patient had been offered palliative radiation and had refused. The patient retorted that he had just been informed that he was going to die, "What the hell good is radiation going to do me?" The physician repeated that the radiation was palliative, and the patient vehemently shook his head. In that moment, I recognized the language barrier. I gently interjected, "Do you know what he means by that?" The patient quieted, and then shook his head again. Nobody had explained to him what palliative radiation was, or the fact that it was being offered for pain management, and not for curative purposes. The conversation took a decidedly more collaborative tone from that point forward, and the patient ultimately agreed to palliative radiation.

Beyond concrete communication breakdowns, the chaplain can be instrumental in serving as a bridge or "translator" between the clinical staff's medical understanding of a situation and the family's spiritual understanding of the same situation. As Kirby observes while engaging in shuttle diplomacy between family and staff members struggling to communicate, "Finally, a light bulb went off in my head. I realized that [the physician] was taking Mary's statement that she was 'dying of a broken heart' literally." She elaborates: "Doctors are trained to listen for data, detail and facts, while chaplains are trained to listen for meta-stories, meaning, and values. In this case, I perceived that the family had spiritually diagnosed a medical crisis, due to their recent experience of traumatic grief."

Kirby's description of the encounter additionally highlights a material difference between the way chaplains typically communicate compared with other members of the team. She writes: "Returning to the ICU, I asked Dr L if she would talk with the family again. She seemed exasperated and said, 'I've talked to them three times!'" There is a meaningful distinction between talking "with" and talking "to" someone. Kirby's intervention to facilitate conversation in which the family and physician talk "with" one another helps to break the impasse and promote a collaborative decision-making process.

Chaplains occupy liminal space in situations where, for religious or cultural reasons, patients or families harbor a deep distrust of the healthcare system. Such distrust may be quite unfathomable to team members who work within the system and are deeply steeped in it. Rosencrans "sought to build a bridge between 'us and them'" in her work with a family displaying a high level of suspicion due to underlying cultural and religious differences.

Chaplains are well prepared to sit squarely in the midst of conflict and consider all points of view. The gray-area quality of their identity is an asset in this context, as chaplains consciously use their "insider" status to promote trust among staff and their "outsider" status to deepen relationships with patients and families. This ability to stand in the breach makes chaplains especially qualified to facilitate potentially contentious conversations, such as goals-of-care conferences. It also helps to explain why, like Kirby and Rosencrans, many chaplains serve on their organizations' Ethics committees and participate in Ethics consultations as part of their professional responsibilities.

Finally, the liminality of the chaplain role enhances decision-making by influencing both the timing of the decision-making process and the appropriate sharing of decision-making responsibility. The chaplains in all three cases describe different ways in which they mediate between staff and family in an effort to pace the medical decision-making process, reflecting an understanding of both the staff's need to move forward with a plan and the family's challenges in processing information and coming to terms with the realities of their situation. Rosencrans attends to issues of moral distress of staff members while simultaneously advocating for decisions that integrate the patient's values, goals, and priorities. She also acknowledges the medical team's clinical and ethical responsibilities, even when in conflict with the family's religious and cultural values, artfully balancing the sensibilities of everyone with a role in decision-making.

The chaplain in human connection

Chaplains influence goal-setting and medical decision-making by entering into healing relationships with those they serve. Chaplains mindfully and authentically connect their own humanity with the humanity of others. While most members of the medical team concentrate on what is wrong with the patient, the chaplain's whole-person assessment focuses on the patient's strengths, exploring how those strengths can be accessed to support coping and optimize participation in decision-making. The chaplain begins from a place that recognizes that patients possess inner resources and abilities to help themselves. Among other things, the chaplain's intervention aims to restore a sense of empowerment in a setting that can be intrinsically disempowering. An enhanced sense of empowerment promotes decision-making that is truly a partnership.

Through collegial and trusted relationships with staff, the chaplain strives to infuse this sense of whole-person care into the collective work of the team. When the medical team in Rosencrans' study expresses concern about "the irrationality" of the family from a medical viewpoint, she broadens their perspective: "Let me tell you about this family."

Sometimes there is suspicion that the patient's assertions around religious or cultural needs are not truthful. Rosencrans alludes to such a possibility in her case study. More often, staff members may try to convince patients that their understanding is mistaken by presenting literature or opinions from religious authorities that align with the goals set by the medical team. Such debates, even if entirely well intentioned, are usually not helpful. At worst, they may be viewed as an insulting act of hubris that can seriously damage the relationships needed for shared decision-making. Chaplains promote collaborative decision-making by respectfully and collegially coaching staff to avert such escalations and by empowering patient and family "truths."

Conclusion

Religious and cultural differences can influence goal-setting and decision-making processes. Chaplains play a central role in ensuring that religious and cultural values are competently and respectfully acknowledged by the care team and accounted for in the care plan developed in genuine partnership with the patient and family.

References

Balboni, T.A., Paulk, M.E., Balboni, M.J., Phelps, A.C., *et al.* (2010) 'Provision of spiritual care to patients with advanced cancer: Associations with medical care and quality of life near death.' *Journal of Clinical Oncology 28*, 3, 445–452.

Koss, S.E., Weissman, R., Chow, V., Smith, P.T., *et al.* (2018) 'Training community clergy in serious illness: Balancing faith and medicine.' *Journal of Religion and Health 57*, 3, 1413–1427.

McCurdy, D.B. (2012) 'Chaplains, confidentiality and the chart.' *Chaplaincy Today 28*, 2, 20–30.

Chapter 15

CRITICAL RESPONSE TO NEGOTIATING RELIGIOUS AND CULTURAL DIFFERENCES CASE STUDIES

A Family Medicine Physician's Response

CHRISTOPHER SMYRE

For many people, religion is a core part of their identity. Religion strongly influences decision-making regarding health and determines the right decision when facing complex situations. As someone who grew up in the American South and in a highly religious family, I have witnessed this degree of religiosity first hand. As an African American, I am also acutely aware of how complex social dynamics, systems, and our history of race and race relations within the US impacts health and healthcare decisions. The history of being denied full access to healthcare or, worse yet, having been made the subjects of healthcare research without consent, continues to manifest itself today in how African Americans and other marginalized groups interface with the healthcare system. The overlay of religion often adds another tension between accepting the reality of illness versus hoping and praying for something that seems idealistic or unlikely to occur from the perspective of medical science.

I pursued a dual degree at the University of Chicago, Pritzker School of Medicine and the Divinity School, with the latter course of study focusing on applying theological ethics to the medical context. The experience equipped me with language to engage patients holistically and comfort in appreciating diverse cultures. My research during my training focused on end-of-life care and on how physicians' religious views influence their attitudes and behaviors toward patient care and the decisions they face. I chose to become a family medicine physician because I am interested in patient empowerment and equipping patients, especially those from vulnerable backgrounds, in navigating the healthcare system. As a primary care provider, I am able to get to know patients over time. Furthermore, because I care for patients over their lifetimes, I also get to engage with them as their values, goals, and beliefs evolve due to life experiences and interactions with the healthcare system.

There is currently a lively debate among scholars regarding what role physicians should play in addressing the spiritual and religious concerns of their patients. The classic objection arises from the argument that physicians neither have the time nor training for this dimension of care (Curlin and Hall 2005; Sloan 2006; Sulmasy 2006). Others argue, to the contrary, that the role of the physician is to treat the *whole* patient and, as such, physicians are morally obligated to attend to the patient's spiritual concerns (Sulmasy 2006). Still others express concern of bias as physicians' own religious views (or lack thereof) have been shown to influence their recommendations about specific medical dilemmas faced by their patients, especially in the areas of fertility, pregnancy termination, organ transplantation, artificial nutrition, and withholding or withdrawing life-sustaining treatment options.

Regardless of where one lands in the debate, a team-based approach is widely accepted as necessary for ensuring patients receive holistic care. Professionally trained healthcare chaplains are now the norm in most inpatient hospital settings and in many outpatient clinics. Studies have found that incorporating healthcare chaplains into the medical decision-making process for patients with advanced illness leads to better outcomes than relying solely on community faith leaders for such guidance (Balboni *et al.* 2013). Other studies have suggested that hospitalized patients are more satisfied with their medical care when someone asks them about their religious and spiritual concerns (Williams *et al.* 2011). Chaplains are experts in attending to the religious dimensions of health, illness, and healing. In each of the cases in this section, chaplains play a role in medical decision-making when religion and culture strongly influence healthcare decisions. These cases demonstrate that the benefits of chaplain involvement stretch beyond immediate care for a specific patient to impact medical culture at large.

Chaplains enter into the process of supporting patients and families in medical decision-making in a variety of ways. In the case submitted by Chaplain Axelrud, the family specifically makes the request for the chaplain. Studies show that the majority of physicians are comfortable including a chaplain if the patient desires it (Smyre *et al.* 2018). In the case submitted by Chaplain Rosencrans, the physician requests the chaplain without prompting by the family. Though the case does not reveal the referring physician's level of religiosity or familiarity with spiritual and religious issues, studies have shown that physicians who are religious or have had training around the chaplain's role are more likely to request their involvement (Curlin *et al.* 2006; Curlin 2008). In the case by Chaplain Kirby, the chaplain is requested automatically via hospital protocol. At some hospitals, admissions to Intensive Care and Oncology Units trigger an automatic referral to the chaplain. Yet, studies have shown that despite the benefits of chaplains being involved in patient care, they are typically underutilized (Sinclair and Chochinov 2012). One explanation suggests that physicians may not think of requesting a chaplain in the moment. Thus, having chaplains automatically consulted alleviates this barrier, and if the patient does not find it helpful, the chaplains can simply sign off.

Regardless of how chaplains are initially consulted, they have intentional and systematic ways of engaging the patient and the family. Interestingly, several of the approaches depicted by these chaplain authors are also the ways that physicians are trained to engage with patients. Axelrud initiates the conversation with the patient's parents using open-ended questions and then validates their experiences and feelings. When speaking with Mohammed, Rosencrans begins her assessment by asking what he knows about the situation, acknowledging this perspective and then proceeds to discuss specific issues or concerns. Physicians classically use this approach when they have to deliver bad news. A notable difference between these two disciplines is that while physicians engage patients with their biopsychosocial lens, chaplains engage patients through a wider lens that includes "spirituality." Chaplains take the time to explore the meaning, values, and context for how a patient understands their illness, priorities, and the decisions they face. Kirby's case study is a prime example of this difference. In eliciting the family's story and feelings, she uncovers their central interpretive metaphor for the illness—the patient "got a broken heart." She asks them to say more about what they mean, and listens to them share and express their grief and anger. In so doing, she uncovers their complex non-medical explanation for their concerns. She does not ask about previous heart problems or redirect them to the current medical problem of the brain bleed as the physician continued to do throughout her interaction with the family.

Chaplains employ an interpretive lens that suggests that, in some way, all people are "spiritual." I understand "spiritual" to include a sense of meaning and purpose, values, and beliefs. Every individual makes medical decisions and frames their interpretation of facts based on their constellation of a set of values and beliefs formed over a lifetime and in interaction with family, culture, and religious traditions. The resulting framework is never monolithic. Note the similarities and subtle differences between how the parents process their daughter's condition in Axelrud's case. Axelrud describes them both as having "complex, nuanced" views that are "rooted deeply in the Orthodox Jewish set of beliefs rather than born of a desperate wish to have their daughter with them." However, the father has a medical background as a vascular surgeon. He is therefore more able to accept the poor prognosis and is less optimistic than his wife. Knowledge of how a particular culture approaches illness and medicine or about the religious doctrines that inform specific normative medical decisions must be refined by an acknowledgement and appreciation of how an individual internalizes and integrates them into their life. Chaplains possess such skill, as these cases demonstrate.

It takes time to learn what the patient and family value and what aspects of their upbringing, culture, and religious tradition inform their current perspective. During emergencies, physicians have limited time before the need to start intervening. Chaplains are able to spend significant time with patients and families. They are thereby positioned to gain comprehensive insight into values and particular understandings of illness and healing. The spiritual lens of chaplains serves a crucial role in ensuring values, religious beliefs, and cultural frameworks are known, respected, and integrated into the medical decision-making process.

I find Kevin Hector's metaphysical understanding of language to be a helpful analytical framework for appreciating the unique role of professional healthcare chaplains. In *Theology without Metaphysics: God, Language, and the Spirit of Recognition*, Hector addresses the ethical problem of silencing or misinterpreting others (2011).[1] Hector's understanding of concept usage is particularly useful when we consider shared decision-making that involves various parties with different values, beliefs, and interpretative lenses.

Silencing can be overt or covert. Silencing is not simply disagreeing but dismissing without engagement. In Rosencrans' case, we observe the medical team framing their language in such a way that the husband's desire to continue doing everything to keep the patient alive is disregarded. In Kirby's case, we see a subtler form of silencing as the physician disregards the family by labeling them as not understanding the patient's current situation. The chaplain gives voice to the family's narrative, ensuring that the medical team engages the family directly. The family is thereby recognized and heard.

When both parties recognize each other as a concept user, silencing is avoided. When one is recognized but does not recognize the other, silencing occurs. If a concept has already been established and understood, it sets a precedent for future recognition. When used again, if it aligns with previous usages, it will be better understood and accepted. For example, football and *fútbol* sound the same, and are both sports played on a field with 11 people. As such, I could engage in a conversation with someone about football or *fútbol*, and it is possible for them to know and use the concept football but not know and be able to use the concept *fútbol*. In football, the play stops when the ball hits the ground and you can use your hand. In *fútbol*, the play would stop if you used your hand, and the ball is mostly on the ground. If the individual's response and conversation didn't match with this precedent use established, then I would not recognize them as understanding football, and may clarify, "Oh, do

---

1   The essentialist-correspondentist framework is a philosophical approach in metaphysics that believes that there are essences that define something in the purest sense. However, when language is used it is true only when the words correspond to the essence of these concepts. The resulting conflict of language known as the ontological problem when speaking of God arises, on how our language can be connected to that which is beyond us. Moreover, classically, once one states how to speak of God appropriately it automatically silences others' approaches toward speaking of God. This silencing of others is seen in the history or religious organizations debating and stating who can speak of God and how they may do so.

you mean soccer?" The other person could also respond, "Oh, you were talking about *fútbol de Americano*," highlighting that despite the misrecognition between them, both understand and can use the concepts appropriately.

Let's apply this to the medical setting using a well-known religious reference: a person may refuse consent for a blood transfusion for a specific procedure. Understandably, this causes the physician to question if they understand the risks, and to wonder why they are refusing a life-saving intervention. But if the patient is known to be a Jehovah's Witness and they decline, it is more easily accepted, as the previous usage of the concept has already been established in this cultural exchange. In both Kirby's and Rosencrans' cases, the conceptual frameworks of the families are unique, rather than well known and accepted. The chaplains are sensitive to this difference as well as the distrust it creates for the families. Kirby, who self-identifies as a lesbian woman, has "experienced similar mistrust within LGBT communities." She takes the family's mistrust as a "'healthy suspicion' of systems that have repeatedly failed minority communities." In Rosencrans' case, she intentionally positions herself to hear the story of the outsider, thus recognizing the family's distrust of the medical system and the importance of their Muslim faith to decision-making. As a result, when the need arises to introduce a new concept usage, the chaplain can function as a meaning broker.

Hector's framework helps us further unpack the complex exchange that takes place when disparate discursive worlds intersect. The very act of going to the hospital demonstrates what Hector calls "concept recognition." Implicitly, patients and family accept they have a health problem even if their causal explanation for illness does not align with that of Western medicine. They grant the concepts of medicine some level of authority just by the act of seeking care. Physicians, on the other hand, are more likely to disregard alternative explanations for illness. Unless the conceptual world of the patient and family is acknowledged, they will be denied the ability engage in shared decision-making.

Chaplains are recognized by physicians as concept users in their area of expertise, spirituality. Kirby explains that physicians "trusted" her after working together for five years and witnessing her "negotiate complex spiritual, cultural, and relational conflicts." Rosencrans is granted this kind of recognition by her medical staff as well. After the medical team describes the Muslim family's desire to continue pursuing life-saving interventions as "irrational if not insane," Rosencrans has the authority to intervene on behalf of the family. She provides a bridge to the foreign concept of suffering as a means to salvation. She explains that the "traumatization, marginalization, and disenfranchisement, caus[es] him to be stuck, unable to make decisions, unable to let her go." This leads the medical team to shift from judgment to inquiry, resulting in compassion towards the family.

When patients or their loved ones make decisions and express their preferences in ways that make sense to the medical team, there is rarely conflict. However, as Rosencrans describes, when the family's concepts do not align with those of the medical team, they "suggested we should turn to the daughter for decision-making as she was 'more reasonable.'" When physicians are determining what is medically appropriate versus inappropriate for a patient, what is reasonable versus unreasonable, they may draw on a history of previous patient encounters as well as their own cultural assumptions. Medical culture prioritizes rationality and reasoned decision-making above all. Approaches to decision-making that fall outside the realm of "reason" are likely to be silenced. The role of the chaplain is critical in expanding what physicians consider appropriate or normative constructs for decision-making. Rosencrans recognizes and reaffirms that the husband, however "irrational," is the medical decision-maker. She recognizes the husband as a concept user whose decisions make sense within his experiential world.

Hector contends, "community is constituted every time one recognizes certain other performances and judgments as authoritative over one's own performances and judgments, and when these others in turn recognize the recognizer as 'one of us'" (2011, p.16). The community becomes very important because the normative trajectories will be influenced by precedence. Those who have gained entry to the community are in a privileged position to open the door for new concepts to be accepted as normative. This then elevates the importance of team members who are recognized as concept users— in these cases, that person is the chaplain.

For example, Kirby explains that the family's concept of a broken heart is not biological but rather metaphorical. "They're saying she has a broken heart, because of her grief. They don't mean it literally. The young doctor looked up, stunned and suddenly empathetic."

The doctor's sudden shift happens because she finally recognizes the family—via the role of the chaplain—as authoritative concept users. This then allows her to honor the family's desire to withdraw the breathing machine that is keeping Alma alive.

As previously stated, by going to the hospital patients (at the very least) are implicitly seeking and yielding to physicians and awaiting reciprocal acknowledgement and engagement. This places them in a vulnerable position. Chaplains' comfort with and ability to yield to patient and family conceptual norms serves a therapeutic role. It can change the dynamics of the typical clinical encounter by elevating the status of the patient or family. It also strengthens and enhances the overall relationship with the medical team by creating a greater sense of safety. This then reduces their understandable defensiveness. Rosencrans humbly receives and holds Mohammed's story of suffering and abandonment. In turn, "Mohammed appeared to soften [and] looked at [Rosencrans] for the first time."

Conclusion

As physicians, we are called to evaluate complex situations and make rapid decisions. As physicians, we have taken an oath to do no harm. What we define as harm within our unique framework may conflict with values, perspectives, or definitions held by our patients and families, or even by our own colleagues. As these cases demonstrate, providing care congruent with our professional values is not always possible. This can be because the family is refusing the plan, as seen in Rosencrans' case, where the medical team feels interventions are now "futile" and are only prolonging suffering. It can also be related to hospital policies or lack of resources to provide appropriate care for a patient. Regardless of the reason, sometimes what is desired and believed to be the appropriate action cannot be taken. This can predispose medical teams to lose patience and understanding for future patients. It can also personally weigh on clinicians. Chaplains can minimize these negative consequences by making transparent the value conflicts at work and validating the challenges of working with patients and families from worldviews that differ from our own.

In our current medical culture, that places such a high value on patient-centered care and shared decision-making, chaplains are equipped to promote these noble aims. Chaplains assist in the medical decision-making process by validating and translating the patient's perspective and preferences to the medical team as well as translating those of the medical team to the patient and family. By engaging patients and their family through a spiritual lens, they sensitize the team to religious, cultural, and patient specific values. They also support the medical team directly in the processing and framing of conflicts that involve religion and culture to promote ongoing well-being. Finally, chaplains not only serve the current patient, but also impact the care of future patients by expanding the range of normative concepts that are considered potentially authoritative in healthcare.

References

Balboni, T.A., Balboni, M., Enzinger, A.C., Gallivan, K., *et al.* (2013) 'Provision of spiritual support to patients with advanced cancer by religious communities and associations with medical care at the end of life.' *JAMA Internal Medicine 173*, 12, 1109–1117.

Curlin, F.A. (2008) 'Commentary: A case for studying the relationship between religion and the practice of medicine.' *Academic Medicine 83*, 12, 1118–1120.

Curlin, F.A. and Hall, D.E. (2005) 'Strangers or friends? A proposal for a new spirituality-in-medicine ethic.' *Journal of General Internal Medicine 20*, 4, 370–374.

Curlin, F.A., Chin, M.H., Sellergren, S.A., Roach, C.J. and Lantos, J.D. (2006) 'The association of physicians' religious characteristics with their attitudes and self-reported behaviors regarding religion and spirituality in the clinical encounter.' *Medical Care 44*, 5, 446–453.

Hector, K. (2011) *Theology without Metaphysics: God, Language, and the Spirit of Recognition.* Cambridge: Cambridge University Press.

Sinclair, S. and Chochinov, H.M. (2012) 'The role of chaplains within oncology interdisciplinary teams.' *Current Opinion in Supportive and Palliative Care 6*, 2, 259–268.

Sloan, R.P. (2006) *Blind Faith: The Unholy Alliance of Religion and Medicine.* New York: St Martin's Press.

Smyre, C.L., Tak, J.H., Dang, A.P., Curlin, F.A. and Yoon, J.D. (2018) 'Physicians' opinions on engaging patients' religious and spiritual concerns: A national survey.' *Journal of Pain and Symptom Management 55*, 3, 897–905.

Sulmasy, D.P. (2006) 'Spiritual issues in the care of dying patients: "It's okay between me and God."' *JAMA 296*, 11, 1385–1392.

Williams, J.A., Meltzer, D., Arora, V., Chung, G. and Curlin, F.A. (2011) 'Attention to inpatients' religious and spiritual concerns: Predictors and association with patient satisfaction.' *Journal of General Internal Medicine 26*, 11, 1265–1271.

Afterword

MARTIN WALTON

A wealth of perspectives

One of the questions that arises in case study research on chaplaincy care is whether a case description does full justice to what was actually going on in the care process. The answer is easy: no. Just as no chaplain, nor anyone else, can ever do full justice to the patient, to his or her family, close ones and all that they are going through, no case study does justice to all involved, just as no chaplain or case study can ever do full justice to the intentions and care investment of hospital staff either. However carefully and movingly the case studies in this collection have been narrated, there is always more than can be conveyed in whatever manner. The intention of a case study lies not in the pretention that it can reproduce some essence or capture the fullness of an example of chaplaincy care; the task is simply to identify critical moments in, and explicate crucial elements of, the care process.

Fortunately for us, the cases presented here have indeed been described and shared, for the sake of our information and learning. We see critical incidents and carefully construed care. What do we learn from them? Well, an epilogue like this can never do justice to the wealth of narrative, analysis, and response offered in the 15 chapters of this book. So I will limit myself to identifying some (critical) issues and ordering some of the wealth of perspectives. I will comment on the use of case studies, on the role of the chaplain in medical decision-making, and on the combination of the two.

Case studies

Most of the case studies in chaplaincy care published until now were individual case studies making a particular case on how chaplaincy care was offered in a given situation. The intention is generally to present a potential good practice of chaplaincy care in order to contribute to a bottom-up approach to developing evidence for the effectiveness of chaplaincy care. Wirpsa and Pugliese let us see another use of case studies in two ways. First of all, the collection has a specific common focus, being the role that chaplains play with regard to medical decision-making. Second, their collection of case studies is not the starting point of their research on the topic, but follows quantitative research by means of a survey on the role of chaplains in shared medical decision-making (Wirpsa et al. 2019). The question to ask is what the case studies contribute in relation to the survey.

The survey listed six chaplain activities: helping patients (families) clarify issues; mediating family conflicts; communicating patient values to staff; supporting patients and families; facilitating advance care; and educating patients and families. The qualitative section of the survey added items such as representing spiritual authority; attending to the whole person and to emotions; serving as a liaison or bridge, etcetera. All of these are recognizable in one or more case studies. It would be quite welcome if, in a future publication, the editors would specifically relate the survey to the case study reports.

It would be too little to suggest that the case studies illustrate the named activities. Even if both the survey and case studies are self-reporting forms of research, the case studies substantiate in their concreteness the roles identified in the survey and indicate specific outcomes as a result of chaplains fulfilling those roles: acceptance of the proximity of death; restoration of the relation between father and daughter; establishing peace between the family and staff; ending meaningless medical care, etc. Wirpsa and Pugliese provide, therefore, an example of how case studies can be employed effectively in different phases of research, and can be helpful in confirming findings in other types of research.

What might be done to further substantiate the contribution of chaplains to shared medical decision-making? One would be to gather feedback on the role of the chaplain in the case study from the patient (or family) and from other involved staff members. Can the description of the chaplain be confirmed, nuanced, or complemented by the feedback? (Of course, another possibility is a survey among other health professionals on the role of chaplains in medical decision-making; see Willemse *et al.* 2018, on spiritual care in the Intensive Care Unit, ICU.) Related to this concern is the fact that the six responses of other professionals to the case studies in this book are elucidating, confirming, and full of additional theory. More critical, evaluative responses would also be welcome.

Another concern is to look at the way the case studies themselves are written. In several of the nine case studies presented here, essential descriptive information on the use of a particular model or on communication with staff is added in the analysis. Occasionally the application of a model is included in the narrative, but not the motivation for doing so, or the effect of the intervention. The considerations, consultations, and decisions by the chaplain in the accompaniment process, and sometimes the specific moments of shared decision-making themselves, could become clearer if included in the descriptive phase. The analysis could then take on a more evaluative character. In all cases Fitchett's admonition in an afterword of one of the case studies volumes he edited is applicable: outcomes need to be described as concretely as possible in terms of (sense) observations and, where possible, confirmations (Fitchett and Nolan 2018).

Shared medical decision-making

The case studies in this book provide rich (though never exhaustive) descriptions of chaplaincy care. In order to keep the focus on medical decision-making I would want to distinguish three things: more *generic care attitudes or postures* (therapeutic presence, empathy and compassion, emotional support or holding, non-judgmental and non-anxious presence, etc.), *spiritual and chaplaincy care interventions* (spiritual assessment and support, focus on meaning and story, addressing grief, etc.) and, third, *specific roles of chaplains in medical decision-making*. In the cases and responses any number of roles, metaphoric or functional, are named: translator, interpreter, negotiator, advocate, authority, (being a) bridge, intermediary, cultural broker, educator, facilitator, plus a few tasks such as linking, empowering, aligning, building a bridge, etc. I highlight three—*intermediary*, *negotiator*, and *facilitator*—that describe crucial functions in shared medical decision-making and that can also be aligned with theological categories such as mediation, conciliation, and service.

Fulfilling such roles requires certain skills. I name three: *critical learning, multi-linguality*, and *multiple partisanship*. *Critical learning* has to do with the ability not just to learn from others, but also to understand their critical position, experience of discrimination, and/or distinct perspectives. *Multi-linguality* is the ability to move between various language games, rationalities, and cultures. *Multiple partisanship* is the ability, or strategy, to view situations from and negotiate the perspectives of the various parties involved.

Conceptualizing the contribution of chaplains to shared medical decision-making in this way—and I hope that my distinctions recognizably reflect what is present in the case studies material—has consequences, it seems to me, for the way chaplains look at ethics. A bioethical approach is strongly led by *principles*. While one might be critical of the (somewhat individualized) culture of rationality in which those principles have been formulated, it should be clear that one cannot do without clear and sharp ethical reasoning, whether with regard to principles, consequences, or virtues. At the same time, ethical deliberation is not just about clearly defined ethical principles, but also about the different *perspectives* of patients, family members, and various professionals. Healthcare professionals can differ just as much among themselves in their perspectives as can family and staff, or as can patient and family. The task is to honor and understand the various perspectives as well as possible (*multiple partisanship*). When it comes to decision-making, the alternatives are often not clear-cut. This means that the decision to be made is not right or wrong, not good or bad, but the act of setting *priorities* with regard to a particular principle or perspective, or set of perspectives.

That process of lending priority has to do with the way convictions, experiences, emotions, and perspectives play a role in some narrative (or poetic constellation). The ability to "hold and cherish opposites", as Segar described, is part of that. The point is that whatever the preference or perspective, people do have reasons for the priorities they set. Nussbaum's understanding of "the intelligence of emotions" can be helpful here (Nussbaum 2001). Creating a dichotomy between rationality and emotions often misreads the situation, because there are reasons for the emotions and because rational principles represent matters that have emotional value. The reasoned decision of the doctor to abstain from treatment is intertwined with their emotional investment in saving lives and reducing suffering. The emotional refusal of family members to allow treatment to stop can be intertwined with the narrative rationality of the family in which caring and indebtedness play a meaningful role. The point is not rationality or emotions, but the hermeneutical reading of both (*multi-linguality*).

In light of this I would like to comment on the issue of *cultural* (or *epistemic*) *humility*. The editors introduce the term in the introduction to Part III and the cases demonstrate it. Such humility, such an assumption of a (*critical*) *learning* attitude, cannot be emphasized enough. For chaplains in a situation of shared medical decision-making, one might also speak of diagnostic (assessmental) humility or ethical humility. At the same time what becomes evident in the case studies is that the *interpretative risk* and *hermeneutical audacity* of the chaplains in asking questions, offering new perspectives, suggesting alternatives, etc., is what often made a real difference in the situation. Such audacity can only be risked on the basis of humility, but the roles of *intermediary*, *negotiator*, and *facilitator* do not live from humility alone. Audacity is also needed.

Case studies on medical decision-making

The editors are to be thanked for their varied research on the roles of chaplains in shared medical decision-making, now especially for the gathering of case studies as substantiation of those roles. As the roles have become clearer and more substantiated, positive effects have become visible. The patience practiced in accompaniment processes over weeks and months is hardly named but evident.

In conclusion I want to point to one small example of how writing case studies on medical decision-making can not only provide examples of good practice but also foster reflection and improve chaplaincy care. In the analysis of his case study Hogg comments that there was likely some miscommunication with Glen "regarding his understanding of hospice." In retrospect, being moved to the hospice seems for Glen to have meant "giving up." Hogg feels as though he might have more adequately addressed Glen's concerns about hospice, if he had understood that. Here we see the hermeneutical task of chaplaincy in a small detail of great proportions, in the questions:

What does hospice mean? What does this or that mean to me and to another, and to yet another? What rationality, whose emotions, are at play? Asking such simple questions can make a world of difference.

References

Fitchett, G. and Nolan, S. (eds) (2018) *Case Studies in Spiritual Care: Healthcare Chaplaincy Assessments, Interventions and Outcomes.* London: Jessica Kingsley Publishers.

Nussbaum, M. (2001) *Upheavals of Thought. The Intelligence of Emotions.* Cambridge and New York: Cambridge University Press.

Willemse, S., Smeets, W., van Leeuwen, E., Loes Janssen, L. and Foudraine, N. (2018) 'Spiritual care in the ICU: Perspectives of Dutch intensivists, ICU nurses, and spiritual caregivers.' *Journal of Religion and Health,* 57, 2, 583–595.

Wirpsa, J.M., Johnson, R., Bieler, J., Boyken, L., *et al.* (2019) 'Interprofessional models for shared decision making: The role of the health care chaplain.' *Journal of Health Care Chaplaincy* 25, 1, 20–44.

Martin Walton
Professor of Chaplaincy Studies
Protestant Theological University, Groningen
The Netherlands

Biographies

Abraham Axelrud is an ordained rabbi and holds a PhD from the Wagner School of New York University. He serves as a staff chaplain at Long Island Jewish Medical Center in New Hyde Park, New York, and is board-certified by Neshama: Association of Jewish Chaplains. He is a member of the of the hospital's Palliative Care team, and with his fellow chaplains, he conducts a seminar for Palliative Care fellows entitled "Spirituality and Its Impact on Illness, Death, and Loss." Rabbi Axelrud serves on the Ethics Overview Committee and has been asked to contribute to the Hofstra University Medical School Certificate Program in Medical Bioethics.

Paul Galchutt is a healthcare chaplain with the University of Minnesota Health Fairview. Among his 15 years in healthcare chaplaincy, 10 of those years were served as an inpatient Palliative Care chaplain. He is currently faculty with the Interprofessional Spiritual Care Education Curriculum (ISPEC) connected with the George Washington Institute for Spirituality and Health (GWish). He completed his Master of Public Health from the University of Minnesota in May 2019. Along with being a former bereavement coordinator, Paul has also been an Evangelical Lutheran Church in America (ELCA) pastor for 23 years.

Keith W. Goheen, MDiv, BCC, serves as a hospital chaplain at Beebe Healthcare in Lewes, Delaware. In addition to providing chaplaincy care directly to patients, families, and staff, he brings a chaplain's perspective to the care of his institution, co-chairing the Bioethics Committee and participating as a founding member of the expanding Thoracic Surgery and Palliative Care teams. Chaplain Goheen is a member of the Association of Professional Chaplains (APC) and chairs its Certification Commission's Theological Education Equivalency Committee. He was ordained by the First Universalist Church in Orange, Massachusetts and is in Ministerial Fellowship with the Unitarian Universalist Association of Congregations.

Jim Hogg, MDiv, BCC, is the Director of Chaplaincy Services at Memorial Hermann Hospital–Texas Medical Center in Houston, Texas. Chaplain Hogg is board-certified by the Association of Professional Chaplains (APC), through whom he has also served as a State Representative. His commitment to evidence-based chaplaincy is inspired and informed by the care recipients he encounters. Chaplain Hogg has experience within multiple professional chaplain specialties, including Palliative Care. He is the recipient of a Best Practice Palliative Chaplain Award through the national PACE (Program of All-Inclusive Care for the Elderly) Association.

Michelle Kirby, MDiv, BCC, is an ACPE (Association for Clinical Pastoral Education)-certified educator and board-certified chaplain with the Association of Professional Chaplains. She serves as the clinical pastoral education (CPE) supervisor with the San Diego VA-DoD CPE Center, educating the CPE residents, Mental Health Fellow, and Certified Educator Candidate at the VA San Diego Healthcare System and Naval Medical Center, San Diego. Chaplain Kirby has served on the Ethics Committees at the VA San Diego, St Mary's Medical Center and Saint Francis Memorial Hospital. She also participated in the Palliative Care teams at Saint Francis, St Mary's and California Pacific Medical Center, all in San Francisco. Chaplain Kirby is ordained and endorsed by the Universal Fellowship of Metropolitan Community Churches, and serves as the coordinator of ACPE's LGBTQ Community of Practice.

Karen Lieberman, JD, MSJS, BCC, is a board-certified staff chaplain at the Children's Hospital of Wisconsin. She has worked in adult and pediatric hospital settings for almost a decade. Previously, Chaplain Lieberman practiced law in both the public and private sectors and served as an adjunct law school faculty member at Marquette University. She has a special interest in the intersection of law, medicine, ethics, and spirituality, and writes and teaches on a wide range of related topics, including the professionalization of chaplaincy, the humanities of medicine, informed consent, and the relationship between spiritual care and patient experience. Chaplain Lieberman has served on various hospital ethics committees for the past 12 years, and is currently completing a Master's in Bioethics and Health Policy.

Debjani Mukherjee, PhD, is the Director of the Donnelley Ethics Program at the Shirley Ryan AbilityLab (formerly the Rehabilitation Institute of Chicago, or RIC) and an Associate Professor of Physical Medicine and Rehabilitation and of Medical Education at Northwestern University's Feinberg School of Medicine. Dr Mukherjee is a licensed clinical psychologist and clinical ethicist. After completing her Bachelor, Master and Doctorate in Psychology from Cornell University and the University of Illinois at Urbana-Champaign, Dr Mukherjee completed two years of postdoctoral fellowship training at the University of Chicago's Maclean Center for Clinical Medical Ethics. She was then invited to spend a year in Paris, France, to help start the first center for clinical ethics in France, the Centre D'ethique Clinique at Cochin Hospital. Dr Mukherjee's interests are in the emotional impact of medical decisions, adjustment to disability, and ethical concerns in rehabilitation. At Northwestern University, Dr Mukherjee has taught undergraduates, Master's students, medical students, residents, and fellows. She has been involved in over 500 ethics consultations. Dr Mukherjee has lectured and published on topics ranging from the dignity of risk to an innovative model of clinical ethics consultation. Dr Mukherjee is also a feature editor and edits a quarterly column for the journal *PM&R*, the official scientific journal of the American Academy of Physical Medicine and Rehabilitation.

Linda F. Piotrowski, MTS, is a board-certified chaplain through the National Association of Catholic Chaplains. After over 40 years of ministry in Education and Nursing Home, Acute Care, Hospice, and Palliative Care chaplaincy, she retired from Dartmouth Hitchcock Medical Center in Lebanon, New Hampshire, where she served as the Palliative Care and Oncology chaplain. Previously she served as a chaplain, Regional Director of Spiritual Care, and participated as an instructor in seminary training programs, led a writing group for oncology patients, and was a sought-after speaker for a variety of conferences. Linda is a graduate of the City of Hope's Achieving Clinical Excellence Program. A strong proponent of interdisciplinary care, she has articles in numerous publications, as well as chapters in *The Oxford Textbook of Palliative Social Work, Professional Spiritual and Pastoral Care*, and *Spirituality and End-of-Life Care.*

Karen Pugliese, MA, BCC-PCHAC, is an advanced practice chaplain in the Spiritual Care and Education Department at Northwestern Medicine Central DuPage Hospital in Winfield, Illinois' western suburbs. Karen holds Palliative Care and Hospice advanced certification and serves as a member of the Palliative Medicine team. She continues to provide spiritual care in Hospice, Oncology, Intensive Care, Women & Children, Neurology, and Emergency Medicine. Karen is recognized for her expertise and a deep commitment to workplace spirituality, professional development, and spiritual enrichment of staff, and is sought after as a retreat, workshop, and seminar facilitator. She contributes to, publishes, and presents nationally on spiritual care research and serves on her hospital's Institutional Review Board. Karen supervises Seminarians and Deacons in formation for the Diocese of Joliet and is a member of the Leadership Team and faculty providing professional development in communication and supportive care for physicians, advanced practice nurses, social workers and chaplains to build knowledge and skills in primary Palliative Care, to expand patient access to quality Palliative Care, and to form a supportive, regional network of Palliative Care champions. Karen received the Distinguished Service Award and served as chair of the National Association of Catholic Chaplains' Board of Directors and was a key advisor to the publication *Making Healthcare Whole: Integrating Spirituality into Patient Care.*

Emily Duncan Rosencrans, MDiv, BCC serves as the manager of Spiritual Care and Education at Northwestern Lake Forest Hospital in Lake Forest, Illinois. In this role she manages a staff of chaplains and volunteers, sees patients, and works with interdisciplinary teams to collaborate for patient and staff care. Rev. Rosencrans speaks on a variety of subjects ranging from end-of-life conversations to moral and ethical issues in the hospital and community. She also preaches, teaches, and leads worship at area churches on a regular basis. She is a board-certified chaplain through the Association of Professional

Chaplains (APC), is certified in Palliative Care chaplaincy through California State University, and is certified in Marriage, Family, and Sex Therapy from the Council for Relationships in Philadelphia, PA. Rev. Rosencrans has a Master of Divinity degree from Princeton Theological Seminary and has been ordained in the Presbyterian Church (PCUSA) since 1987.

Nora Segar, MD, is an internal medicine physician practicing primary care and Palliative Care. She works at Erie Family Community Health Center and at the Jesse Brown VA Medical Center. As part of her work, she reads poetry with veterans on the Palliative Care consult service in the Poetry for Patients Project referred to in this volume. She graduated from The Mount Sinai School of Medicine and Yale University's Primary Care Residency Program, where she developed an interest in Medical Humanities and Narrative Medicine. Dr Segar completed a fellowship in Palliative Care at Northwestern, where she works as a faculty member in the fellowship training program and teaches ethics and humanities to medical students.

Christopher Smyre, MD, is a resident at Northwestern McGaw Family Medicine Residency in Humboldt Park, Chicago, Illinois. He received his Bachelor of Arts at Wake Forest University, his Master of Arts at the University of Chicago Divinity School, and his Doctor of Medicine at the University of Chicago Pritzker School of Medicine. His interests are in medical education, ethics, patient empowerment, and community development.

Melanie Swofford, MDiv, BCC, serves as a clinical chaplain for the Cape Fear Valley Health System in North Carolina. She is board-certified through the Association of Professional Chaplains (APC). Chaplain Swofford has advanced certificates in Palliative Care studies and regularly presents on topics related to Palliative Care in critical care, family communication in Intensive Care Units (ICUs), and advance directives. Recently, Chaplain Swofford worked with a team that utilized evidence-based practice to create a new program that improves the quality of family care in the ICU to help prevent post-traumatic stress in families after the death of the patient. Her continued research and collaborative work centers around helping families during the crisis surrounding the death of a patient and finding ways to utilize spiritual development research to improve the provision of spiritual care across the lifespan. Chaplain Swofford is an ordained United Methodist Elder and acts as the ambassador, president, and educator for the Western North Carolina United Methodist Chaplain Association. She is also the chaplain representative of Cape Fear Valley Health System's Ethics Committee, Donor Services Committee and Internal Review Board on research related to clinical care.

TeresaMarie T. Vilagos, MDiv, BCC, is the manager of Spiritual Care & Education at Carolinas Rehabilitation, in Charlotte, North Carolina, and is responsible for spiritual and emotional support for patients, families, and teammates. She co-facilitates their Brain Injury Support Group and Trauma Survivors Network, which fosters post-traumatic growth (PTG) and resilience for patients and their families. She is an ordained Elder in the United Methodist Church and is board-certified by the Association of Professional Chaplains (APC). She is also a member of the Professional Advisory Group that provides advice and consultation on program planning, development, and evaluation for the Department of Spiritual Care & Education at Atrium Health. Chaplain Vilagos is a co-author of research in the *Journal of Healthcare Chaplaincy*, and her essay, "Coping in the Face of Daily Trauma," was featured in APC *e-News* in May of 2015. She is co-facilitator for the North Carolina Chaplains Association Research Journal Club, promoting research literacy and involvement. Chaplain Vilagos was the first chaplain to deploy with the Atrium Health MED-1 mobile hospital in response to Hurricane Florence, where she provided compassionate care to encourage PTG and resilience for the residents of the coastal and inland areas of North Carolina.

Anne Windholz is staff chaplain at AMITA Health Alexian Brothers Medical Center in Elk Grove Village, Illinois. Recipient of fellowships from the Andrew W. Mellon Foundation and the National Endowment for the Humanities, she holds a PhD in English from the University of Illinois-Urbana. She earned her Master of Divinity from the Catholic Theological Union in 2012 and is board-certified by the Association of Professional Chaplains (APC). A published author and scholar, her work has most recently appeared in *New Theology Review*, *Vision*, *US Catholic*, and *St Anthony Messenger*. She is currently one of six chaplain interventionists nationwide contributing to Ascension

Health's study "On Demand Spiritual Care with CHF Patients," led by Beth Muehlhausen and David Peacock.

M. Jeanne Wirpsa, MA, BCC, HEC-C, is a professional healthcare chaplain, clinical ethicist, and educator with over 25 years' experience providing spiritual care in the areas of pediatrics, end of life, and oncology. She currently has a dual role at Northwestern Memorial Hospital in downtown Chicago, serving as research chaplain for the Department of Spiritual Care and Education and as program manager and clinical ethicist for the Department of Medical Ethics. Out of her concern to promote interprofessional collaboration and increase attention to religion and spirituality by the healthcare team, Chaplain Wirpsa teaches a course she developed on the interface between religion and medicine in healthcare practice, a requirement for all students in the Feinberg School of Medicine, and co-facilitates the Religion, Bioethics and Medicine Course in the MacLean Center for Clinical Medical Ethics at the University of Chicago. Chaplain Wirpsa developed a creative program to support institution-wide advance care planning and is involved in several initiatives to promote the moral agency of bedside clinicians. She is principal investigator for the mixed-methods study, "The Role of the Chaplain in Medical Decision Making," that includes the case study research in this volume.

Subject Index

Author Index